# THE SUMMER HOUSE

# THE SUMMER HOUSE

## LAUREN K. DENTON

**THORNDIKE PRESS**
A part of Gale, a Cengage Company

Thorndike Press, a part of Gale, a Cengage Company.

**ALL RIGHTS RESERVED**
Thorndike Press® Large Print Christian Fiction
The text of this Large Print edition is unabridged.
Other aspects of the book may vary from the original edition.
Set in 16 pt. Plantin.

LIBRARY OF CONGRESS CIP DATA ON FILE.
CATALOGUING IN PUBLICATION FOR THIS BOOK
IS AVAILABLE FROM THE LIBRARY OF CONGRESS

ISBN-13: 978-1-4328-8063-7 (hardcover alk. paper)

Published in 2020 by arrangement with Thomas Nelson, Inc., a division
of HarperCollins Christian Publishing, Inc.

Printed in Mexico
Print Number: 03      Print Year: 2020

*To Anna and Holly.*
*And Voxer.*

# ONE

The morning Worth left, something pulled Lily from her sleep, though at first glance nothing seemed out of place. The light coming through the bedroom window was soft and hazy. Above her the ceiling fan ticked and swayed, and outside a lone bird sang, trying to rouse its friends. Everything else was still and quiet.

She sat up in bed and smoothed her hand over the empty space next to her, the sheets on Worth's side twisted and tangled as usual. It was Friday, thankfully, the end of a long week, one she and her husband had both hoped would go better. Worth had spent twelve-plus hours each day this week at his new real estate job, giving himself a crash course in the company and coming home each night tossing out terms she didn't understand — things like metes and bounds, plats and surveys.

For her part Lily had spent an equal

amount of time trying, mostly in vain, to brighten up their drab rental home just off Highway 59 in Foley, Alabama. She'd also dodged phone calls from her mother-in-law, Mertha, who'd taken to calling Lily every few hours once she'd accepted that her son was avoiding her calls. "Just checking in," Mertha would say, wanting to know the state of everything from Worth's job to his mood to his laundry.

Lily had never been so glad for a weekend. She hoped they'd be able to take some time on Saturday to drive around and look for a more permanent place, a house they could make their own, though for all Lily knew, Worth may have been planning to work right through until Monday.

With her mind still fuzzy with sleep, she rose from the bed and made her way down the short hall toward the kitchen. That's when she realized what was wrong. She usually woke to the scent of strong Colombian roast coffee wafting from the kitchen into the bedroom, luring her with a warm, heady promise.

Their fancy Bonavita coffee maker, a wedding gift from Worth's best man, was the first thing he had unpacked two weeks ago when they arrived in Foley from Atlanta, and he'd made a steaming pot of extra-robust coffee every morning before he left for work. It was a small token, especially when everything felt so upside down, but Lily had long grown used to feeling off balance, and she took the daily gift of hot coffee for what it was — his way of offering sustenance, love, and maybe a little hope, all in her favorite mug.

This morning, however, the gleaming silver coffeepot was cold and quiet. She was still tying the belt of her thin robe around her waist when she saw the note propped up against it. A mechanical pencil lay next to it.

Lily, I can't do this anymore. You deserve more than what I can give you. I'm so sorry.

Puzzled, she stared at the piece of paper, waiting for the words to transform into something different, something that made more sense. But they didn't. She blinked hard, pressing her eyelids together until she saw white spots. She turned her head side to side, the muscles in her neck stretching and releasing. But when she opened her eyes, the words were still there. That's when she noticed the packet on the other side of the coffee maker. The thin white envelope almost blended into the counter. Her full name — Lily Chapman Bishop — was typed on the front of the unsealed envelope. With the tips of her fingers, Lily reached inside and slid a piece of paper out a few inches. She scanned the top of the page.

State of Alabama, United Judicial System.
Complaint for Divorce.
Plaintiff: Ainsworth Madison Bishop IV

She pulled the paper out farther, unbelieving, until she saw his name signed at the bottom. It was his handwriting, no doubt — small, mostly capital letters, the ink pressed hard into the page.

Then, like a current of cold water pouring over her, a thought rang in her head, clear and sure. *It's finally happened.* She pressed her palms to the cool surface of the counter.

She realized she'd been waiting for this, probably since the day he slipped a ring on her finger and asked her to marry him. Maybe even since the day they first met. Their union had seemed improbable from the very start, but they'd stubbornly defied everyone and clung so tightly to each other, there had been no room between them for doubt, not a sliver of space for any misgiving or hesitation.

She lifted her head and spread the note out in front of her, smoothing out the creases. Underneath his words, he'd written something else, then erased it. The paper there was gray and blurry, as if he'd tried several times to add more words but kept second-guessing himself. Finally, below the smudge, he'd added his name.

Worth

That was it.

She braced herself against the counter, the edges biting into her hips and the skin of her hands, and took a deep breath.

The evening before had been beautiful — one of those spring nights when the air managed to feel both crisp and warm at the same time. She'd made dinner for them to eat on their small patio out back, with the wild roses climbing over the privacy fence and the sky a constantly changing landscape of pink, orange, and lilac.

As she tossed together a salad to go with their pasta, she'd felt optimistic — hopeful even. Maybe something good would come from this move to sunny south Alabama. Maybe this would be where they could create something lasting — for them, for their marriage, for their life.

She'd planned to bring up the subject of house hunting, but when she joined him outside and glanced at him across the rickety wrought iron table, the sight of his red, tear-rimmed eyes pushed away all her prior thoughts. She was stunned. In the year and a half she'd known him, she'd never seen her husband cry or even come close to it.

"Worth?" She set down her fork and reached across the table. "What's wrong?"

The shape of him was so familiar to her — the slope of his shoulders, his flyaway blond hair, the way his calf muscles narrowed down to his ankles. This evening he'd crossed one leg over the other knee, and his foot bopped up and down. His face, body, even the air around him seemed to quiver with tension. For being so attuned to his body, she wished she knew his mind and his heart half as well.

"What is it?" she repeated.

He took a deep breath and blinked a few times. "I'm sorry I brought you here." His voice trembled as he spoke. "To this new town. This" — he lifted his hand and gestured behind her — "this ugly house. I've completely uprooted you. And for what?" He laughed, but it was devoid of humor.

"Babe, my life was uprooted long before you came along." She smiled to show she was kidding, but they both knew her words were true. "And what do you mean, 'for what'? We came here for your new job. A new start. For both of us. Right?"

He rubbed one eye with the heel of his hand and cleared his throat. "I haven't been a very good husband to you."

The sadness in his eyes almost undid her. She opened her mouth to speak but found she had no words to offer that could fix things. That could fix them.

He gently pulled his hand out from under hers and began to eat, and after a moment she did the same. They didn't talk about looking for houses; they didn't talk about his job. They didn't talk about much of anything.

He remained on the patio long after she cleared the dinner dishes away and wiped the last smudges from the kitchen counter. When he finally came to bed hours later, the scent of whiskey on his breath, he curled his body around hers, his chest pressed to her back. His hand found hers, and they lay like that for a long time, the only sounds their mingled breaths.

Something in his silent embrace felt different from the usual way he held her. It was only now, standing at the counter holding his note, that she put her finger on what exactly she'd felt as he'd tightened his arms around her the night before. It had felt final. He'd been saying goodbye.

That night Lily poured herself a glass of wine and carried it to the patio. Sitting in the same chair she'd sat in the night before, she gazed across the table at Worth's seat, empty but for a single dragonfly perched on the back. Its iridescent wings glimmered, reflecting the light of another sunset.

She'd spent the day absorbing, digesting, and reframing Worth's disappearance to the best of her ability, yet she'd come up with nothing more than this: she was alone. Again. But this time there was no one else to jump in and save her. Her mom was gone, everything she had that had been connected to her was gone, and now Worth had left too, effectively pulling off the bandage that had been covering up all those wounds. Lily was the only one who remained.

She closed her eyes and took a long sip of her wine, willing it to dull the day's sharp edges. Letting herself sink would be so easy, just like falling asleep. She could cover herself in grief like a blanket and never get up again. But all day something had been prodding her, way at the back of her mind like a dream she'd mostly forgotten. Whatever it was, it was the thing that kept her from sinking. From letting go.

She slowed her breathing and stilled her movements. She felt the weight of her arms and legs, the substantial *there*-ness of her body. Her pumping heart, the breath in and out of her lungs.

*Everyone else is gone, but I'm here. I'm still here.*

That night when Mertha called, Lily answered.

"What do you mean, he left you a note?" Mertha asked. "What did it say?"

"The note was for me, but he did leave me a stack of papers. They're divorce papers, Mertha." The steadiness of her own voice surprised her, and she leaned into it, thankful for the stubborn resolve that coursed through her.

Mertha was quiet, and Lily could imagine the shock and fury criss-crossing her mother-in-law's face as she tried to formulate her thoughts. "That's . . . that's insane," she finally managed. "You must be mistaken."

"It's hard to mistake something like this. He's signed his name, so I think he's pretty sure about it."

15

"He can't be sure about it. Bishops don't get divorced, Lily. We make things work." She let out a short, hard breath. "This is so unlike him. Did you do something? In all his years, Worth has never gone this long without talking to me, and it just happens to be right after the two of you up and moved away. I knew something was wrong."

Lily pinched her lips together, willing herself to remain calm. "Mertha, your son is thirty years old. He's a grown man and he's making his own decisions. Trust me, I'm not standing in the way of him talking to you. I'm not standing in the way of him doing anything."

"Have you called him? Why don't I try calling him again?"

Lily had called him, in fact. Only once. The call went to voice mail, and she hadn't left a message. What was there to say? After that, she called Worth's office, but no one there had seen or heard from him.

"If it makes you feel better, try calling him," Lily said. "Maybe he'll answer you this time."

"I'll do that. I'll give him a call and see what in the world is going on. Just go easy on him." Mertha paused. "With this new job and the sudden move, he's been under a lot of stress. If you do talk to him, have him call me."

Lily sighed. "We both know you'll hear from him before I will. And when you do . . ." Lily paused, but the impulse to say the words was still there, so she continued. "Tell him not to come back."

There. The words were out. She was done. She'd expected anger, and it was there, in part, but what she felt most of all was relief.

Mertha was silent, and her shocked breaths whispered through the phone. When she finally spoke, her voice was icy. "You don't mean that."

"I do." Lily's retort was a jab of assertion. And it was true. She did mean it. She almost laughed at her unexpected boldness.

"You *don't,*" Mertha jabbed back. "You don't get to tell my son to stay away. He made a serious misstep when he married you, but what's done is done and we make the best of it. You do what you need to do to calm yourself down, but when all this blows over — and I will make sure it blows over — you'll need to be able to pick up the pieces, put them back together, and move forward. Trust me on this. You're his *wife.*"

"But I'm not," Lily said gently. "Not anymore."

# TWO

The secretary tapped lightly on the door, then opened it a crack.

"Lily Bishop is here. Are you ready?" Her voice was perky, her eyebrows planted high on her forehead.

"Send her in, please," Lily heard from the other side of the door.

With a flourish, the secretary opened the door a few feet and gestured with her free hand. "Go right on in." The woman's smile was wide and tight. Behind her, Lily saw another receptionist furtively glancing in their direction.

"Thank you." She cleared her throat and put one foot in front of the other. As she crossed the threshold, she eyed the temporary nameplate on the wall next to the door. Worth hadn't been there long enough to get a real nameplate. Instead, his name was written in Sharpie on a sheet of paper.

It was strange to walk into her husband's

office and see Harold Pender sitting behind the desk. Mr. Pender, a fixture back home in Atlanta, had recently hired Worth to head up the south Alabama branch of his real estate development company, Pender Properties, despite the fact that Worth had no real estate experience. The Bishop business was lumber, and everyone in the family had their fingers in it, including Worth, right up until the day he told his mother he wanted out.

Mr. Pender's jacket was draped across the back of the desk chair, his briefcase open on an adjacent seat. It was as if Worth had never been there at all. But there on the table under the window was the fern Lily had given him on his first day of work. When she bought it, the fern had vivid green leaves and healthy stems. Now the poor plant was in need of a good watering and dry leaves were scattered across the tabletop.

Mr. Pender motioned for her to have a seat across from the desk. When she was settled, he pushed aside a laptop and propped his hands on top of a pile of papers on the desk. She took in the deep red smudges beneath his eyes, the defeated slump of his shoulders. Instead of being back in Atlanta, presiding over council meetings and land acquisition dealings, Worth's boss was here, in Foley, Alabama, cleaning up Worth's mess.

"I'm sorry for the . . ." He gestured to the stacks of papers. "I was in the middle of a lot of projects back home when I heard what had happened here. This was a good deal for Worth. I'm still not sure what . . ." He rubbed the back of his neck. "I'm sorry. I know I don't need to rehash all this with you."

He paused, clearly waiting for her to speak, but she didn't have anything to say. After an awkward moment, he continued. "Things were already behind schedule when Worth arrived, and this new . . . situation . . . has slowed things down even more. There's a deal that's pending, and if I don't have someone here to handle it in the right way . . ." He spread his hands out on the desktop. "I'm sure you can see the difficult position this puts me in."

She tilted her head. "This must be very hard for you."

Mr. Pender reached up to his tie and loosened it. "I'm sorry. It's difficult all the way around, I know. I can't begin to imagine what it must be like for you. Worth didn't say anything to you about where he might have been going?"

She'd been asked that same question so many times in the days since he'd left, in so many different variations. At some point they were all going to have to accept that being Worth's wife did not make her privy to his interior life. His thoughts. His plans.

When she didn't answer, he reached for a folder and tapped it against the desk, then laid his hand on top and met her gaze. "Bottom line is I have to hire someone else to fill this position and I need to do it quickly. I have two guys interested, one who can start next week. I'm leaning in his direction." He paused and took a breath. "I've held off on this in the hopes that Worth would show up, but . . . I'm afraid I can only give you through the weekend to make living arrangements."

"Living arrangements?" Her mind spun into top gear. "What do you mean?"

"The house, in Pelican Cove? The new guy will live there. That's what the house is for. For quick starts, just until new hires can have a chance to look around and find a place that fits them."

"But that's — We rented that house. I know it's just temporary, but we were doing just what you said — living there until we found something else. I haven't had a chance to look around, but surely . . ."

She stopped when Mr. Pender propped his elbows on the desk. With one hand he took off his glasses, and with the other he pinched the bridge of his nose. Sweat pricked at Lily's hairline and under her arms as realization dawned on her.

"Mrs. Bishop —"

"Please stop calling me Mrs. Bishop." The words came out sharper than she intended. "That's my mother-in-law," she said, softer now. "I'm Lily. And the house is yours, isn't it?"

He sighed. "Lily, your home belongs to Pender Properties. It was a corporate lease, month-to-month, with the agreement that if Worth did not fulfill his job duties for whatever reason, the lease would be terminated. Unfortunately, that's the situation we're now in."

She thought back to the evening Worth signed the papers at their carved cherry dining table in their stately Tudor home in Atlanta. He'd even bought a small cake and stuck a candle in it, his attempt to make the move six hours south seem celebratory and exciting. Signing papers on a house! Starting a new job! At the beach! It was going to be great.

She knew the house was temporary, but she'd known nothing about a company lease with strings attached. She wracked her brain trying to remember his words, what that piece of paper looked like, but as usual he'd taken care of it all and she'd gone along with it. Why hadn't she asked more questions?

Lily stood abruptly. Mr. Pender looked up in expectation. His face was so hopeful, as if waiting for her to say something to take away his guilt at being the one chasing her out of her house. But she had nothing to say. He wasn't the guilty party, and she had no attachment to their house anyway. It would be easy to leave.

"Thank you, Mr. Pender." Lily stuck out her hand and waited for him to take it. They shook as if closing a deal, which, when she looked back on it, they kind of were.

He stood and rested his fingertips on the desk. "So . . ." He shoved his hands in his pockets, then pulled them out again.

"If you can give me a few days to make arrangements, I'll be out as soon as I can." She turned and moved toward the door.

Before she opened it, he spoke again. "I don't mean to pry, but I just want to make sure you're going to be okay. I assume you'll go back to Atlanta? I know Mertha will want to help." His eyes were softer now. "If you need any assistance with the move, you just let Debbie know and she'll make arrangements for you."

Lily nodded. "I'll be fine."

Outside the air was warm and thick against the unusual chill on her skin. She turned the corner, and when she was sure she couldn't be seen by anyone who might have been watching her through the office windows, she paused and inhaled, then blew the air out slowly.

In the week and a half since Worth had been gone, she'd made phone calls, taken pointless drives in the car, and paced back and forth, front door to window, expecting to see his car drive up.

Expecting it and fearing it at the same time.

She'd stayed up late into the nights, considering the unanswerable questions swelling up within her. Where was he? Would he change his mind? Did she want him to? What would she do now? His note was at the very back of the drawer in her bedside table, and she'd pulled it out and read it so many times its edges were becoming soft.

I can't do this anymore.

*Thank you, Worth. Neither can I.*

24

Standing on the sidewalk in front of Worth's office — his *former* office — with a closed door behind her and a hazy, unrecognizable path in front of her, Lily closed her eyes and thought of her mother.

*You be brave now,* her mother had whispered to her toward the end, her grip still strong and sure. She wished she could talk to her mom again, wished she could hear her soothing words and soak up her wisdom like dry desert sand.

Instead, she opened her eyes and found her car, climbed inside. She lifted her hands to the steering wheel. Through the windshield, she noticed a V of seagulls soaring overhead. A bird at the back of the V trailed off the end, separated from the bunch. As she watched, the gap between the lone bird and the group widened until the bird was alone in the sky, his wings flapping lazily, seemingly unconcerned by his solitude.

Lily tightened her fingers around the steering wheel as truths solidified in her tired mind, one by one.

She was not going back to Georgia. She had three days, at most, to find a new place to live. And she needed a job.

# THREE

When she walked into Rouses Market, the aisles of the tiny store were jammed with ladies sporting faintly purple hairdos and clip-on earrings. Everywhere she looked, small clusters of folks were comparing coupons and newspaper circulars. Near the front door, two women peered at a display of Pyrex dishes.

Lily eyed her quickly scrawled grocery list and started down the first aisle. A few minutes later her cart held buttermilk, flour, eggs, butter, and a package of bacon as she pulled into the produce section to grab some fresh fruit. She added a handful of kiwis to her cart, but as she turned toward the front of the store, she bumped into someone kneeling on the ground. Before she realized what had happened, lemons tumbled around her feet and clear across the tile floor. Lily peered around her cart and saw a broad woman dressed in a starched white apron staring back at her. The woman wore a hairnet pulled firmly over tight black curls.

"I'm so sorry," Lily said as she bent down to grab the runaway lemons. Just as she reached for one that had skittered under the apple display, a pair of purple tennis shoes with silver Velcro across the top paused in her field of vision.

"Don't you worry a thing about it," said the woman attached to the purple shoes.

Lily straightened. This woman was petite and wearing a jogging suit as purple as her shoes. In her ears were tiny silver earrings in the shape of airplanes. "Roberta's just in a hurry, and she gets clumsy when she goes too fast."

The large woman in the hairnet, who Lily assumed was Roberta, was shoving lemons in her cloth bag, her back to them. "I beg your pardon, Tiny," she said. "I am *not* clumsy. It's hard to hold on to a dozen lemons when someone rams you from behind."

Lily opened her mouth to apologize again, but Tiny shook her head. "You didn't ram," she whispered. "Gentle nudge." Then in her regular voice, "Looks like you have the makings of a darn good breakfast. Let me guess — waffles."

"Close. Pancakes. My mom's recipe."

The woman nodded. "I have a knack for these things. Oh, and you have kiwis. Did you know kiwifruit is named for a bird?"

"I did not know that." Lily couldn't keep the smile from her face.

"They are! These fuzzy things look so similar to a little brown bird in New Zealand that they named the fruit after the birds. Kiwis!"

Behind Tiny, Roberta let out a deep, throaty laugh. "Tiny Collins, is there anything you don't know?"

Tiny threw a look back at Roberta. "I know nothing about cooking. Not a smidgeon. That's why I show up at your café seven days a week." Turning back to Lily, she smiled. "Kiwi birds. Look it up when you get home. I'm sure you have the Google. Do you travel, hon?"

"Not really. Before I got married, I'd hardly left my hometown."

"And where was that?"

"North Georgia. A little town called Fox Hill."

Tiny paused, pondering. "Nope, never heard of it. But no matter. You're young. Plenty of time for New Zealand later. Did you know the Europeans used to ship their criminals off to New Zealand?"

"That was Australia." Roberta shook her head and dropped her bag of lemons into the cart. The bag was practical canvas with sturdy handles. It had a picture of a broken egg with an orange sun popping out of the eggshell. Cheery red letters across the top spelled out Sunrise Café.

Tiny noticed Lily eyeing the bag. "Have you ever been to the Sunrise?"

Lily shook her head. "I just moved here. Is it close by?"

"Oh no," Tiny said. "It might as well be in another country. You take a right at the airport, down West Boulevard, over the bridge, and around the bend. You can't miss the sign — it has this same sun, just like the bag. It's in Safe Harbor Village, where we live." When Lily didn't speak, Tiny continued. "It's a community for . . . well, I guess for old folks like us." She gestured to herself and Roberta. "It's right on the tip of Safe Harbor Island, looking out over Bon Secour Bay. It's a beautiful place, though I'm a little biased because it's home."

Behind her, Roberta rubbed her forehead. "Remind me not to take you shopping with me again. She could be an ax murderer and you've just told her where we sleep at night."

Tiny smiled, the apples of her cheeks as pink as a baby's. "She doesn't look much

29

like an ax murderer."

"They never do." Roberta pulled on Tiny's elbow and directed her toward the cash registers at the front of the store.

As they passed a rack of sunscreen and aloe gel, Tiny called out, "You should stop by sometime. We can continue our chat. You can tell me more about Fox Hill."

After stopping for a carton of milk, Lily paid for the groceries and walked toward the door. Along the front wall, a bulletin board held several layers of flyers and notes, all thumbtacked and flapping gently in the breeze that whooshed in every time the glass doors opened. She passed the board without a thought, then paused and took a step back. One flyer at the bottom corner might as well have jumped off the wall and pinched her.

"Help wanted," it read. "Hairstylist at Safe Harbor Village. Experience necessary."

The image came back to her in a rush, a great flood of memory. She closed her eyes and let her mind drift back to that frozen flash of time — the steamy heat, the clean scent of washed hair mixed with the chemical tang of dye and permanent solution. The headiness of women's camaraderie. Lives lived out in animated conversation, laughter, and tears. Oh, how she missed it. How she missed being a part of that whirlwind of life and love.

A moment later a cash register dinged. Lily opened her eyes and she was back in the grocery store, the glass door sliding open and closed, carts wheeling past her.

Outside, she put her hand up to her forehead to block the sun pouring through the high clouds. There, along the edge of the parking lot, Roberta was loading bags into the back seat of a blue Subaru. Tiny sat in the passenger seat checking her hair in the pull-down mirror. Lily hurried across the lot toward them.

"Excuse me. You said you live at Safe Harbor Village, right?"

Roberta looked up at the sound of Lily's voice and sighed. "I did not say that. Tiny did. Please tell me you're not going to kill us in our sleep."

"No, I just . . . I saw a note on the bulletin board." She gestured back toward the building. "About a hairstylist position?"

"That's right." Roberta's eyes narrowed.

"Is the position still available?"

Roberta pointed at her hairnet. "Does it look like I know anything about a hair salon?"

Lily tilted her head and shrugged. "Actually, with those curls, I'd guess you've spent a fair amount of time in a hairdresser's chair."

Roberta put a hand to her curls and patted them softly. "Well, maybe." She grabbed the last bag and shoved it in the car, then slammed the door. "What? You looking for a job?" Her eyes swooped over Lily, head to toe.

Lily fought the urge to beeline out to her own car. Instead, she squared her shoulders and sucked in her breath. "Maybe I am."

Roberta's eyebrows lifted, just a millimeter. She opened the driver's door and stepped one foot inside. "Stop by and talk to Rose," she said just before sitting down and pulling the door closed behind her. She cranked the engine, then pressed a button to roll down the window. "But watch out. She's got thorns."

Roberta backed up as Tiny waved from the front seat. Lily remained rooted where she was, her thoughts racing until a horn honked close by, startling her and making her jump back. She realized she was standing in the middle of the row, blocking a string of sedans trying to exit the parking lot. She waved an apology and walked across the lot to her own car.

On the drive back to the house, questions hovered around her like a fog she could almost see. Doubt and possibility slipped through her mind. Fear and hope mingled together.

Could she really look for a job here? In this unfamiliar beach town where she knew no one? She couldn't go back to Fox Hill; she'd ended that part of her life when she closed the door to Lillian's Place for the last time and handed the keys to the small house over to the new owners. There was always the option of going back to Atlanta, though it had been her home for only a short time. If she moved back there, she'd be closer to Mertha, closer to the people who would no doubt think Lily had done something to run Worth off. Looking at it that way, Alabama was preferable. Could she try to make a fresh start here? Wasn't that what she wanted?

Hunger grumbled in her stomach, reminding her of her mother's pancakes, which was the whole reason she'd gone to the store in the first place. With all the packing and unpacking over the last several weeks, she hoped she could locate the recipe.

The courtyard behind their rental house was comprised of two squares — one of concrete supporting the rusty wrought iron table and two plastic chairs, and the other of thick St. Augustine grass in need of a good mow. Lily had been in charge of cutting the grass at the house she shared with her mom back in Fox Hill, but in Atlanta, she and Worth had employed a landscaping service that took care of all their lawn needs. Not only did they not own a lawn mower, but Worth had never learned to operate one. Needless to say, no lawn mower had made the trek to the rental house in Foley, but their patch of grass was so small Lily could have cut it with a pair of kitchen shears. Not that it mattered now. In three days she'd be gone. She just didn't yet know where.

After dinner she sat in one of the plastic chairs and pulled her knees up to her chin. The air around her was tepid, like bathwater that had cooled just enough to make you want to get out and grab a towel. Above her she could barely make out the Little Dipper in the dark sky splotched with gray clouds.

Lily closed her eyes and ran her thumb across the paper resting in her lap. *Help wanted.* A flash lit up around her, and a moment later thunder rolled in the distance. The man who'd rung up her groceries at the store that afternoon had mentioned rain coming in. "After this, the heat will crank up. You just wait." More thunder, louder this time, then a breeze as soft as a baby's exhale lifted strands of hair around her face.

She lowered her knees and leaned forward on her elbows, staring at the piece of paper. She hadn't given a real haircut in well over a year. Trimming her own floppy auburn waves didn't count, and Worth always preferred to go to a ritzy gentlemen's barber shop, one that offered steamy towels and a shave with a straight-edge razor.

Lily's father had died when she was twelve, leaving her mother to try to make ends meet. As a house painter, her father had never made much money, definitely not enough to put any into savings, and after paying for the modest funeral, Lillian had to do something to keep the lights on. She started her salon with only a few female clients, offering trims and styles at their home in Fox Hill, a small mountain town fifty miles north of Atlanta.

Fox Hill was full of scrappy women who worked hard, mostly blue-collar jobs. Many of Lillian's customers were waitresses, some drove buses, some worked at apple orchards or in nearby towns touted as "great family getaways." Those women worked long shifts, then came home tired and bedraggled, and often found their way to Lillian's salon for a haircut or just for the camaraderie. These

35

were women who would rather go years without a cut than set a toe in one of the fancier places, those downtown salons offering ninety-dollar trims and a side of Botox.

Lillian made a place for these women. A place that felt comfortable, where they belonged. Her mother had a way with hair, drawing something out of a woman that had been hidden before. Something about the way she angled her scissors, brushed out a lock of hair, or added a curl or wave made her customers sit up straighter and lift their chins. They lost the hard edges around their mouths, their lips curving upward in a shy smile. Lily had seen it so many times, her mother's magic.

As word of Lillian's Place spread, more and more women came to the salon Lily's mom had set up in the back room off the kitchen. The space was small but it had a big, light-filled window that overlooked the vegetable garden and the chicken house. As she was able, Lillian added a second chair, then a sink and a second dryer. What had started as nothing more than a way to make money turned into a respite, a bright spot in women's otherwise hardworking days. The clean scent of shampoo and wet hair and baby powder against the simple dresses and worn shoes. The sharp *snip-snip* of her mother's silver scissors, her prized possession. How she blew the lock of curls out of her eyes as she cut and pinned and combed.

Lily helped out after school and on weekends. She started with sweeping the floors, washing hair, and checking ladies sitting under the hooded dryers, but she was always watching her mother's hands. As she learned the cuts and angles, the strokes and techniques, her mother let her do more and more, and when she was sixteen, she started cutting hair too. She even had some ladies request her when calling to make an appointment. Lillian was so proud. *Every woman needs a gift, Lily,* she said one day above the roar of a hair dryer. *This is yours.*

Thunder rolled, yanking Lily back to the present. A fine mist had begun falling from the sky, but still she sat. She wondered about the skill — *the gift* — her mother had been so proud for her to have. Would her mom still be proud knowing Lily had let that gift lie dormant for a year and a half? When she mentioned to Worth in the first year of their marriage that she was considering looking into renting a chair at a salon downtown, he'd been confused. "Rent a chair? And do what? Be a barber?"

"A barber is for men," she'd said with a

smile. "Women go to *hairstylists.* Salon Nouveau is a nice place. It's where your mother gets her hair cut."

"I know that, but don't you think . . . Well, she might be a little embarrassed to have her daughter-in-law working at the place where she gets her hair done."

"Embarrassed? What's embarrassing about being a hairstylist?" When he didn't respond, she shrugged. "Okay, so I'll find another place. There are other salons around here. It's not like I don't have the time."

"Lily, I — You don't have to do this, you know. You don't have to get a job. That's why I work hard — so you can stay home."

He never did understand that "staying home" wasn't her goal. She'd been working for more than ten years by the time she met Worth, and sitting still wasn't something she knew how to do.

"Look, if you really want to work," he added when she began to object, "tell my mom. She's been looking for someone to work in the front office a few days a week. You'd be perfect for it." His tone indicated his pleasure at having solved the problem, and Lily let the matter drop. Now she wondered why she'd let it go — let her gift go — without a fight.

On the table next to her, her phone buzzed with a text. It was from Mertha.

When are you heading back this way? Harold probably can't hold the house for you much longer.

Lily rubbed her forehead. Of course Worth's mother knew the details of their corporate lease. She probably knew the details of their entire marriage. Possibly even where he was at this moment, although she'd denied any knowledge of his whereabouts every time Lily had asked.

The guesthouse will work for you just fine, her mother-in-law's next text read.

Just until you and Worth sort things out.

*Sort things out?* The sorting had been done as far as Lily was concerned. And why was Mertha offering Lily a place to stay? Lily assumed Mertha would be glad to be rid of her, considering Mertha had never wanted Worth to marry her in the first place. Lily pressed the button on the side of the phone and darkened the screen. Then, on second thought, she opened the text message and tapped out a quick response.

I'm not coming back.

Mertha's reply was instant:

Don't be stubborn. Worth would want you

back here with family.

*Not family,* Lily thought. *Not anymore. If they ever were at all.*

Worth lost his say when he filed for divorce.

This time she turned the phone off entirely.

It had been a little over two weeks since the morning she woke up to his absence, and regardless of what Mertha said about him needing time to sort things out, Lily felt in her bones, in her blood, that he wasn't coming back. That they really were done. Hour by hour, minute by minute even, she seesawed between fizzy bubbles of relief in her chest — a relief that surprised her every time it showed its giddy face — and a terror so solid and thick she could feel it threatening to suffocate her.

But as she had for the last two weeks, she swallowed the terror, stuffed it down into a small space in her overcrowded heart, and mentally took the next step. She smoothed her hand across the front of the flyer once more. *Safe Harbor Village.*

Early the next morning, in the quiet stillness of her rented house, Lily called the number on the flyer before she could change her mind.

"May I ask why you're calling?" the

clipped voice on the phone asked. "Are you a potential resident?"

"Oh no, I —"

"I have to ask because we only have a couple cottages open at this time, and we require a detailed background check, personal references, and a phone interview before we invite potential residents for an on-site tour. I'd hate for you to drive all this way for nothing."

"I see. Do you require all that for the hairstylist position?"

"Hairstylist." The woman's voice flattened.

"Yes, ma'am. I saw the flyer at the grocery store and . . . someone told me to come see Rose."

"Is that so?"

"It is. I used to cut hair. And I'm looking for a job." Lily nibbled on her thumbnail.

"Well. That was fast." She sighed as if disappointed to have a job candidate. "I suppose I could see you around two o'clock today. Do you have a pen? I'll tell you how to get here, but you'll have to pay attention."

Lily jotted down the directions and kept herself busy until it was time to go. Her stomach was a knot of nerves, fluttery and vaguely nauseated, but she tamped down

41

the butterflies. She knew nothing about this place or the people who lived there, but it was a job she could do. She could cut hair. She generally liked people. And she didn't want Worth's money anymore. She needed a way to make her own.

Lily turned right just past the sign for Jack Edwards Airport, then took another right. The road ahead was long and empty, straight as an arrow, and lined on both sides with tall trees and thick brush. The woman on the phone had said this road would feel too long, like she'd taken a wrong turn.

"Stay the course," she'd said. "The road only leads one place, and we're at the end."

Lily gripped the steering wheel, the sun's heat sinking into her palms, giving her courage. The thing that had been needling the back of her mind since Worth's disappearance, the thing that kept her hanging on instead of drifting away, now stood at attention in her mind. She was alone, but she was enough. No one was coming to her rescue, but maybe what would save her was inside her. Maybe it had been inside her all this time.

# THE VILLAGE VINE

## Your Source for Neighborhood News

May 9, 2018
Compiled by Shirley Ferrill

## GOOD DAY, SAFE HARBOR VILLAGE!

### TIDES
High tides will be in the 6:15–7:45 p.m. range, while low tides will fall somewhere between 4:10 and 6:20 a.m. Make your fishing plans accordingly.

### WEATHER
Summer is cranking up early with temps in the mid-80s during the day but falling pleasantly to the mid- to upper 60s at night. If you take an evening stroll, consider bringing a light sweater.

### MARINE LIFE
A manatee has been spotted by more than one concerned villager in recent weeks. It seems the large mammal is trying to swim toward the Bon Secour River, but the current is pushing it back. Attempts to direct it toward the bay have been unsuccessful. Marine authorities have been contacted, and I will update you again as soon as I find out more.

## SAFE HARBOR NEWS

- The Summer Kickoff Party will be held the last Saturday in May. I know it's a few weeks before the meteorological start of summer, but as we all know, temps creep up as soon as the white pants come out, and the beginning of another summer season is a reason to celebrate.

- For months now we've been hearing about a possible new resort, Island Breeze, coming to the island. The name may be apropos, but can you imagine the trucks that would tear up the roads and the commotion a building project like that would stir up? I assure you, villagers, I was ready to stand all day with my picket signs if necessary, but the powers that be have elected to build their fancy resort elsewhere. It seems people are learning about our quiet little haven here on Safe Harbor Island. Next time someone asks you where you live, consider telling them about the odor from Humphrey Hammond's infernal crab traps.

### RECREATION

The paddleboats Coach ordered should arrive any day now. As soon as they're in, he will plan a guided tour of Bon Secour River for interested parties. You'll find the sign-up sheet on the clubhouse bulletin board. I feel it is my civic duty to inform all of you that the last time Coach was on a nonmotorized vessel, he and everyone in the boat capsized. Sign up at your own risk.

## REMINDERS FROM MANAGEMENT

- Please keep the homeowners' association guidelines in mind as you make decisions regarding outdoor décor. Yard art is strictly forbidden. This includes, but is not limited to, dolphin-shaped mailboxes, concrete or plastic figures (flamingos, deer, garden gnomes, etc.), and oversize bird feeders. Remember, if it detracts, give it the ax!

- Dogs are tolerated in the village, but not their droppings. If your canine friend must relieve himself or herself, do us all a favor — pick up the waste and dispose of it properly. And not in the marina! There is a $100 fine for every violation. (Any money collected will be added to the bingo pot.)

Lastly, *The Village Vine* received a letter this week, and as editor, I feel compelled to share it with all of you:

To Whom It May Concern,

With last year's departure of Beverly Pine and the resulting closure of the village hair salon, I would like to request that management hire a replacement. I understand that some people think a village hairstylist is unnecessary, but those of us who have been traveling all the way to Mobile to get a decent haircut would disagree. Other than an hour of travel time, our only other option is Coach Beaumont, who says he cut the hair of his whole fraternity during his college years. We ladies feel it is within our rights as Village homeowners to have access to a reasonably proximate and qualified hairstylist, no offense to Coach.

Sincerely, and with solid trust in management's excellent decision-making skills,
Tiny Collins

# SUNRISE CAFÉ MENU

## May 10–May 16

Mains: spaghetti & meatballs, shrimp & grits, Mississippi pot roast
Sides: honey-glazed carrots, fried okra, butter beans, macaroni & cheese
Desserts: chocolate icebox pie, layered lemon cake, peach cobbler

# FOUR

Rose Carrigan woke to the sound of singing. It was far off, but it was insistent. Deep. Male. Perky.

She groaned and pulled the pillow over her head, then shoved it away when she realized the voice still trickled through the layers of cotton and down. Exasperated, she sat up, rubbed her face, and threw back the blanket. The tile floor was cool on her bare feet, and she was glad she hadn't put down carpet like so many of the other residents had done in their own cottages. Carpet harbored all manner of untidy organisms she'd rather not have camped out around her toes. Hard tile floor suited her just fine.

Before she yanked open the French doors of her second-floor balcony, she spotted Coach's red hat bouncing on the other side of the tall grass alongside the water. All she could see of him was his hat, but it moved swiftly back and forth, telling her he was in his canoe again, rowing. He continued to warble, his voice winding its way inside her bedroom even though the windows were firmly closed.

She wrinkled her nose and exhaled. He was so doggone cheerful it sometimes made her stomach ache. The man was known to burst into song at any given moment, as if he couldn't bear to keep his happiness — his exuberance at nothing more than plain old life — to himself. Then he had the gall to try to spread it around.

She turned for the stairs, grabbing her cotton robe off the end of the bed on the way. Downstairs she tightened the belt around her middle before opening the back door and tromping out onto the damp grass. At the water's edge, she waited for Coach to round the bend.

"Good morning, Rose," he huffed when he saw her, his cheeks pink with exertion. "You're up bright and early today."

She crossed her arms and tried not to look at his chest, bare as the day was long. "I am up early, Coach Beaumont. Any idea why?"

He paused in his rowing and let the canoe coast for a moment before breaking into a grin. "I don't have the foggiest. Lady problems?"

She tightened her mouth. "Is there any

reason you are outside my bedroom window singing this early in the morning?"

"Rose, I am not outside your bedroom window." He spread his arms toward the bay, smooth and silver as a mirror. "I'm out here enjoying the beginning of a brand-new day in the most beautiful spot on God's blue earth." He shook his head. "I can't help it if your bedroom window just happens to be within earshot of my enjoyment of the morning."

"Just . . . try to enjoy yourself a little quieter. I'm going back to sleep." She started back for her house, then whirled around again. He was still watching her. "What's that song you're singing, anyway? It sounds teenagery."

"It's John Mellencamp, sugar. And he's not teenagery — he's one for the ages." Coach picked up his oars and resumed rowing. " 'It's a lonely ol' night,' " he sang, his voice nicer than she cared to admit. " 'Can I put my arms around you?' "

She sighed and turned again, stepping firmly through the grass, wishing it were something harder so she could emphasize her displeasure with the sound of stomping feet. *Silly old man.* Making her feel like a squirmy teenager. Rose Carrigan wasn't about to let anyone put their arms around her, and she surely did not allow herself to feel ruffled by a man who went by the name Coach and wore flip-flops every day but Christmas, and some years, even then.

She was in charge of this place. The keeper of the keys, as it were. For the moment at least. The unexpected message in her inbox a few days ago had gone a long way toward redirecting the way she saw her future.

But until she made a decision, she was the village owner.

Back inside her spotless kitchen, she flipped on her four-cup Mr. Coffee and grabbed a pad of paper and a pencil. If she wanted to add another rule to the *Safe Harbor Village Handbook,* she could certainly do so. While coffee dripped into the glass carafe, Rose stood at her counter and wrote a note in her careful penmanship.

No loud noise — including singing — before 7 a.m.

"There." She ripped out the page, folded it once, and slid it into an envelope. She'd stick it in Shirley Ferrill's mailbox after breakfast.

When the coffeepot stopped dripping, she poured a cup and sat down at her kitchen table. It wasn't until she saw Coach rowing back toward shore that she remembered she'd meant to go back to sleep.

She sighed and sipped her coffee, but its heat burned her tongue. She set the mug down with a thud and a bit sloshed over the edge. As she wiped up the mess with a dish towel, she watched Coach out the window and huffed.

Twenty minutes into the day and he'd already ruined it.

After her too-early start, Rose felt off. Not her usual self. Her body felt tired, though her mind was a hive of activity. She tried to settle herself with a cup of lemon tea and a chapter of an old Anne Rivers Siddons novel she'd picked up secondhand at Beach Reads, and when that didn't work, she found herself in the same place she always ended up when she felt out of sorts — her rose garden.

She knew it bordered on cheeky to have a rose garden when one's name was Rose, but the bushes were planted for her as a gift, and Rose had come to accept her prickly relationship with them. They were as much a part of her life as her elevated blood pressure and newly overactive bladder. Many times she'd considered asking Rawlins to pull them out and plant something simple in their place. Some low-maintenance shrubbery — Mexican sage maybe, or plumbago. Something that wasn't so needy. But each time, she reconsidered, then picked up her pruning shears or her bottle of fungicide, and slipped on her gardening gloves instead.

Sometimes she thought of them as her thinking gloves, because often as soon as she pulled them on and took her place in the flower beds, her mind settled, discarding unnecessary worries and elevating those that needed her attention. And today what needed her attention, what was causing her mind to vibrate on overdrive, was that email.

Rose, I know we haven't spoken in a while, but I can only hope the news I have to share with you will be of the welcome variety. We've finally been offered a chance to sell Safe Harbor Village, and for a pretty penny too. You and I would both be set, and you could do whatever you like — stay in the village under the new ownership or take your money and move elsewhere. The world is your oyster.

Let me know your thoughts. Terry

She'd read the email so many times she

could recite it word for word, though she hadn't spoken of it to a single soul in the village. No need to start a panic when she hadn't decided what to do.

But somewhere down deep, underneath everything else piled on top that covered up truth and honesty, Rose knew what she wanted her answer to be. She wanted to say yes to Terry. She had nowhere else to go, but looking back over her life, she never could have imagined she'd be alone at nearly seventy years old and in charge of a bunch of people just as old as she was. This was where life had placed her, but she never thought she'd stay as long as she had.

She was reaching down to check a stem for signs of the black spot fungus that arrived each humid summer, when she heard rapid footsteps on the street. She turned to see Peter and Ida Gold fast-walking toward her, their slim hips swiveling in tandem, arms pumping, sweatbands around their foreheads as if it were already ninety degrees out.

Peter held up a hand as they approached. "Morning, Rose."

Rose nodded. "Peter. Ida."

The Golds were the healthiest residents at the village. As bronzed as pennies twelve months out of the year, they walked three fifteen-minute miles every morning and snacked on sunflower seeds and rice cakes. Peter was still a proud six feet tall with thick hair and a *Magnum, P.I.* mustache, though his was silvery white.

A former set designer, Ida was obsessed with Old Hollywood and had even been cast as an extra in several Rat Pack movies. These days, as dementia began to take root, she often thought she was on a movie set, even going so far as to talk to "the director" about where she should stand when she entered a room.

In deference to Peter's commanding presence and his unflagging love and devotion to Ida, everyone in the village obeyed his instructions not to question or correct her but just to go along with whatever she said.

This morning Ida seemed clearheaded. She walked over and stood next to Rose, hands on her hips, dainty sweat beading on her top lip. Estée Lauder perfume rolled off her in waves, and Rose turned her head for a quick moment to take a breath.

"They're lovely, Rose. You really have the touch."

"Well." Rose swallowed the compliment as if it were vinegar. "I don't know how far that touch will get me later in the summer when these leaves are coated in black spot."

"But you won't let that happen. You work your roses like Ginger Rogers danced." When Ida leaned down to smell a Sweet Juliet, Rose lifted her eyes to Peter, who smiled and shrugged. He checked his watch.

"You're usually already gone by the time we pass your house," he said. "Are the Bubbas not meeting this morning?" The Bubba Club was the group of men who met weekly in the main clubhouse to discuss everything from politics to prostates over coffee and Krispy Kreme doughnuts.

"Fred had an early doctor's appointment in Mobile. I'm heading up there soon to open the door for the rest of them."

"Wouldn't it be easier if you just gave them a key?"

"I can't hand out keys like candy. Someone has to make sure no one tries to pull any funny stuff."

Peter's laughter was booming and jovial. "Some funny stuff is good for the soul every now and then. You should give it a try."

Rose snorted.

He touched Ida's shoulder. "We need to get moving if we want to be back in time for Kelly and whichever young man is sitting in the chair next to her these days."

Ida straightened up. "Oh, it's that Ryan Seacrest. I could listen to him talk all day."

"Well, let's get you on home then. He's on in twenty minutes." Peter put his hand on the small of his wife's back as she turned and blew a kiss back to Rose.

Rose watched them as they walked away, and something in her heart clenched. So many residents had found community within the gates of Safe Harbor Village. Enjoying life together with other people had never come naturally to Rose. More often than not, she found herself on the outside of everyone else, wishing she could be a part of things, never willing to admit it bothered her that she wasn't.

Maybe it *was* time she moved on. Hang up her visor, hand over her keys, and watch as a well-oiled company came in, rewrote her handbook, and took control. No one would miss her one bit.

# FIVE

After a quick bite to eat, Rose changed clothes, then hopped on her bicycle — a navy blue Schwinn she'd had for decades — and headed for the clubhouse situated near the entrance to the village. As a common area for residents, the clubhouse served as the backdrop to daily game show viewings, intense chess matches lasting for hours, and all manner of book clubs, card games, recipe swaps, and general gossip sessions.

With the village office attached to the clubhouse, separated by only a thin wall and a glass door, Rose was literally in the middle of the hubbub whether she wanted to be or not. "Not" was her standard preference.

She opened the door and winced as the bell clanged, announcing her presence to absolutely no one. On a whim, she untied the ribbon attaching the bell to the door and dropped the whole thing in the trash can. The clang was satisfying, but it felt even better to see the bell sitting there at the bottom of the plastic bag, the gong silenced by a ball of tissue.

Rose flipped on the lights and twisted the plastic rods on the blinds. There. The place looked a little less barren with some sunlight streaming in. Rose preferred to work with minimal distraction, and therefore the small office held only two desks, a computer and printer, a telephone, and a file cabinet. The white walls were bare except for a framed print from a 1950 *Farmers' Almanac* showing the phases of the moon from the month of her birth.

If the office was stark, the clubhouse just on the other side of the glass door was its polar opposite. Over the years, residents had filled the space with countless kitschy beach baubles and decorations. A wooden replica of a shrimp boat and multiple dolphin statues and coral reef snow globes dotted side tables, and several old printers' boxes hung on the walls holding a beach-worth of seashells. A huge, chemically shined sailfish adorned the wall over the TV, and the tabletop lamps were in the shape of seahorses.

Facing away from the riot of color, Rose settled into her ergonomic desk chair behind the larger of the two desks and flipped on the computer. When she opened her email, she was dismayed by the number of new messages that had come in overnight. A small group of residents — mostly new, and therefore unaccustomed to the way things worked at the village — were in the middle of a spat over whether they had the right to drape beach towels over the lounge chairs by the pool to save them for later use. Now everyone was up in arms about one neighbor's use of the word *entitled.*

Occasionally she wondered if the work was too much for one woman. She wasn't above admitting her mind wasn't quite as sharp as it used to be when she and her husband — *ex*-husband — Terry, had first started out, but she hadn't had the best luck with office help. Their first receptionist, Joan, turned out to have questionable morals and fled the village with Terry without a care in the world, her hair blowing in the breeze.

A few years ago she hired another assistant who, thankfully, was fifty years old and built like a Ford F-150. Aside from being an ace on a riding lawn mower, Marge helped with office duties — mostly fielding questions, complaints, and suggestions from the residents in the village and scheduling appointments with electricians and plumbers.

The job also involved the more delicate work of keeping up with the village calendar, but Rose always reserved this particular duty for herself. It was one thing to answer phones. It was another thing to work the schedule in just the right way to make sure groups like the Jesus and Jewelry crafters didn't meet at the same time as the Rowdy Romance Readers. The atmosphere in the clubhouse could deteriorate rather quickly if the schedule was not handled properly.

After Marge moved away, Rose took on the bulk of the responsibilities herself. She could have hired someone else, but there were very few people in the world whom she trusted — especially when it came to fine-tuning the inner workings of her business — and none of them resided in Safe Harbor Village.

She'd been working through the emails for an hour when the phone rang. The voice on the other end was young, which was unusual. When the woman asked about the hairstylist position, Rose propped an elbow on the desk and rubbed her eyes. As if the village needed a hairstylist. An on-site hair salon had never been in the plans, but back when the village was pristine and new, a group of residents — mostly female, though there were some vocal men in the group too

— had lobbied for one, saying when they decided to buy homes here, it was under the agreement that the village would provide many of their daily needs.

"That means shelter," Rose had patiently explained. "Access to food. Medical care. Those are your basic necessities, and you have them here. Hair care is just . . . luxury."

"And what's wrong with that?" one woman had argued. "We're in the prime of our life, with retirement dollars to spend, and if I want to be able to get my hair done twice a week, is that too much to ask?"

Rose had finally caved and recruited Beverly, a hairdresser from the Supercuts down Highway 59, to be the village hair guru. At the residents' insistence and under Beverly's direction, Rose agreed to outfit the bottom floor of one of the empty cottages with a hooded dryer, a swivel chair, and a basin sink for hair washing. Rose thought the matter was closed, but it wasn't long before the residents started complaining of Beverly's manner of work.

"She washes hair like she's scrubbing a casserole dish and chops like a drill sergeant." And that came from a male customer.

"You asked for a hairdresser and you got one," Rose told them all. "Beggars can't be choosers."

They'd accepted Beverly's particular manner of scalp cleansing and her back-to-basics haircuts because they had to, but when Beverly started talking about moving away to be closer to family, no one tried to talk her out of it.

After almost a year of no hair service, Rose agreed to hire another hairdresser, if only to quiet everyone's ranting and pleading. Tiny Collins wasted no time slapping up flyers on every window and bulletin board from Loxley to Orange Beach. And now someone had answered the call.

She wanted to ask the woman on the phone what her qualifications were, but she'd included right there on the flyer, in black-and-white, "experience necessary." The woman did say she used to cut hair, but Rose wouldn't put it past a person in desperate need of a job to inflate trimming one's own bangs into a full-fledged hairdressing career. If the woman was applying with no experience, then that was her own bag of bad apples.

With a hard knot in the center of her stomach, Rose agreed to see the woman at two o'clock.

Rose waited on the porch of the office at

1:55, cup of coffee in hand. When she saw the unfamiliar white car pull slowly into the small parking lot, she stepped behind a wide sago palm so she could get a stealthy look at the prospective employee.

The woman sat in the car for a long moment with the engine running. Sunlight glinted off the windshield, making her face a mess of shadows and light. All Rose could tell was that the woman was sitting very still. Finally she cut off the engine, opened the door, and stood.

Rose sighed. She didn't know what she'd been hoping for, but it wasn't this. Demure white blouse with short sleeves fluttering in the breeze, pale blue skirt, flat shoes. Hair the color of burnished copper pulled partly up on one side, revealing a curve of cheek and the soft scoop of neck. Young. Lovely.

*Of course,* Rose thought.

Rose watched her for a moment, then stepped out from behind the palm. "Over here," she called.

The woman shielded her eyes from the sun with her free hand. "Rose Carrigan?"

"That's me. I assume you're the one who called about the hairdresser position."

"Yes, ma'am."

Rose opened the glass door, but when she looked behind her, the woman wasn't following. "We can't very well do the interview out here in the parking lot. It's too hot. You might as well come on in."

Inside, the woman stood behind the chair across from the desk. "I'm Lily Bishop. Thank you for letting me come," she said, lowering herself to the seat.

Rose brushed nonexistent dust off the surface of her desk, then clasped her hands together and sat back in the chair. She anchored her feet firmly to keep the chair from swiveling and aggravating her vertigo. "I have to admit, you're not quite what I expected."

Lily's eyebrows rose a fraction. "Why's that?"

"It just seems that someone so . . . young . . . would want to work with people your own age. Most of the people who live here are more than twice as old as you. You're, what — twenty-five?"

It was probably frowned upon — if not downright illegal — to ask a potential employee her age, but Rose needed to know. She had a knack for correctly assuming other people's ages, as well as their personality type, and the only time she'd been wrong on both counts was with the original Safe Harbor Village receptionist, the scandalous Miss Joan Temple. She was not going to be wrong again.

"Twenty-eight."

Rose lifted her chin. "Ah." Close enough. "As I was saying, the residents here are all decades older than you. Most are over sixty. We have one who just celebrated his ninety-first birthday. Are you sure you would be comfortable cutting hair in this environment?"

Lily opened her mouth, but it took a moment for her to formulate words. "So this is . . . What type of village is this?"

"Did you not see it on the sign? Safe Harbor Village is an active lifestyle community." Rose enunciated carefully to make sure the girl understood. "There are no rules per se dictating that people must be over a certain age to apply for residence, but you would be the youngest face around here by . . . well, by a large margin."

Lily nodded. Her hands were in her lap and she was twisting a thin gold band around her ring finger. Rose could already tell what was going to happen. Any second now Lily would stand, thank Rose for her time, and walk out. Why would a woman like her choose to work among a bunch of old coots in a moss-draped spit of land miles away from any kind of activity frequented by the young? Nope. Lily Bishop was not it. Rose had a hunch for these things.

Lily took a deep breath and sat up straighter in her chair. "That doesn't bother me at all."

Rose cleared her throat. "Why don't you tell me about yourself. Your family, where you live . . . ."

She smiled. "I'm from Georgia. Fox Hill. But more recently I lived in Atlanta. I moved here with my —" She stopped, as if the words froze on her lips, then exhaled.

"Are you okay?"

"I'm fine." She gave a little shake of her head. "I moved here with my husband — Worth — but . . . well, I'm on my own now."

She waited, as if to give Rose a chance to comment, and when Rose remained silent, Lily continued. "My mother had a hair salon at the back of our house when I was young, and I started cutting hair when I was a teenager. My mom passed away five years ago. I kept the salon going as long as I could, but I ended up having to sell it, and I moved to Atlanta to look for another job. A way to support myself a little more securely. Instead, I met Worth."

"I see," Rose said, although she didn't see anything clearly. Not yet, anyway. "I'm sorry about your mother."

67

A small smile and a quick nod. "Thanks. It was quick. Unexpected. At least I didn't expect it."

"Yes. Death is always unexpected, even when we know it's coming." The words slipped out before Rose had a chance to bite them back. Lily's eyebrows rose, recognition flooding her face. Rose mentally chastised herself for letting her guard slip. There was no need to invite personal confidences in a business interview.

She cleared her throat. "So you're from Georgia, and you moved down here for . . . work?"

Lily nodded. "Worth took a new job in Gulf Shores — well, he said it was in Gulf Shores, but it was actually in Foley. I haven't had a chance to see much of the beach."

"How long have you been here?"

"Just a few weeks."

Rose raised her eyebrows. "You're very new in town. And your husband isn't with you?" Something was going on — Rose could smell it. She wondered if she should be entertaining the idea of hiring someone with so much obvious baggage.

"It's . . . it's a bit of a complicated story, Mrs. Carrigan. If it's okay with you, I'll tell you about it at another time. If you decide to offer me the job."

"Okay. Well, if you can't tell me anything else about yourself, why don't I tell you a little more about our village here. My ex-husband and I built this place from the ground up a little over forty years ago. I'm the owner — well, co-owner. Terry is considered a silent owner. But for all practical purposes, I'm in charge. I'm also the manager, and as such, I do all the hiring and oversight. We do have a homeowners' association to take care of things like landscaping, collection of dues, facilities maintenance and upkeep, and rule enforcement. However, I'm the head of the HOA, so I still have the final say-so."

There. Rose always felt better once she'd established she was the boss.

"We had a hairdresser here until about a year ago. Beverly. She was . . . sufficient. But she moved away to be closer to her grandkids and I, for one, don't blame her. I imagine grandchildren far outweigh the joys of washing and setting Roberta's curls once a week."

Lily smiled. "I think I met her in the grocery store. Does she work at a café?"

"She doesn't *work* at a café. She owns Sunrise Café. She has one employee, a young man who takes food orders and tends the bar. Roberta does the rest, including cooking the food. She's a very capable woman." Rose liked capable women, though most of the ladies she met did not qualify as capable. Capable of backing their cars into mailboxes, maybe, giving Rose one more thing to have to fix, but at the first sign of turmoil or trauma, most of the women she knew would crumble and break.

"Do you have grandchildren?" Lily asked.

"Excuse me?"

"You said grandkids would be better than doing hair. I was just wondering if you have any."

Rose shook her head. "No. I don't. Now, correct me if I'm wrong, but it sounds like some time has passed since you've given a proper haircut. Is that right?"

Lily paused. "Well . . . yes."

Rose sat back in her chair just as Lily leaned forward. She rested her hands flat on Rose's desk, fingers spread. Her nails were short, stubby, the skin around the edges pink and raw. A small Band-Aid wrapped her left pinkie nail. When Lily noticed Rose staring at her hands, she pulled them back into her lap. Rose looked up and met Lily's gaze.

"I need this job, Mrs. Carrigan."

Rose shook her head. "It's Rose. Just Rose."

"I can cut hair, Rose. It's like riding a bicycle. If you have the skill, it's not something you forget." She tucked her hair behind her ears. Her face was bare, just a hint of pink in her cheeks and smudges of deeper pink just under her eyes. So many emotions were written across the peaks and valleys of her face — anxiety, sadness, hope. Desperation, stark and familiar. Rose fought the urge to reach across the desk and take Lily's hands in hers.

Instead, she opened a file folder sitting on the edge of the desk, just to have something to do. "I assume you've kept your license to cut hair current and up to date?"

"Yes. It's current. It's in the car — I can run out and grab it if you'd like to see it."

"It's not necessary at this point." Rose exhaled and stood up. Lily followed the older woman's movements, her eyes piercing. For a brief moment, Rose saw a flare of determination. It had bubbled up from somewhere, and Rose was glad to see it.

She closed the file folder on the table in front of her and slid it back to the edge of the desk. "Let's take a walk."

Outside, the sky was pale blue with high wispy clouds skirting around. A few people

71

from the maintenance team knelt in the flower beds on the side of the clubhouse, and the smell of freshly cut grass and the tang of motor oil filled the air. Rose cast a quick glance down to the marina to where Humphrey Hammond was baiting a crab trap with chunks of dead fish, an odor she could never stomach.

Instead of the boardwalk, she guided Lily toward the sidewalk running alongside Anchor Lane. They paused a moment to let the mail truck pass by. Next to her, Lily tilted her face up to the sun for a moment, eyes closed against the brightness. She inhaled deeply, a tiny smile playing on her lips. *My goodness,* Rose thought. *The woman is blooming right in front of me.*

When the truck moved on, they walked and Rose pointed out various residents' cottages lining the road. Each one was painted the same shade of white; the only variation came in the color of the wooden shutters — lime green, pink, mango, turquoise. Up ahead, the road came to a T at Port Place, with more cottages to the left and shops to the right.

When Terry first mapped out the site of Safe Harbor Village, he said it would be different from previous planned communities he'd built. "It has to fit the contours of the land, and with the island coming to a point here, we're going to have to go with a single road, rather than a more spread-out neighborhood feel. You sure you're still okay with this?"

Rose remembered how, all those years ago, she'd nodded, the fire in her belly smothering the knot of nerves formed by the idea of forsaking her family's land.

"It's not a bad piece of real estate, honestly," he'd admitted. "I think you made a good call. Sunset views of the bay, peace and quiet. Not your regular tourist destination, that's for sure. It'll attract a different kind of crowd."

Walking down Anchor Lane, toward the bay that offered such wide sunset views, Rose thought of the "crowd" that had gathered at the village in the years since Terry had been gone — those with more years behind them than ahead. Those looking for one more shot at a type of childlike freedom, despite the havoc age wreaks on a body and mind. Here, along this quiet shore, these people were hoping to find a second chance at happiness.

Was the village successful? Not many people moved away, and if they did, it was usually because of family demands, not dissatisfaction. That said something about the community here, didn't it? Rose liked to think this village was the one good thing she'd done in her life — the only thing she hadn't messed up. She may not have been a part of the community, never quite fitting into the social life of the village, but she was happy that in some way she'd helped create it. And with Terry's email hovering at the edges of her mind, she wondered if that community would remain even if the ownership were to change hands.

Lily paused with her hands on her hips and looked down the road. "You said everyone who lives here is . . . older. An active lifestyle community. What exactly does that mean? Is everyone healthy? Or are there nurses and doctors or . . ."

"Most everyone is healthy. We do have a clinic, just up there with the rest of the shops." Rose pointed ahead to where the road veered right. "A nurse is in the office three days a week to assist those who need help managing their medications. She'll do a basic workup — check blood pressure, cholesterol, bone density, weight. She can do hearing and vision tests. If anyone comes down with a bug, it's easier for them to stop in and see her rather than make an appointment with a doctor in Gulf Shores or Foley. For the most part, though, everyone is healthy and vigorous. This is just like any other neighborhood. It just happens to attract people who are a little more seasoned."

"I see. And you mentioned the shops. That's where the hair salon is?"

"That's right. The salon is across the street from Sunrise Café. We have a secondhand bookstore, Beach Reads. Shirley Ferrill manages that. There's a clothing store, the Pink Pearl. That's Janelle's domain. Fran Metzger runs the Masthead, but it's back by the office. It's not much more than a general store, but she keeps a few shelves stocked with basic items — some grocery staples, first aid supplies, laundry detergent, that sort of thing. Keeps people from having to drive all the way into Gulf Shores if they run out of coffee or Metamucil."

"So you have pretty much everything you need right here." Lily's smile faltered. "It seems like a really nice place."

Rose straightened the visor on her head. "Do you have —"

Before she could continue, she heard the unmistakable purr of a golf cart on the road behind them. Rose closed her eyes for a moment, then turned.

Coach Beaumont had bought himself the golf cart a couple of weeks ago, and he'd wasted no time decorating it with flowered leis as if this were the South Pacific. She'd tried to rule against the cart in last week's association meeting, but once Coach told the members it was street legal, even going so far as to volunteer to bring in a Baldwin County police officer to swear to it, they overruled Rose's complaint. Peter Gold even asked if Coach would give him and Ida a ride home in the ridiculous thing.

Today there were some additions to his decorations: two fuzzy coconuts hanging from the rearview mirror and Janelle Blackmon sitting on the seat next to him, just as pink and perky as she could be.

Coach beeped his horn, as if they hadn't already noticed him. When he pulled up to a stop next to them, the coconuts knocked together like wooden wind chimes.

"Hello, Rose." He grinned and ran his hand through his windblown hair. His white button-down shirt was open at the neck, revealing tan skin. Rose quickly forced her gaze away when she realized she was staring. Next to him, Janelle smoothed the front of her skirt, which was a couple inches shorter than Rose would have preferred. Her ample chest pushed against the confines of her bubble gum–pink blouse, defiant of her age. It was a shame Rose's jurisdiction didn't extend to residents' attire.

"Coach. Janelle."

"Lovely to see you, Rose," Janelle chirped. She patted her hair, piled up on her head Brigitte Bardot–like, with bottle-blonde waves curling and swirling everywhere.

Coach turned to Lily. "Well, who do we have here? Rose, do you have family we don't know about?"

"This is Lily Bishop. She's applying for the hairdresser position," Rose said pointedly. "I'm giving her a little tour."

Coach rapped his knuckles on the dashboard. "That's great. I know this old mop on my head could use a trim, although I don't like it to be too short. Makes me look a little too serious."

Beside her, Lily gave a small laugh through her nose.

"I doubt there's much of anything that could turn you into a serious person," Rose said. "Definitely not a haircut."

Coach's face fell a bit, like she'd pricked a hole in his balloon and all his hot air fizzed out. She felt something in her rushing out too.

"You're probably right about that." He drummed his fingers on his knee, then said to Janelle, "What do you say I get you on back to your cottage?"

"Whatever you say, Coach. I'm putty in

your hands."

Rose rolled her eyes.

"I found Janelle up the road teetering in those high heels," Coach said to Lily. "I thought the least I could do was offer her a ride home."

Lily smiled. "How gentlemanly."

Coach laughed. "Thank you, my dear, though I'm sure Rose would argue with that estimation of me." He turned the key and the engine leaped to life again. "I hope you take the job," he said to Lily. "We could use some young energy around here. Let me know when you start. Maybe I'll swing by."

He tooted the horn again and waved as he drove off toward Janelle's cottage on Port Place.

"He seems like a nice man," Lily said.

"I suppose. If you like that sort."

When Rose and Lily reached the end of the street, Rose led them to the right, where the small shops sat close to the road. The area was quite charming, when it came down to it. Years ago someone had strung twinkle lights between the shops, so at night the area glittered, even after the shops were closed. It was especially quaint during the holiday season, when Roberta hung wreaths in all the shop windows and piped Christmas music through speakers hidden in the flowerpots.

Rose stopped in front of the closed salon. Two stories, stained wooden porch posts, shutters and front door painted a bright turquoise. Like all the other cottages, it had a long porch across the front with a swing at one end, painted in the same turquoise hue. Clematis climbed over the eaves and cast the porch in deep shade. *Those vines will pull the gutters right off the house.* She made a mental note to have Rawlins trim them back before anyone moved in.

A piece of poster board taped to the door proclaimed the salon Closed Until Further Notice. The faded sign curled at the edges where the tape had worn away.

"Here we are." Rose pulled her key ring from her pocket and unlocked the door, pushing it open. Sunlight flooded in through the large front window, illuminating the swivel chair, a hooded dryer, and a deep sink. A wicker cabinet held small baskets. Red smocks hung from hooks along the wall, and on a small rattan side table sat a pitcher, a discarded paper cup, and a vase with a single long-dead sunflower.

Lily stepped inside and ran her hand along the chair back and the large clear dome of the dryer. "Did Beverly not want to take any of her things with her?"

"We bought it all for the salon, so when she left, all she took was her scissors. And all her personal belongings from upstairs, of course."

"Upstairs?"

"Yes. Beverly lived upstairs. She was living all the way in Spanish Fort at the time, and it was easier for her to stay here rather than make the drive in every day. But you live in Foley, right? So driving in wouldn't be a problem for you."

Along the baseboards, dust motes gathered in the corners and blew against the wood, disturbed by the breeze from the open door. Rose grabbed a broom standing up against the wall. "It won't take much, just some elbow grease, and it'll be ready for customers."

She swept dust and old sprigs of hair into a small pile before realizing cleaning the floor would take much more than a quick sweeping. She grabbed the dustpan to corral some of the debris, then opened the back door of the tiny kitchen and tapped the pan against the inside of the trash can sitting behind the cottage.

That was one thing she'd been sure to tell Beverly — don't take the trash can. The county had agreed to extend garbage pick-up service inside the gates of Safe

Harbor Village on the condition that everyone used their city-approved garbage cans. Rose thought the rule was ridiculous, but being a rule follower herself, she insisted all the residents obey it. Years ago a resident had shoved her garbage can into the back of her moving van when she'd relocated, so determined was she to keep the ugly thing. Said she'd never had a can with such ergonomic handles. Rose had to admit she was right about the handles.

The back of each of the cottages in the village looked the same. Just outside the back door was a small patio ringed by palm trees and a flower bed. A white picket fence lined the edges. Through a gate in the fence, residents could walk down a slope of grass to the boardwalk that edged the marina. Each cottage had its own short dock and space for a boat.

Before going into the cottage, Rose glanced around the fenced-in patio. Beverly hadn't been much of a gardener, and the beds along the fence were as sad and empty as they were when she had moved in. The guidelines were such that as long as no one else could see it, residents could do what they wanted with their personal space, including the patios. There was only so much a manager could legislate.

Inside, she found Lily sitting in one of the chairs in the waiting area, her hands tucked under her thighs. Her shoulders were drawn up under her ears, but when she saw Rose, she exhaled, stood up, and crossed the floor to the middle of the room.

"I need to ask you a favor." Her hands were by her sides, one fingernail digging into the soft flesh around her thumbnail. "Woman to woman."

Rose swallowed hard. "And what is that?"

"I need this job." For all her fidgeting, her voice was surprisingly sure and steady. "And not only that, I need a place to live."

Rose hadn't expected that. "You . . . I thought you lived in Foley."

"I do, but only for the next two days. After that . . ." Lily held up her hands. "Well, I'm pretty much homeless." She gave a small laugh, though Rose couldn't see what in the world was funny about either her words or her situation.

Lily's gaze swung from Rose to the front window and the afternoon light beyond. For a brief moment — just a flash, really — her face tightened. Some kind of dark emotion pushed to the surface, and she covered her lips with her fingertips. Then, just as quickly, it was all gone. She passed her hand over her hair and straightened her shoulders, her voice steady as a sailboat sitting on dry land.

"Even if it's just for a little while. I know you don't know me, and I'm not sure you even like me very much, which makes this all the more crazy, but I'm asking you anyway. I can do the job. I promise. I can cut hair well. I can make clients happy." She paused and swallowed. Then her voice picked up a notch. "I can even do more. You must have a lot on your plate being the only manager, from what I can tell. I can answer phones, run errands, do any tasks you need me to do around here. I'm not afraid to work hard. I just . . ." She breathed in a breath as big as the world, then blew it out and shrugged her shoulders. "I just need a place to live for a while. Until I figure some things out."

Rose pursed her lips. She should let her down easy, and now. Say her qualifications weren't enough to offer her the job. And it was true. She'd be foolish to hire someone like this, practically on a whim, to take care of the hairdressing needs of a gaggle of mouthy seniors. Now, the extra work she spoke of — Rose could use that kind of help.

But a certain level of trust was necessary to bring a new person into the life of the village. She couldn't hire just anyone, no matter how much the woman needed a job.

Rose adjusted the visor on her head and crossed her arms, thought for a moment. She wanted to tell the woman she was indeed crazy, asking if she could move in five seconds after driving through the gates, expecting Rose to roll out a red carpet when she could be anybody — a thief, a spy, or one of those telemarketers who takes advantage of old people. Who knew?

Rose looked away and pinched the bridge of her nose. She sighed. "Well, you don't look crazy."

"I'm sorry?"

"Say I do offer you this job. What happens if your circumstances change and you have to leave just as quickly as you got here? Am I going to be in this same position in a month, having to look for yet another hairdresser to work here because you left us high and dry in the middle of the night?" She propped her hands on her hips, her best attempt at intimidation.

"I won't do that to you."

"But how can I trust you?"

"You can't." Lily shrugged. "Not yet. All I can do is promise not to leave you high and dry. I *want* to work here. I won't let you down."

"Can you afford to live here? The rent isn't cheap in this area. And I can't possibly let you stay free of charge."

"I don't expect you to, and I do have a little money. And maybe if you let me help in the office, my pay could go toward my rent instead."

"Rent," Rose repeated. She rubbed her forehead and chewed on the inside of her cheek. "Honey, where's your husband?"

"I don't know." Her eyes were red but not damp, and a fire burned in them, like an ember that refused to die out. She swallowed hard. "But he's not my husband anymore. Or he won't be as soon as I sign the papers."

Rose closed her eyes and tried to gather her thoughts. *This girl's a grade A mess. No doubt about it.* But then she sighed. She didn't know everything about the residents in her village, but she knew most people's lives were messy to some degree. And her own life? One mistake after another.

*She may be a mess, but aren't we all?* Who was Rose to deny this young woman a place to land for the summer, a chance to breathe and figure out whatever needed figuring out? Her answer to Terry could wait a little bit.

She spoke before she could change her mind. "I suppose the space upstairs is just sitting empty. Having someone living up there would keep the mold from setting in."

Lily laughed, a quick burst. "So does that mean . . ."

"I've haven't seen you cut a single hair, but Lord help me, I'm going to give you the job." Lily grinned and Rose held up one finger. "We'll start with a trial period. We'll see how things go. If you like it and everyone likes you — and be warned, this crew can be quite particular — then we'll move forward. But I wouldn't count your chickens yet."

"Understood."

Pausing for a moment of mental reshuffling, Rose waited for the dust to settle on her new reality. She suspected Lily was doing the same.

"Do you mind if I look around upstairs?"

Rose held out her arm in the direction of the corner stairs. "Be my guest."

While Lily ascended the steps two at a time, Rose stayed behind in the makeshift salon. She took off her visor and smoothed her hands over her bun pulled tight at the back. What in the world had she just gotten herself into? And what was she thinking, welcoming this unknown person — and whatever past she was dragging behind her — into her carefully constructed life? She'd been just fine with her obstinate roses, her stack of paperbacks, and her Monday night dinner dates, yet here she was inviting trouble. Not just inviting it, but opening wide the gate and practically ushering it in.

But Rose couldn't deny the ache she'd felt emanating from Lily as she'd stood there in the center of the salon, asking for help. Rose had felt that ache as if it were her own. The very blood in her veins had thrummed in anguish, as if for a moment she were Lily. She'd be lying if she said it hadn't rattled her, and she wasn't in the habit of lying to herself.

Lily's footsteps thumped on the steps and she appeared back in the kitchen. She looked around and inhaled deeply. "I can see the water from the front bedroom. I like that."

Rose nodded and slid her visor back on her head. "Waking up every day and seeing the water does something to a person. Something good."

"Mrs. Carrigan —"

"It's just Rose. Please."

"Rose. Thank you."

Rose cleared her throat and pointed out the front window to the cottage across the street. "That's the café. Roberta makes the best gumbo you've ever tasted."

"It'll definitely be the best. I've never actually tried gumbo."

"Never?"

Lily shook her head. "I'm not quite sure what all is in it. Isn't there an oyster at the bottom?" She wrinkled her nose.

Rose raised her eyebrows. "Good grief, girl. You have a lot to learn about living this far south. Now, let's get you back to the office. I need you to fill out some paperwork so I can make this official."

"It's a trial period, though, right?"

Rose waved her hand. "Right, right. But I still like to do things the proper way."

She ushered Lily outside and locked the door behind them. She looked at the key in her hand. "I'll just hang on to this for now." She slipped it back in her pocket. When she turned around, Lily was facing the bay, her head tipped back, the sun bathing her face in gold.

"Welcome to Safe Harbor," Rose said as she passed Lily with purpose, leading the way back to the office.

*Your Source for Neighborhood News*

May 19, 2018
Compiled by Shirley Ferrill

## GOOD DAY, SAFE HARBOR VILLAGE!

I'm sending out this special weekend edition of *The Village Vine* to tell you Rose has hired a hairdresser! It all happened very quickly. As you know, Tiny Collins distributed flyers this past Monday, and just yesterday Rose made the decision to hire Lily Bishop, a native of Fox Hill, Georgia, though a more recent resident of Atlanta. She will be moving into the vacated space above the salon as soon as possible.

Lily will start seeing clients as soon as she is settled, so you're free to book appointments now for future dates. She'll have her hands full, but she is young and fresh, and I, for one, have full confidence in her abilities! Neighbors, please do all you can to help make Lily feel welcome here in the loveliest village on the bay.

### UPDATE FROM MANAGEMENT

A new rule has been added to the village handbook:

- No loud noise — including singing — before 7 a.m.

The paddleboats are in! The first tour will be up to Captain's Chair on Bon Secour River this Friday. If you're interested, please meet at 9:30 a.m. on Coach's dock. He suggests you bring bottled water, bug spray, sunscreen, and a camera. He also strictly forbids selfies. (I'm not one to point fingers, but I think that's how he capsized last time.)

# Six

On Monday morning Lily woke up with a chest full of panic. She turned her head toward the empty spot in her bed, the spot where Worth should have been, with his sleep-thick eyes, blond hair sticking up in little-boy cowlicks, and pale scruff that made his chin scratchy. He always woke up with such languid ease, stretching like a cat and curling his arm over her stomach. Lily loved the early mornings the best, those moments before he remembered whatever it was that burdened him during his waking hours. The burdens that made him jumpy and unpredictable. He rarely shared that weight with her, but when she got glimpses of it — little peeks when his guard was down — it was easy to see his mother was at the root of it. Her and the family name and all the various expectations that went along with it.

But his burdens were no longer her trou-

91

ble. He'd packed them up and taken them with him when he walked out their door. She wondered if another woman — a better wife — would have been able to offer him a different kind of help. The kind that could have made him happy.

Lily threw the covers from her legs and looked at the clock by the bed: 7:27. She stood and crossed the room toward the bathroom. On the way she stepped over boxes of winter clothes she hadn't unpacked yet and other boxes she'd filled over the weekend. Her life spread out before her in various states of readiness and disorder.

She splashed cold water on her face, the water dripping down her wrists and forearms, making small puddles on the vanity. She turned off the faucet, held a towel to her cheeks, and stared at the pale, thin woman in the mirror. What if Worth came back? What if he decided he'd made a mistake and hurried home from wherever he was, only to find her gone? All the certainty — all the bravery — she'd felt as she drove away from Safe Harbor Village on Friday fizzled, leaving her limp and nervous.

Back in the bedroom, she threw on yesterday's clothes and walked down the hall to the kitchen. She was just about to pick up the phone to call Rose to — what? Admit to a hefty dose of last-minute panic? Apologize for making promises she couldn't keep, only to back out? — when someone knocked on the door. Startled, Lily whirled around and smacked her hip into the corner of the kitchen island. The unexpected pain brought tears to her eyes, and she was still blinking them away when she peeked through the window next to the front door.

A man stood on the front stoop, hands in his pockets, eyes turned down toward his feet. Another man stood at the curb next to a long flatbed trailer attached to a pickup. The man on the porch — taller than Lily and not much older than her — checked his watch and shifted his ball cap.

They must've been looking for Marie, the lady who lived next door. In the short space of time they'd been living in the house in Pelican Cove, Lily had seen a variety of workers pull up outside and knock on Marie's door — a yard service, a handyman, a housekeeper, a dog walker. Even a laundry service. Lily often wondered what the woman did all day while her husband was at work.

Lily opened the door a few inches, aware of her just-out-of-bed appearance. "Hello." She kept one hand on the door and rubbed her sore hip with the other. "Are you look-

ing for Marie DeAngelo? She's next door."
She pointed to the house. Just as she was
about to close the door, the man spoke.

"Actually, I'm looking for Lily Bishop. I'm
Rawlins Willett. I'm here to help you move."

"You're who?"

"Rawlins." He stuck out his hand. Caught
off guard, Lily just looked at it, and after a
second he let it drop. "My aunt was supposed to call you," he said slowly. "But by
the look on your face, I'm guessing she
hasn't."

Lily shook her head. "No, I —"

Just then her phone rang back in the
kitchen. For a moment she didn't move.
When it rang a third time, Rawlins pointed
through the doorway. "Are you going to get
that?"

"Uh, yes. Can you — I'm going to . . ."
He nodded and she closed the door, lock-
ing it behind her. She ran into the kitchen,
giving the island a wide berth, and grabbed
the phone. "Hello?"

"Lily, I'm glad I got you. I've asked my
nephew Rawlins to come help you get
packed up today. Now, I told him the earlier
the better, so you might want to go ahead
and start looking for him."

"He's standing on my porch, Rose.
There're two of them. I wish you'd given

me some warning before they showed up."
Lily shifted a little so she could see the men
through the window. The one on the porch,
Rawlins, had taken off his cap and was tapping it against the side of his leg. His hair
was dark and stuck up in a few places where
the cap had been. His face was freshly
shaven.

"Giving you warning was the purpose of
this phone call. He just came a little earlier
than I expected. And the other one — is he
a big black man, looks like a linebacker?"

"Ah, yeah. That fits."

"That's Canaan Halsey. He's a friend of
Rawlins — a friend of everyone, really. I
didn't know he was coming, but he'll be
good help."

Lily sighed. "Rose, I . . ." She leaned
against the wall and rubbed her eyes. What
was she doing? It was all too fast. "I don't
know if I can —"

But Rose pushed on. "Now, word of you
has gotten out, though I tried to keep it
quiet. Coach spilled it to Tiny Collins, who
told Shirley, who put it in *The Vine,* and
now everyone knows. I hope you have a
sweet tooth."

"What? Why?" Nothing Rose was saying
made any sense.

"Oh, you'll have some welcome treats

95

showing up soon as you get here. I don't know how young women eat these days, but if you won't eat them, I'm sure you can pass them along to Rawlins and Canaan."

"Okay, but . . . Rose —"

"Good. Now, like I said yesterday, the place needs a little spiffing up, but nothing a wet rag and a sturdy broom can't handle. Edna offered to do the cleaning for you — she was a housekeeper before she retired — but her hip has been acting up again."

Lily glanced again toward the front door. Through the window, Rawlins lifted his eyebrows in question. She held up a finger.

"Lily?" Rose asked. "Are you there?"

"I'm here."

Silence stretched between them until finally Rose spoke again. "I'm going to let you in on a little secret. Sometimes the hardest step is the first one. After that, it can only get easier."

Lily took a deep breath and exhaled through her nose.

"Let Rawlins do the heavy lifting. I'm sure he brought that trailer. It may smell like shrimp, but it'll do the job. Now, get cracking."

"Can I try this again?" he asked when she opened the door. He extended his hand and

96

this time Lily took it. "Rawlins Willett, Rose's nephew." He jerked his thumb behind him. "This is my friend Canaan." Canaan did indeed look like a linebacker — wide shoulders like big boulders and a torso thick with muscle. He wore a floppy, wide-brimmed hat that said "Best Hooker in Town" in red letters across the front. Lily's eyes lingered on the words.

Canaan laughed and pointed to the hat. "It always catches people off guard. I drive a tow truck when I'm not on the boat with this guy." He nudged his chin toward Rawlins, who rubbed his eyes with the heel of his hand.

"I'm sorry about that — he forgets he's wearing it. I told him to leave it in the truck."

Lily gave a small laugh, more air than noise.

"If you want us to go, I understand. I told Rose no one would want two total strangers in their house at eight o'clock in the morning. But she insisted, and you know Rose . . ."

"Actually, I don't know her well. We only just met. But I'm beginning to see that she can be very persuasive."

"To say the least. My father could come up with a few more choice words, I'm sure."

His eyebrows pulled together. "You just met? And you're moving in?"

Lily hesitated. "It would seem so."

He shrugged. "It takes most people weeks of interviews to get a foot in the door at the village, whether you're looking for a place to live or a job." Rawlins studied Lily's face. "She must like you."

"I don't know about that. She may just feel sorry for me."

Rawlins glanced past Lily into the house. "So is your husband helping today or . . ." He stopped when she didn't fill in with the expected information. "I'm sorry, I —"

"No, it's fine. It's just — I . . ." The words piled up in a jumble in her mouth. "It's just me."

He held up his hands. "I'm sorry, it's none of my business. I'm just here to help you move. If you want the help, that is. If you don't, we're out of here and you don't have to see us again."

She put her hands on her hips, then reached up to block the sun that had just risen high enough to pierce through the trees with bright, fresh rays.

At the street, Canaan waited with one thick leg propped up on the back of the trailer. Rawlins was watching her, his cap pulled down low, his dark brown hair sticking out around the edges, in need of a good trim. Under the bill of his hat, his eyes were soft as he raised his eyebrows.

*Staying or going?*

Staying was out of the question. Mr. Pender had already told her that. In a few days someone else would move in and unpack his own family, the new occupants' fears and worries and hopeful dreams filling the cracks and corners of this house, making it their space, no longer Lily's. Or Worth's.

However, *going* was an even greater unknown. But wasn't it better than looking backward?

She took a deep breath and summoned the resolve she'd felt a couple of days ago. Finally she met Rawlins's gaze. "I still have some packing to do."

He smiled. "Well then, it's a good thing you have some help, isn't it?"

When Lily and Worth moved into the Pelican Cove garden home almost a month ago, they'd unpacked the necessities — some clothes, toiletries, kitchen items, books. Pillows for the couch and chairs. Bedding. But most of their stuff remained in boxes in the back guest room — things like winter jackets, their good china, and Worth's collection of scrapbooks, eighteen of them in total, each one meticulously crafted by his mother, showing his best and brightest achievements from birth through high school. Lily couldn't imagine dragging an entire childhood of milestones and triumphs clear into adulthood, as if to remind yourself that all your life's success had already happened.

Lily had procrastinated in unpacking that back bedroom, not feeling any urgency since, according to Worth, they'd be looking for a new place once he got settled in at the new job and they had a chance to drive around and scope out the neighborhoods and towns up and down Highway 59. Why unpack just to pack it all up again so soon?

Anytime she asked Worth how long he planned for them to stay in the house, he'd say, "I just need a little more time, Lily." Or "Why don't you look around on your own? See what you like and come back and tell me. Maybe we can look together this weekend."

It never happened, though. He kept putting it off, and Lily kept accepting that it was all fine. That there was nothing to worry about. That the move and the new job had been wise, and that their marriage would eventually right itself now that they were out from under Mertha's thumb. But all that happened was Lily exhausted herself by keeping her thoughts and concerns inside her own head all day, and Worth's pensive, worried demeanor when he came home each night did nothing to show that things were getting any better.

And now, here she was, finally moving out, but the reality was quite different than she'd imagined. Instead of moving with Worth into a new home they'd chosen together, she was wrapping dinner plates and skillets in newspaper and shoving clothes back into suitcases while two strange men loaded her belongings onto a flatbed trailer that did indeed smell a lot like shrimp.

She'd already packed up most of the den and all of the kitchen, so she asked Rawlins and Canaan to start there while she headed off to strip the sheets off the bed in her room and cram last-minute things into boxes.

Amid the muddled snatches of conversation and the heavy footsteps of the guys carrying boxes from the kitchen and guest room, Lily stood in the doorway to her and Worth's bedroom and surveyed the space. Bins of Worth's clothes and shoes sat against one wall. His dresser still held the clothes he'd carefully tucked into the drawers the night they'd moved in. She wondered again what he'd taken with him when he left; she hadn't yet peeked inside to see what, if anything, was missing.

She pulled a hair tie from her wrist and yanked up her hair into a ponytail, tucking loose pieces behind her ears, then started on the bed. After pulling off the pillows and squeezing them into an empty plastic bin, she stripped off the duvet and sheets and dropped them in a pile on the floor. Down on her hands and knees, she slid out the under-the-bed boxes where she'd packed clothes, picture frames, and shoes when they'd left Georgia. Sitting back on her heels, she noticed a piece of newspaper sticking out from underneath Worth's night-stand. It was from the Life section of the *Atlanta Journal-Constitution,* a page showing a single photo and headline: "Atlanta Native Makes Her Mark in Hollywood." Next to it were the words, "That's our girl," written in Mertha Bishop's spidery penmanship.

The photo was of Delia Park.

The first time Lily heard Delia's name was in Mertha's living room during Lily and Worth's engagement party. Most of the glowing couples in the Bishops' social circles had several engagement parties, thrown over the course of their engagement, held at homes of friends and family. Because Worth and Lily's romance had been a whirlwind and their engagement much shorter than Mertha thought appropriate, they only had one party.

All of Worth's childhood friends, along with his entire family, had filled the Bishop family's Buckhead home, laughing and drinking the evening away. After unwrapping all the gifts — monogrammed wine and whiskey glasses, serving pieces in the Bishop family's Reed & Barton sterling pattern, and four different ice buckets complete with gold and silver ice scoops — conversation swelled and Lily sat back, listening in on all the stories. Later, as fatigue began to manifest itself in a headache behind her eyes and Lily stood to tap Worth on the shoulder, the voice of his friend Patton carried loudly over all the others.

"If only Delia could see him now, right? Look at Worth. Another girl by his side, working his way up the ladder. Delia, man. She missed out." His wife next to him had tried to shush him, but as the other conversations in the room dimmed and the gaze of almost everyone in the room found her, Lily knew she was not the only one who had heard Patton's words. And that those words held significance.

Worth squirmed in his seat, shot a death look at his friend, then turned his face up to Lily, who had moved to stand next to him. His eyes, his mouth, the set of his jaw — all of it combined to paint a picture of a man who had lost something. Someone. A man who was making do with the next best thing.

But then he rose from his chair to wrap his arm around her waist, his face wiped clean of discomfort. He kissed her cheek, and she tried to let the warmth and solidness of his body push her fears and doubts away.

Later she'd asked, "Who's Delia?"

"She's no one." He shrugged, nonchalant. "Why?"

"She's not no one. Her name stopped conversation."

"She's just . . . someone I used to know."

"Used to date?"

"Something like that." He shrugged again. "Our families were friends. But, Lily — you're the woman I'm marrying." He kissed her, and again she let his smile, his charisma, wash away her doubt.

A few days after that, at a shop near their house, Lily ran into Patton's wife. She apologized for her husband and the "spot

of awkwardness" — that's what she called it
— at their engagement party.

"Worth's old girlfriend," she'd said when
Lily asked who Delia was. "I can't believe
you haven't heard anything about her.
Though not being from here, I guess it
makes sense. Worth and Delia had been
together practically since they were in
diapers. Everyone thought they'd get married right after graduation, but she kept putting it off. Then she broke up with him. I
hear she's a big shot in Hollywood now."
She stopped when she saw the look on
Lily's face. "Worth's just crazy about you,
though. We're all so happy for you."

After that, Delia was never far from Lily's
mind, though she hadn't mentioned the
name again. Worth sure hadn't. Yet there
she was, smiling up from the black-and-
white photo Worth's mother had torn from
the Atlanta newspaper and mailed to her
son.

*That's our girl.*

The date at the top of the page showed it
was from a little over two weeks ago. Just
before Worth disappeared.

Lily carefully folded the page along its
original creases and set it on top of his
nightstand. She stood and looked around
their room. Her toiletry bag sat on the

bathroom counter next to a bottle of Worth's shaving cream. Her slippers were on the floor next to his tennis shoes. Everything physical intertwined, except for the deepest parts of their hearts. Those they kept locked away from each other. It had made their life together easier in some ways but harder in the ways that really mattered.

She shoved the pile of sheets into an empty laundry basket, dropped her toiletry bag and slippers on top, and propped the basket on her hip. She trailed her palm down the wall of the hallway as she passed through to the living room, taking it all in — the cream-and-pink silk pillows on the chairs, the expensive but uncomfortable couch, the carved cherry dining table and monogrammed dining chairs, all picked out by Mertha. It all had to go.

When she opened the front door, Rawlins and Canaan, both sitting on the top porch step, turned to her. "We would have started on the living room furniture, but I didn't want to do anything without asking," Rawlins said. "But if you're ready . . ."

*If you're ready.*

Her eyes burned and she had to look away. "Lily?"

She blinked once, twice, then looked back to Rawlins. "I'm ready."

He rubbed his hands together and nudged Canaan with his elbow. "Let's get going then."

"No, I'm finished. I'm done." She shifted the basket on her hip. "This is it."

His forehead wrinkled in confusion. "But your furniture . . ."

She shook her head. "I don't need it. I've got everything I want to take with me."

His mouth worked though his lips stayed closed. She could tell he wanted to ask, to question her rashness, her decision-making skills. But then he held up his hands. "Whatever you say."

She grabbed her purse, locked the door behind her, and walked to her car in the driveway. When the two men didn't move from where they stood on the porch, she gestured toward their truck. Rawlins shook his head and walked to her car, stopping next to her.

"You sure about this?" he asked quietly.

Lily bit her bottom lip and nodded.

"Okay then."

As he turned away, she hesitated, then called out to him.

"Rawlins? Do you mind if we make a quick stop on the way?"

"Just show me where."

They made a haphazard convoy pulling out of the neighborhood, with Lily's car, Rawlins's truck, and the small flatbed trailer piled with an assortment of Lily's things. She took a left onto Highway 59 and didn't look back.

A few miles down the road, she spied the small building that had caught her eye the first week they'd arrived. The sign said Mary's Antiques and Thrift. The building itself looked shabby but loved, with rocking chairs on the long porch, pink flowers cascading out of terra-cotta pots, and two cats lying in a spot of sunshine in the grass out front. To the side of the shop was a collection of old shutters and cast-off architectural pieces — corbels, columns, pieces of old gates. It was the type of place she loved to browse, but knowing Worth couldn't stomach thrifted items in their home, she hadn't yet made a stop at Mary's.

She turned on her blinker and pulled into the small parking lot in front of the shop. Rawlins followed, but unable to fit the truck and trailer into a parking space, he pulled alongside the building and rolled down his window. She rolled down her passenger window.

"This is where you wanted to stop?" he called.

"Do you mind? I'm just going to take a quick look around."

The place reminded her of the types of places her mother liked to shop. Never one to pay full price for anything — and unable to do so, even if she wanted to — Lillian Chapman had always found just the right things at thrift and secondhand stores. Most of the furnishings in their home had once graced the homes of other families, families who upgraded into nicer things and donated their castoffs, not knowing they would end up in Lillian's home, adding to the warm, cozy, mix-and-match atmosphere Lily grew up in. The atmosphere she didn't realize she loved until she was firmly ensconced in the world of her husband, who couldn't abide anything secondhand or less than perfect.

Now that Lily had left most everything behind in the rental house, she had hardly a stick of furniture to her name. She hoped to find a few things at Mary's that would make the cottage in Safe Harbor Village feel like home.

When she opened the door to the shop, a

wind chime hanging from the ceiling announced her presence.

"Come on in," came a woman's voice from another room. "Make yourself at home."

Lily meandered between furniture in all sorts of styles — mid-century chairs next to cannonball bed frames, simple pine dining tables standing close to rich mahogany ones. Dried flower arrangements, lamps, framed artwork, vases and cups holding old silver spoons and serving utensils. A rusty wheelbarrow filled with wreaths made from pieces of driftwood. And everywhere her eye landed, palm trees — ceramic, glass, concrete, even crocheted.

The wind chime jangled again, and just as Rawlins walked inside, a woman came up from the back, wiping her hands on a towel. "Looking for anything specific today?" She looked like Mrs. Claus, with short gray hair, glasses perched on the end of her nose, and a bright red T-shirt. When she saw Rawlins, she stuck her hands on her hips and smiled. "Well, look who the cat dragged in."

He gave the woman a hug. "Good to see you, Mrs. Mary." He nodded his head toward Lily. "I think my new friend here needs a little help."

"Is that so?" She straightened her glasses

and peered at Lily.

"Yes, ma'am. I'm moving and I need some new things. Well, new to me at least. And it's a small place, so I don't need much."

"Okay." Mary rubbed her hands together. "So, are we talking accessories? Knick-knacks and whatnot? I just got some new mirrors in and a whole bunch of baskets. Let me show you what I have back here —"

"Actually, I need furniture."

"Well, even better. What kind of things do you need?"

"A bed, for starters," Lily said. "And a kitchen table and chairs. Maybe a small couch."

Mary propped a hand on her hip and stared at Lily. "Sounds like you're starting over."

Lily nodded. "I am, actually."

The older woman appeared to think for a moment, then exhaled. "Okay then. Follow me."

Lily looked back at Rawlins, feeling like she should explain, but he'd already turned back toward the door. "I'll wait outside."

Within minutes, Mary had walked Lily through the entire shop, all five winding, twisting rooms and hallways, and had stuck a piece of blue painter's tape on a handful of items: a blond wood kitchen table with four spindle-backed dining chairs, a deep-seated chair in a pretty watermelon color — "a great reading chair," Mary said — a cream loveseat with floral pillows, and a full-size four-poster bed. She even had a mattress for it, still wrapped in plastic.

"I hope you know what a steal you're getting with all this stuff. A lady came in just yesterday and unloaded almost a whole house-worth of furniture. She's starting over too, but with a new husband who lives on Ono Island. I imagine she'll be getting much nicer things . . . not that this stuff isn't nice."

"No, I think it's perfect, actually." The furniture they'd picked out felt cheerful and cozy. She hadn't felt that way about most of the things that had already filled up Worth's house when she moved in.

"I'm glad to hear it. We got you fixed up, for sure. And lucky you, you've got someone here to help you get it to your new home."

Lily found Rawlins and Canaan on the porch outside the shop. "Do you mind giving us a hand with a few more things?"

An hour later they were back on their way, the trailer now full to capacity. Lily's back seat was full too. Mary had added a few lamps, two area rugs, several panels of eyelet lace curtains — "call me if they're not the right length. I'm handy with a sewing machine" — and two white Pottery Barn end tables, priced at $20 each.

"Seriously?" Lily had asked. "You should probably charge more than that."

Mary shrugged. "I set my own prices. For you, they're $20 apiece." Then she leaned closer and whispered, "I started over once too." She winked. "It wasn't easy, but it was the best thing I ever did."

Back on the road and headed to the village, Lily pondered Mary's words. *The best thing I ever did.* No way could Lily say that right now. Part of her felt like she should be back at the house in Pelican Cove, sticking close in case Worth came back. Calling his cell and demanding some sort of explanation from him. Or at least clarification.

But she had a hunch things were as clear as they were going to get. And even if she did talk to him, what would she say? She couldn't deny the number of times over the course of the last year she'd wondered what freedom would feel like — the freedom to do things differently, to choose another path for her life. Maybe even pack her own bag and slip away.

If she'd followed through on her middle-of-the-night musings and anxiety-fueled dreams, though, where would she have gone? For better or worse, she'd linked herself with Worth, and where he went, she followed.

Except this time he left and following was impossible. Part of her wished she had someone around to tell her what to do, but at the same time she thrilled at the thought of being in charge of her own life. Her next steps were up to her, solely and completely. And here she was, buying secondhand furniture to fill a small cottage by the bay where she'd live and work among strangers. Given the alternative, she felt pretty darn good about it.

# SEVEN

It took Lily, Rawlins, and Canaan far longer than they'd thought to unload his truck, her car, and the trailer. Almost every time they brought in one box or piece of furniture, they'd walk outside to find yet another neighbor standing in the driveway or on the front porch of the cottage. Having read about Lily's imminent arrival in Shirley's special edition of *The Village Vine,* they all came bearing food. A petite woman named Ida brought a pot of corn chowder, and the man on the golf cart she'd met last week — Coach something — showed up with a platter of fried chicken. None of them stuck around — they just said hello and handed over the food and often a bottle of wine or pitcher of tea — and by late afternoon her kitchen table was full of disposable aluminum containers and Tupperware bowls. "If nothing else, you'll eat well around here," Rawlins said, sidestepping the heavy-laden kitchen table to bring in a dining chair.

"You're welcome to take any of this." Lily gestured to the wild assortment of food and drink. "You two haven't stopped all day, and I didn't even think about lunch. I should be a better hostess."

"You haven't stopped either. And I'd say moving day is a good reason to set aside any hostess duties."

With the final box unloaded and the last lamp in place, she sat in her new pink chair tucked into a corner of the den and rubbed the balls of her feet. Across the room, Rawlins lifted one side of the loveseat and smoothed out a wrinkle in the rug underneath.

"Mrs. Mary was really helpful. Is she a friend of yours?"

"She's a family friend. Her husband worked with my dad for a long time. Hank was one of the best shrimpers around."

"Shrimper?"

"Yeah. Shrimp boats." He shrugged a shoulder. "Hank worked mostly on the *Mary Lou,* but he'd come out with me from time to time."

"So you're a shrimper too?"

"Yep. The season starts next Monday."

Through the French doors at the back of the cottage, they heard Canaan's booming voice. "Time to roll, Boss."

Lily stood and faced Rawlins, who was already at the front door, looking like he was ready to wash his hands of Lily and all her furniture. "I can't thank you enough for your help today. Both of you. I'm not sure how I would have managed all this on my own."

"It's nothing. I'm glad we could help."

"It's not nothing. You don't even know me and you gave up your whole day with nothing in return. I want to pay you for your time." Lily reached for her purse lying on a chair by the door.

"No, no. Really."

"What about some food then? Are you sure you don't want to take anything?" Lily gestured toward the table. "I'll never be able to eat it all before it goes bad."

He smiled. "Nah, it's okay. I'll be out on the water most of the week."

"I thought the season didn't start until Monday."

He rubbed the side of his face. Fatigue showed in his eyes. "It doesn't. Not officially. Sometimes I'd just rather be on the water than on land."

"Does your boat have a name?"

A corner of his mouth lifted. "*Miss Stella.* My mother's name."

"Are all the boats named after women?"

"We only name them after the good ones."

Lily smiled, and then Canaan opened the door and stuck his head through the doorway. "Sorry to interrupt, but I gotta get moving. Elijah's at the Land tonight."

"Right." Rawlins turned back to her. "We're off then." He tapped his knuckles on the side table by the loveseat. "If you need anything else, Rose knows how to get me."

"She sure does," Canaan chided, one eyebrow lifted. "And she doesn't hesitate to call on you whenever she needs any little thing."

"As if you don't come running too."

"That's just because she gives me roses to take back to Lea. Gets me out of the doghouse for running off to help an old woman instead of sticking around to help my own wife." He tipped his floppy Hooker hat. "Nice to meet you, Lily. I'm sure I'll be seeing you around."

Rawlins followed him out. On the porch, he paused. "Folks around here can be a little feisty. The men as much as the women. But they're nice. I think you'll like it here."

"Thank you."

He hesitated, and the moment stretched a hair longer than was comfortable. To break the tension, Lily spoke the first words that popped into her mind. "Let me know if you need a haircut."

He lifted his ball cap and ran a hand over his hair. "I'll do that."

From the doorway she watched him climb into the truck. He cast one more glance toward the cottage, where she stood in the falling light, before driving away.

The night of Worth and Lily's one-year anniversary, Mertha planned a party, though it had nothing to do with celebrating their year-old marriage. Instead, it was to fete Bishop Lumber's longest-standing clients, a way to thank them for years of business.

"She's only doing it to butter them up, fill them with Sazeracs and hope they'll divulge the names of any friends who might be good leads," Worth said as he struggled with his bow tie in front of their bedroom mirror. Of course the party was black-tie.

"It makes good business sense," he continued. "I just can't believe she planned it on our anniversary."

Lily had no trouble believing it. When Worth had first brought it up to Mertha — "Seriously, Mother? You could have picked any other night" — Mertha had apologized profusely.

"I don't know where my head was, forgetting your anniversary like that. And I hate that it can't be moved. It's the only date I could book the caterer and the sommelier at the same time. You two can celebrate another night, can't you?"

Her words had been sweet as honey, but Lily heard the satisfaction in them.

Lily reached over to straighten his bow tie, and Worth grabbed her hand. "I'm really sorry. I wish tonight could just be about us," he said, remorse written on his face in the thin crease between his eyes and the worry at the edges of his mouth.

Lily kissed him there. "It's fine."

That night, once the dessert trays had made the rounds and after-dinner drinks were poured, Mertha and Worth's sister, Lydia, cornered him as he and Lily stood to the side of the bar set up out back.

"Did you hear about John Albright?" Mertha asked, her tone sharp. "He's decided to go with Dixon Lumber." She kept a tight smile on her face as her gaze slid to the small knot of guests to their right. It would not do for the host of the party to appear distressed.

Worth's eyebrows hitched up. "What?"

"We're not getting the contract," Lydia said pointedly.

"Yes, I get that, but what happened?" Red splotches rose in Worth's cheeks. "I thought we had them. They told us —"

"It doesn't matter what they told us. What matters is where they signed their names. And it wasn't on our contract." Mertha lifted a glass of brandy from a passing tray and smiled a hello to a woman in a dark mink stole making her way to the outdoor fireplace. A stack of kindling nearby had dwindled during the evening as party guests fed the fire to ward off the chill of the early spring evening.

"We needed them, Worth. If we're going to keep Bishop Lumber at the top of the food chain, we can't lose clients like the Albrights."

"I know. I know." He took a long swig of his bourbon, neat.

"They're close friends with the Dennis family," Lydia added. "Who knows if the Albrights went straight to Jack Dennis and told him they'd changed their minds. What then?"

Worth hung his head. He seemed so despondent, Lily spoke up.

"He's trying," she said. "He works so hard for the company. It was just, what, three weeks ago that he secured the deal with

Carrier Whiting? That was a big deal, wasn't it?"

"It was good," Mertha said slowly, "but Carrier Whiting is not the big league. That's where we operate." She turned back to her son. "Worth, Jack Dennis is standing in my kitchen at the moment talking golf with Dave Skillen. I want you to take a minute and compose yourself, then go in there and calm any concerns he may have. I'm leaving it in your hands."

"Mother," Lydia started, but Mertha silenced her with a look.

"It's up to Worth. He can handle it."

She tossed one last penetrating glance over her shoulder at Worth, and then she and Lydia moved as one toward a group of men laughing near the stone steps that led down to a lower terrace.

Next to her, Worth exhaled deeply and a curse slipped out.

"You okay?" Lily asked.

He shook his head, but before he could speak, the small three-piece band Mertha had hired for the night struck up a jaunty Frank Sinatra tune. A smile tweaked the corner of Worth's mouth, and then it stretched into a grin.

"You remember this song?" he asked before singing a few bars adorably off pitch.

122

" 'The best is yet to come and babe, won't it be fine?' "

Lily laughed. "Our wedding dance."

He glanced across the yard to where his mother and sister had joined the group of men, their backs turned toward him, and then he took her hand and gave a tug. "Come on. Follow me."

"Worth, I don't have anything to talk about with Jack Dennis."

"We're not going to talk to Jack Dennis."

The Bishop home was situated on an acre of natural gardens, and while the inside of the house was crammed with stuffy centuries-old antiques and paintings, the outside was airy and relaxed with gently manicured rows offering winter honeysuckle, snowdrops, and daffodils. Worth led her past those to a large cherry tree in the corner. Standing on the other side of its low branches, they were mostly hidden from the guests but could still hear the music.

He pulled her toward him, circled her waist with one arm, and took her hand. As they swayed, he hummed the tune softly in her ear. She waited a bit, enjoying the quiet peace of the moment, before she questioned him.

"Are you not going to —"

"Shhh," he'd said.

"But . . . what are you —"

"Nothing. I'm doing nothing, except dancing with my wife. It's our anniversary, isn't it?"

"It is. And I appreciate the gesture, but . . ." She trailed off as Worth turned them in a slow half circle. Lily rested her cheek against Worth's shoulder and closed her eyes. "I just know your mom and . . ."

"It's okay," he whispered. "I don't care anymore."

When she opened her eyes a moment later, Mertha was watching them from across the yard, her mouth rigid with disappointment.

Eighteen days later Worth told his mother he wanted out of the family business. A few days after that, Lily was packing boxes for their move south. And tonight, two months after their last dance, she signed the divorce papers her husband had left in the kitchen for her to find.

After making up the bed with clean sheets and sinking down on her soft pillows, Lily picked up her phone and called Worth. He didn't answer, though she hadn't expected anything different. Next she called Mertha, who did answer, just as Lily knew she would. This time Lily skipped the polite niceties that usually started off their phone conversations.

"Mertha, I know you know where he is."

"What makes you say that?" Her voice was taut.

"You've been hyperaware of every step of your son's life, and I'm sure you know about this step as well."

Mertha sighed. "At this moment I don't know exactly where he is, but I have a general idea."

"If I can't find him, I can't get these papers back to him, so that means you're going to have to do it for me."

"Excuse me?"

"I've done my part. I've signed my name. It's all over now. I'll mail the papers back to you, and it'll be up to you to get them to Worth."

"I think you're being hasty. I told you Worth just needs some time . . ."

As Mertha rambled, blood rushed in Lily's ears. In and out, breaths and blood. She began to count slowly as Mertha told Lily all the things she was doing wrong in this situation. All the things she should have done differently to make this easier on Worth. As Lily breathed, she reminded herself she was done with Worth and his apologies, his unpredictability. His meddling mother. His secrets.

"Lily, are you hearing me?"

"Does this have anything to do with Delia Park?"

Mertha paused. It was so short, most people wouldn't have noticed, but Lily was well versed in Mertha's quick, confident answers, and she knew a hiccup in her mother-in-law's composure when she heard one. "Lily. You have to understand —"

"You know what? Never mind. I don't care." She was surprised to realize she actually meant it. The jealousy that should have been there . . . wasn't. Anger? Yeah, a little. But also comfort. A strange sense of lightness. "I don't need to hear your explanation. Worth, Delia — it doesn't matter anymore."

She ended the call and set down the phone on the table beside her. Under the sheets she pointed her toes and extended both arms out to the sides, stretching herself as far as she could. She inhaled deeply and let the air out slowly.

In her stilled mind she turned the page.

# EIGHT

Having lived alone for the better part of forty years, Rose generally didn't mind her housekeeping duties, but cleaning the kitchen after preparing a meal was another thing altogether. If she made the switch to microwave dinners or cans of soup and crackers, she wouldn't have as much to clean and put away, but she refused to eat like she was a sad old woman. She was neither sad nor old. Plus, she liked cooking. She learned a lot from the Food Network. That Bobby Flay taught her how to add some Cajun heat to her fish fillets, and she'd started sprinkling Parmigiano Reggiano on most of her roasted vegetables thanks to Giada with the big smile.

Tonight was different, though. Instead of her usual cleaning-the-kitchen scowl, she had a smile on her face as she waited for her guest. She didn't mind scrubbing the pot or rinsing the baking pan after making

chicken, buttered rice, and roasted aspara-
gus. As she wiped her skillet dry, she
hummed to a song she'd heard on the radio
earlier in the day.

She'd even considered making a little
extra chicken this evening and taking it
down to Lily, but Rose knew the woman
would probably be buried under a mountain
of welcome food and didn't want to be a
burden. Rose was about as Southern as one
could be, her family having been rooted in
the same few square miles of coastal Alabama land for generations, but no matter —
the Safe Harbor villagers, most of whom
came from parts much farther north, had
her beat when it came to bringing food to
help smooth life's curveballs. Births — of
grandchildren, of course — deaths, welcoming or going away, the residents had an itchy
trigger finger when it came to food. Rose
had never grown comfortable with inserting
herself into someone else's joy or pain.
Instead she usually let someone else step up
and do that particular job, and around here
there were plenty of willing volunteers.

As Rose leaned down to set the skillet in
its place in a lower cabinet and hang her
dish towel on the oven handle, she heard a
knock at the door. Three quick raps, then a
fourth. She smiled and glanced at the clock

on the microwave: 7:30. She was almost embarrassed by how much she looked forward to this evening each week — the one night she cooked for two, though tonight she'd eaten alone, as her guest had called to say he'd be late.

Rose twisted the lock on the door and opened it to see Rawlins standing under the porch light. "Sorry I missed dinner," he said. "I figured you'd appreciate me taking the time to shower before I came."

"I do appreciate it. And I saved you a plate." She opened the door wider and he stepped in, leaning down to give her a quick kiss on the cheek as he passed. He smelled of soap, like a little boy fresh from the bathtub. "I'm sorry I went ahead and ate without you. You know how my stomach acts up if I eat dinner too late."

"No worries." Once inside, he passed straight through to the glass doors overlooking the grass, then the bay. She gave him a moment as he silently greeted the living, breathing thing that was both his friend and foe. He tucked his hands in his back pockets and exhaled.

"Season opens next week." She pulled the foil off his plate and set a fork next to it. "How are you feeling about it?"

"It's hard to say. Canaan and I are going

129

out early tomorrow to have a look. See how the water feels."

"How early is early?"

"We'll be on the water by five thirty."

She looked at her watch. "What about your bedtime, young man?"

"Bedtime?" He turned away from the door and sat at the table, pulled the plate toward him. "Don't worry, Aunt Rose, I'll keep an eye on my bedtime." A crack of a smile. "Make sure it doesn't run off on me."

"Oh, you." She scoffed and reached over the table and pinched his shoulder as he dug into his chicken. "I know you're not little anymore. You're a grown man. Sometimes it's hard to see you that way, though. Especially with all that scruffy hair." She reached up and smoothed the curls that flipped up at the back of his head.

"Lucky for me, Canaan doesn't care what my hair looks like."

"I imagine you're right about that." As he ate, she took the wax paper off her pound cake and set it on a tray, then cut two slices. "How's Hazel doing? Is she still trying to pull her own tooth?"

"She's fine, and yes. She's determined that it's loose. I keep telling her it's not coming out anytime soon."

"She's with her mom for the weekend?"

Rawlins nodded. Rose didn't press. She knew he missed Hazel when she was gone.

She let him eat in peace while she grabbed two glasses from the cabinet and filled them with milk. When he finished eating, he set his plate in the sink, then grabbed two small plates. Rose slid a slice of cake on each one and added a fork, and then picked up the two glasses of milk and followed him out the back door.

All of the cottages in the village had sunset views, but Rose's cottage was situated away from the others on the tip of land that pushed out into Bon Secour Bay, making her view unparalleled. A large swath of grass led directly down to the water, and without a neighbor on either side like the rest of the cottages lining the marina, her view was unbroken. No fence or flamingo bird feeder in sight. Just wide, blue-gray water.

Two Adirondack chairs and a small table were in the middle of the grass facing the bay. Sitting there, her back to the rest of civilization, with nothing in her sight except water and sky, it was easy to imagine she was an explorer, perhaps the first person to have stumbled on this particular slice of beauty.

But of course she wasn't. Her great-grandfather had been the first, all the way back in the 1800s, long before anyone knew the water around this jut of land was teeming with brown, white, and pink shrimp. They figured it out quickly though, and subsequent generations of Willett men, and a few women, had traveled the water by trawler, seeking its bounty and goodness.

At one point in her life, many moons ago, Rose thought she'd be one of those women, one strong and brave enough to stand with the men, haul in the nets, gather the shrimp, bring them to shore. She wanted to help carry on the Willett tradition. But life had beat that particular ambition out of her, setting her on a path that culminated in Terry. It was only fitting that the man she married took a chunk of Willett land to build himself a village.

*Oh, come off it, Rose,* she chided herself. At this point in her life there was no reason to sugarcoat or soften blows. She couldn't blame it all on Terry. Or even half of it.

Regardless of how it happened, the village was built, and now, and for the last several decades, when Willett shrimpers navigated back home — through the gulf waters, back to Bon Secour Bay, and continuing along the narrow passageway of the Bon Secour River — the village flaunted itself right there, on the tip of the land, in all its landscaped, sunscreened glory.

Rose had long ago accepted her lot as owner of this village, the creation of which had so angered her family. People who had no knowledge of the Willett family and all that had happened before had flocked to the village from far-flung places, seeking their own type of bounty and goodness from these waters and this land. Who was she to ask any of them to give that up? At sixty-eight years old, she was just like them, seeking all manner of things from what she saw around her. Solace and comfort. Forgiveness. Redemption.

She stabbed her cake with her fork and pulled off an unladylike hunk. She hesitated, then went ahead and popped it in her mouth.

"You're quiet tonight," Rawlins said.

He'd stretched his long legs out in front, one ankle crossed over the other, his head tipped back in the waning blue glow. Eyes closed. His slice of pound cake sat untouched on the table between them.

"I could say the same about you," she said.

He shrugged one shoulder, then reached up and rubbed both hands over his face as he sat up in his chair. He picked up his fork and took a bite. "Mmm." He tapped his slice with the fork. "Something's different."

"Good different or bad?"

He paused, swallowed. "Good. Definitely good."

She pressed her lips together as her cheeks tried to stretch into a grin. "I added orange flower water."

He stared at her a moment, then took another bite. "Huh. I didn't know oranges had a flower. Or flower water. But I do taste orange."

"See what you would've missed if you'd changed your mind about coming?"

"I wasn't going to change my mind. I told you, I just needed a shower. I was moving furniture and boxes all day. As you know, since you volunteered me for the job."

The hint of a smile on his face betrayed his testy words.

"And I'm very thankful. I wouldn't have asked you to help if I thought she had anyone else. I think there's a husband, but something tells me there's trouble."

"Something? How about her leaving half her furniture behind and filling in the gaps with secondhand gems from Mrs. Mary?"

"You don't say."

"I do. I don't know what's going on there, and I didn't ask any questions. I just did what she said."

Rose nodded, pensive. "That was probably the best course of action." She sighed and leaned back in her seat. She decided not to mention what Lily had said about her husband not being her husband anymore. Something that big was best kept between the two people doing the deciding. "I don't know what all's going on with her, but she has some gumption, I'll grant her that. Whatever predicament she's in, she'll figure it out on her own."

She felt Rawlins's gaze on her face. "What?"

He chuckled. "Nothing. It's just not like you to take in strays. You don't typically . . . like people."

"I do too. I like you plenty. Usually."

"I know. It's just . . . It usually takes you a while to warm up to people. Look at Mr. Beaumont. He's been here, what, five years? And you still wrinkle your nose every time he comes around."

"That man is nothing but an annoying ray of sunshine. They don't make SPF high enough for him."

Rawlins stared at her, then laughed. "See what I mean? And here's this woman you met five minutes ago and she's already moved in."

"Okay, okay, I get it. It's . . . unlike me. But who said anything about liking her? You don't hire someone to do a job because you like her. If that was my hiring practice, I would have hired you to be the new hairdresser. How'd you like that? You feel okay trimming Peter Gold's mustache every week? Or covering up Janelle's grays?"

He smiled again — they always came easier once he let the first one go — and shook his head. "You're impossible."

"I'm not either. But I am a good businesswoman. I hired Lily because she came along at the right time. She needed a job, I needed a hairdresser. It was a business decision, pure and simple."

But darn if there wasn't more to it. Rose couldn't deny it, though she wouldn't admit it to Rawlins or anyone else. Watching Lily in the middle of that empty salon as she made her case for the job and the living space, seeing the fire in her eyes — it was obvious she needed an escape. What kind of woman would Rose be if she turned her down?

Despite all her willy-nilly emotions, Rose had done her part. She'd gotten Lily here, provided her with a job and a place to live, and now Lily was on her own. It was a trial run and it was up to her if she made it out the other side.

Rose turned her face back to the water

and stretched her legs out in front of her like her nephew. The sun was a blazing fraction of light now — partly there, mostly gone. She'd seen countless sunsets just like it, and more than half of them from this very spot, but they never failed to put her in her place.

"Business decision, huh?" Rawlins set his empty plate on the table just as the last sliver of sun drifted below the horizon. "If you say so."

Rose set her plate on top of his and noticed his empty milk glass. "How's that milk treating you?"

A half smile. "Just fine. I seem to be drinking a fair amount of it these days."

"Well, it's good for you, you know. Good for your bones."

"That's what I hear. Good for keeping me out of trouble too."

She made a noise of assent that she hoped was encouraging. She didn't want to shut down his talking, his enjoyment of the evening, by saying the wrong thing.

"You doing okay?" she ventured. It was always easier talking about trivial matters — pound cake, Coach Beaumont — than real things. She knew to be careful of unseen cracks in the path.

Rawlins exhaled, leaned forward, and

rested his elbows on his knees. "I'm fine."
He turned to her when she didn't respond.
"Really, Aunt Rose. I'm good."

"Well, I'm glad." She reached over and
squeezed his shoulder. "I'm always here for
you. Whatever you need. I know your dad
and I haven't . . ." She let the words trail
off. After all this time, there was nowhere
for them to go.

"I know. You haven't." He hung his head
and studied his thumbnail. "I've never
understood it." He looked back up at her
from under the brim of his cap. "You're
adults. Why can't you just talk it out and
move past it?"

Rose clasped her hands in her lap and
squeezed. The naïveté of the young. To think
she and Jim could just have a little chat and
put it all behind them.

"You should try to talk to him," Rawlins
said.

"He doesn't want to talk to me. I've tried
over the years. What happened between
us . . . Well, it was a long time ago."

Rose fell silent, remembering the day in
the somber church as if thirty-two years
hadn't passed by in a blink. When the
service was over, the sanctuary had been
still except for the sound of her brother's
weeping that bounced off every surface and

soul-wounded everyone within earshot. She used to be glad Rawlins had only been two at the time, too young to know what was really happening, but lately she'd been thinking about how much he had missed out on, not having his mother around as he grew up. Rose cared for him now — and Hazel too — as well as she could, but she knew she didn't take the place of a real mother.

Rawlins rubbed his palms together and stood. "He mentioned you the other day. Maybe the ice is thawing." He grabbed their plates with one hand and reached the other one down to help her up.

She thought of the last time she'd seen Jim. She'd run into the five-and-dime store on the island to look for a cheap tablecloth to cover the burn mark on the clubhouse card table, left there after Violet Abernathy's sewing machine caught fire. He'd been reading the label on a bottle of Formula 409, his reading glasses perched low on his nose, his hair as gray as hers and just as thick. She'd almost burst into tears there in the cleaning supply aisle, thinking of her brother's long years without Stella, as well as her own long years without him.

She turned and hurried out of the store without speaking, unable to withstand the possibility of seeing him turn away from her again.

"Maybe you should come see him," Rawlins said. "Call first, though. Probably best not to catch him off guard."

Rose chuckled. "You think?" She picked up their empty milk glasses and followed him back into her cottage.

He set the plates in the sink. "What do *you* think?"

"About what?"

"About calling Dad?"

"I think that ship has sailed. I think it's long gone by now."

"Don't be so sure." He pulled keys out of his pocket and moved toward her front door. "Don't you . . ." He hesitated, his brow creased, then shrugged and reached for the doorknob.

She stopped him. "Don't I what?"

He shrugged. "He's your only family. Other than me and Hazel. Do you really think my mom would want the two of you to still be fighting like this?"

*It's not a fight if we're not talking to each other.*

"Just think about it, okay?" He opened the door and stepped out onto the porch. The eastern sky was dark purple and studded with pinpricks of light. Crickets

140

hummed in the trees. Rose's favorite time of day.

"Let me know if she needs any more help?"

Rose shook her head in confusion. "Who?"

He raised his eyebrows. "Your new hire. Lily."

"Oh. Right." She picked up the gardening gloves she'd dropped by the door that morning, hitting them against the side of her leg. "I'll do that."

He nodded. "Let me know if you need anything too. It's a busy week, but I'm around if you need me."

Rose found herself fighting a lump in her throat, so she just nodded. She almost mentioned Terry's email and the proposition it held, letting him know things around here might be changing, but she bit her tongue. "Don't forget about this weekend. Saturday night."

"Summer Kickoff. How could I forget?"

"Everyone will expect to see you there."

"All they care about is making sure I bring shrimp."

"That's true. But the ladies like you. I think you're the main reason Janelle Blackmon comes. Well, you and the dancing. She doesn't turn down a chance to shake her bottom in front of a crowd of people."

He closed his eyes. "That woman. Last year she wouldn't quit pinching my . . . well, nowhere a grown man wants to be pinched."

Rose laughed. "Citronella spray. Use it liberally. She hates the smell."

His eyes widened. "I'll do it."

When he was halfway to his truck, she called to him. "Thanks for coming. It always does me good to see you."

"I know. That's why I come every week." He turned and walked the rest of the way to his truck. At the door, he called over his shoulder. "It does me good to see you too." His smile — easy, honest, laying bare his tender boy's heart — was a gift. "See you in a few days."

She waited until he started his truck and drove off, one arm out the window in a wave. Back inside her neat, clean, uncluttered cottage, she felt its quiet — its solitude — as both a comfort and a wound.

# NINE

Dear Stella,

Rawlins came over tonight. He's a good boy. A *good* one. I don't know what that Chrissy was thinking — there are no greener pastures. And right after he'd talked to me about giving her your ring. Praise the Lord for small blessings, she left before he handed it over. He's too good for her anyway. His heart is too pure. Don't worry — I'd never say that to his face. He'd get all quiet as he does sometimes, head off on that boat of his, turn off his GPS, and we wouldn't hear from him for a week.

There's a new girl here. I just hired her to take Beverly's place at the salon. If it appears she can do two things at once, I'm hoping to use her in the office at some point as well. The older I get, the less I seem able to juggle all I need to. You sure would've been better at all this than I am. Everyone here would've just eaten you up. You'd probably get Christmas cards and book club invitations. Shoot, you'd probably be first in line to do Coach Beaumont's silly paddleboat tours. Everyone would love you.

But instead they get me. And who knows, maybe they'd be happy to hear someone is interested in buying the place from me. From me and Terry. That's right, I have a chance to let this village go, which would probably be a nice full-circle moment, seeing as how this place came to be because of another letting go. A bigger one. Maybe I should just tell Terry yes now, hand the new owner my keys, and bid my farewells. I don't know yet.

I often think about our choices back then. *My* choices, I mean. I think about mine. Mine were the ones that got all jumbled and turned sour.

Do you remember when we first met? That day is seared in my mind with such clarity, as if it happened only a little while ago. Jim and I were eating lunch at that little café on Gay Street. I remember how sticky the menus were and how famished Jim was after the drive up to

Auburn from the island and unloading his truck at my apartment. He was so hungry he ordered two cheeseburgers. He'd already eaten the first one before you showed up standing next to our booth with a sweet smile, saying you recognized me from our biology class.

I remembered you too. You were the girl who always sat in the front row, your blonde hair in a perfect long braid, always raising your hand with right answers. When I asked if you wanted to sit down, Jim got so flustered he knocked over his Coke bottle. Do you remember that? You probably thought he was just clumsy, but that wasn't it. My little brother may have had appalling table manners and a bad habit of leaving piles of stinky, fish-smelling clothes in the bathroom, but he was careful and methodical to a fault. Shrimpers have to be. No, he was nervous, his heart already beating with affection for you, even on that very first day.

He barely noticed when Terry Carrigan sat down out of the blue, introducing himself and shaking hands like he was the mayor, thanking us for offering him the very last seat in the entire restaurant. We found out about his family money later, but even in the moment, I think all three of us knew there was something different about him. Something that both attracted and repelled us.

Sometimes I think back on that day. That random day when all four of us just happened to end up at the same booth, all thrown together by a hand we couldn't see. What if I'd had lunch ready for Jim at the apartment when he arrived? What if Terry had grabbed a burger down the street, or if the only open seat had been at someone else's table? Would the four of us have become friends? Would our lives have turned out differently?

That's a rabbit hole if I've ever seen one, and I often have to haul my mind out of it or I'd be lost forever. It's tempting to ponder the possibilities, though. Especially the thought of what would have happened had Terry never sat down. If he hadn't, you and I might be sitting at my kitchen table — or yours — having this conversation over a cup of decaf instead of me writing these letters, mooning over things that happened so many years ago they shouldn't even matter.

But they do matter. I know they do. And I live with the regret of it all.

Love,<br>Rose

Rose stood from her kitchen table and walked quietly up the stairs, though there was no one around to disturb, even if she'd stomped hard on each step. Sometimes she wanted to do just that — stomp, jump, even dance her way up the stairs and back down, just because she could. But she'd yet to summon the nerve.

The dresser in her bedroom used to belong to her mother. After Rose's actions all those years ago, she figured she'd be cut entirely from any inheritance she might receive when her mom passed away, but surprisingly, her mother left her several pieces of her best furniture. *Best* in this case was a loose term, as nothing in her parents' home would be featured in any catalog or department store showroom. But her mother did have a few nice things, items passed to her from her own parents, furniture that had stood the test of time and would no doubt continue to do so because it was well made by capable hands.

Rose's favorite piece was the Victorian highboy dresser that sat against the far wall of her bedroom, positioned between two windows. Solid oak with dovetail joints and a hazy mirror on top. In the bottom drawer, way in the back behind the carefully folded sweaters she kept in case the temperature dipped below sixty, was the manila envelope. She pulled it out and smoothed her hand over the top, feeling the various lumps and bumps inside. She slid tonight's letter inside with all the rest and patted the top, then tucked it away again, back into the drawer.

*Your Source for Neighborhood News*

May 23, 2018
Compiled by Shirley Ferrill

## GOOD DAY, SAFE HARBOR VILLAGE!

### TIDES

The next low tide will fall in the 3:15–3:30 a.m. range, so please set your alarm clocks. Last Tuesday when the tide was at its lowest, a certain villager strolling along the shore was startled to see a complete set of dentures lying in a clump of seagrass. This made me wonder what other treasures may have been dropped, accidentally or otherwise. If we could all take a quick peek at this next low tide, it'd do a world of good to clean up our shores. (And if the owner of the dentures would like them back, let me know. I'm keeping them in a mason jar under my sink.)

### MARINE LIFE

If you missed it in last Monday's newsletter, a large manatee has been spotted in the mouth of the Bon Secour River, causing no small amount of worry. The marine authorities are at work, attempting to lure the poor lost creature back out into the bay rather than risk being bumped by a shrimp trawler or one of Coach's paddleboats. If you happen to see the manatee, please give him a wide, respectful berth.

## RECREATION

The inaugural paddleboat tour was a success! No capsized boats and no belongings (or people) overboard. A big thank-you to Coach Beaumont, who worked so hard to secure the paddleboats for the village and for showing us the sights on the river. There was only one slight hitch — one of the boats hit a hidden cypress knee, which tore a tiny hole in the hull. Coach says not to worry. He can fix it with some epoxy.

## SUMMER KICKOFF — THIS SATURDAY NIGHT!

- Festivities will kick off at 6:00 with Old Enough to Know Better starting at 7:00.
- If you're bringing food, please have it ready no later than 5:30. We all know how antsy certain residents get if dinnertime is pushed back too far.
- As usual, Toots Baker is in charge of the cocktails, though this year she's keeping mum on her selections. I've already

asked her to go ahead and make an extra pitcher.

# TEN

In the dead dark of night, something pulled
Lily from sleep. She shot up in bed like a
spark, scanning the strange room, the
mounds of clothes and shoes and boxes, and
it took several long moments before she realized where she was.

A new place. Again.

What had woken her? Rain splattered
against the window, but it was a soft,
nonthreatening patter. Her mind swam with
vague shapes and faces, everything mingling
together until she wondered, *Dream or not
dream?* Thunder rumbled overhead, long
and deep. Just as the echo faded, she heard
something else, something softer, inside the
house. A rustle, a stirring. Worth?

She flung the sheets away and swung her
legs to the floor. In a second she was out
the bedroom door and down the hallway to
the stairs. She started down them quickly,
but she slowed as she reached the bottom,

unsure of what she hoped to find. Her thin nightgown swirled around her knees, the cotton as light as breath, and her heart thumped.

Downstairs was even darker, and the rain came harder now, a steady thrum like a fast-moving river. The rustle was still there, coming and going, though she couldn't tell from where. She glanced around as shadows danced in the corners. When the sky lit up with a zip of lightning, the shadows retreated. Misshapen lumps became her new loveseat, the small kitchen island, the hooded hair dryer. And the rustle revealed itself to be a magazine lying on a side table, its pages stirred by the breeze from the ceiling fan. She wrapped her arms around herself as her heart's rhythm slowed.

It had rained the night Worth left. It had started sometime after he'd come to bed, after she'd fallen asleep with his arms around her and his damp cheek against the back of her neck. She never heard the rain, though. For that matter, she hadn't heard Worth leaving either. She was oblivious to both until the next morning when she woke up to a rain-washed world outside her window and his note next to the coffee maker.

Lily walked to the front door. When she

pulled it open, heavy, moist air rushed in. The rain was starting to slack again to a drizzle, and the light drops made a soft *pat, pat, pat* against the grass and leaves. She sat on the porch swing and took a deep breath, inhaling the salty scent of the bay mixed with the earthy, water-cleansed air of this new and strange land. *Bon Secour. Safe Harbor.*

As the rain faded into mist, a tall, thin woman walked by on the street, passing under the streetlight. She held a leash, and at the end of the leash was the smallest dog Lily had ever seen. It wore a bright yellow rain jacket and hat with a strap under its chin. As Lily stared, the woman slowed and held up a hand in greeting. Lily waved back, and then the dog yipped and the woman hurried along behind it.

Lily sat for several more quiet minutes, letting the cool night air wash from her mind the disorientation she'd felt moments before.

*This is home,* she reminded herself. It may not be permanent, but nothing was, really. She was sure of that. All she could do was rest in the peace she already felt in this place. The certainty that this was the right step for right now. *And that's enough.*

Back in bed upstairs, she thought of her

first home. A few miles from their house in Fox Hill, a hiking trail ran through the woods and ended at a breathtaking cliff. Down below was a sparkling blue-green lake fed by a waterfall that spilled from the rocks and plunged with enormous strength into the waters below. It scared Lily the first time she found it. Everything about it seemed dangerous — the loud, crashing water, the rocky places wet and slippery with algae, the prickly, ragged bushes that surrounded it. But one day she found her spot — a dry rock, warmed by the sun, the edges covered in a soft fur of moss. It was a bare area, a little space carved out of the wild just big enough for her. And there she'd rest, legs outstretched, her back against a boulder, the crisp, clean air filling her senses.

Lying in bed inside her cottage, Lily closed her eyes and imagined she was high on that cliff. Behind her everything was covered in thorns and briars, all poised to pierce and hurt and bruise, and ahead was nothing but the great wide open — birds flying in lazy loops, high white clouds in a blue sky, a distant echo. It was remote and scary, and below were dark depths, but this spot was warm and comforting. A soft place to land if she could just keep her eyes focused on all that open air.

■ ■ ■

The next morning Lily awoke as soon as daylight pricked the edges of the blinds and spilled into the crevices of her bedroom. On the kitchen counter in the back of the cottage she found the coffeepot and the few mugs she'd nestled into a box and brought with her. She plugged in the coffee maker, found her bag of coffee in a box on the stairs, and pressed the Start button. With her bare feet chilly on the old parquet floor, she stood by the counter and waited for the scent to rise.

An hour later Lily was elbow-deep in the kitchen sink, the basin full of hot, soapy water. While drinking her second cup of coffee on the front porch, she'd decided everything she'd brought into the cottage — everything she'd shoved into a box or a reusable grocery bag — needed a good cleaning. Utensils, plates, laundry, life. It would all start over fresh.

When she finished washing, she wiped her hands on a damp dish towel hanging from the oven door and surveyed the rest of the cottage. There was much to do.

She worked for the rest of the morning — dusting, sweeping, and mopping the floors.

She opened the windows to let in fresh air and arranged and rearranged the sparse furniture they'd brought in the day before. At some point she stopped to eat a corn bread muffin with homemade butter a neighbor had brought by, and she turned on some music on her phone when her energy lagged. The sun had popped out, and by noon she was singing along to the Avett Brothers as she went around the room on her hands and knees, wiping the baseboards with damp rags.

Just as the song ended, someone knocked on the open door. Lily swiveled her head and saw Rose standing in the doorway holding two small, lidded containers.

Lily stood and wiped her hands on the sides of her shorts as she walked to the door. Behind Rose, a handful of people milled around the café across the street, casting curious looks in their direction.

"Good morning." Rose glanced at her watch. "Afternoon now. I heard your music from the street. Sounded like a party in here." She leaned her head in and peered around. "You've been hard at work."

"Yes, ma'am. I figured I'd go ahead and start getting things straightened up so I'm ready for customers soon. I'm not sure when people are expecting me to be up and running . . ."

"Maybe take this week, and then start on Monday. Everyone knows you're here, so take any longer and my phone will start ringing with complaints. The minute you say you're open, you'll have a string of ladies lined up at the door, I have no doubt."

"What about you? Will you need a haircut? As the boss, you could skip to the front of the line."

She expected a smile, but Rose pressed her lips together. Rose gave off the appearance of severity — gray-streaked hair pulled back into a bun with a visor low over her eyes, practical khaki shorts, white tennis shoes — but something in her face suggested a gentle beauty, though she tried her best to snuff it out with sternness.

"You just let me know when you're ready, and I'll spread the word. I assume you'll need to make some purchases. Shampoos and . . ." She shrugged. "Other necessities?"

Lily nodded as a breeze lifted tendrils of the climbing vine growing up the corner post of the porch. "There's a beauty supply store in town. I should be able to get most of what I need there."

"Good." As if remembering what she held in her hands, she thrust the Tupperware containers toward Lily. "I made some

158

spaghetti. It's nothing special. And there's some cucumber salad too."

"Thank you. That's very thoughtful."

Rose shrugged. She looked past Lily into the house again.

"I still have some work to do," Lily said when Rose remained silent. "I want it to feel comfortable for people."

Rose looked at her, one eyebrow cocked. "It's a hair salon, not a spa. People just need a wash and trim, right?"

"Well, yes. That's true. But it doesn't hurt for the place to feel a little special, right?"

"I suppose. I've never given much thought to how a trip to the hairdresser is supposed to feel."

"I'd say it should make you feel like a new man," boomed a deep voice. Together the women turned to see a man strolling toward them from the cottage next door, a shop called the Pink Pearl. "Or a new woman, in your case," he said to Rose with a grin.

Lily recognized him as the man from the golf cart, the one who'd brought her fried chicken. Coach. His dark gray hair was windblown, like he'd just gotten off a boat, and he wore a sky-blue fishing shirt with the top couple of buttons undone. On his feet were leather flip-flops. His appearance and general ease made Lily smile, but Rose

159

cocked a skeptical eyebrow.

"A new man? You get all that from a haircut?" Rose asked.

"Oh yes. A hot towel on my face, a shave with a straight razor, and an inch of cold whiskey in a glass next to me." He closed his eyes and let out a sigh.

"For Pete's sake," Rose muttered. Small splotches of pink rose in her cheeks. "I don't think Lily will be serving whiskey in her salon." She eyed Lily. "Will you?"

"Ah, no, I don't think so. And I'm sorry to say I've never shaved anyone with a straight razor. But I have cut men's hair."

"Good to hear, although I don't actually get haircuts that often." He put a hand to his hair and ruffled it a bit. "Makes me a little nervous to go under the scissors."

Rose rolled her eyes, but Lily laughed. "I understand. I'll be open soon if you want to swing by. I promise not to do anything dangerous."

He laughed. "Have you been to the pool yet? It's a good day for a swim."

"No, not yet. Honestly, I'm not even sure where my bathing suit is at the moment."

"It's just as well," Rose said. "Tiny's grandkids are here for a couple days. I saw them at the pool on my way here."

Coach chuckled. "Rose is right. Best to

steer clear while they're around. The granddaughter is fine, but you have to watch out for the little boy. The rascal punched his sister's tooth out last summer. Of course he said it was an accident."

"How do you accidentally punch someone's tooth out?"

"The tooth was already loose," Rose said. "And he swore he was trying to brush a yellow jacket off her head. But you know boys."

Coach winked. "Boys are always up to no good." He turned and headed for the street where his golf cart was parked in front of the café. Sitting on the front seat like a passenger was a pink plastic pelican with a lei around its neck. "I'll see you ladies later." He paused in the grass. "You're coming to the party Saturday, aren't you, Lily?"

"Party?" She looked at Rose, who sighed.

"It's the Summer Kickoff picnic. But don't feel obligated to come if you don't want to."

"Are you kidding?" Coach boomed. "Lily, you won't want to miss it. It's the party of the year."

"You just say that because everyone compliments your barbecue."

"And my ribs are reason enough to come, even if Lily didn't have a whole village of people to meet. There's food, music, swimming. Games set up on the grass. You name it. And you're coming if I have to come pick you up in my golf cart myself."

Lily smiled and shrugged. "I guess I'll come. Do I need to bring anything?"

"Nothing but an appetite."

Lily looked at Rose. "You're coming too?"

"No, I don't usually —"

"Nod your head, Rose," Coach instructed. "Yes, she'll be there." He tapped two fingers to his forehead in a salute. "Ladies. Until we meet again. Oh, and, Lily, even if you don't want to go swimming, the pool deck is especially nice as the sun sets." He crossed the street, whistling some tune Lily faintly recognized, and climbed in his golf cart.

Rose patted her hands along her head, though no hair was out of place, and straightened her shirt. "If you go, follow the road that way," Rose said, pointing. "You can't miss the pool. It overlooks the bay. Keep your eyes peeled — when my nephew is working a night shift, he usually heads out around sunset."

"On the shrimp boat, right? He mentioned it yesterday."

Rose's eyebrows lifted and she nodded. "That's right. Shrimping is our . . . Well, it's *his* business. His and his father's, actually.

It's the family business."

"He just said he worked on a boat. He didn't say anything about a business."

"He wouldn't. He's about as humble as they come. Willett Fisheries. It's down the river a ways. My family has owned it since the early 1900s. Rawlins is a third-generation shrimper." Lily heard the pride in Rose's voice, though her face gave nothing away.

"You can't miss his boat. It has a bright green stripe down the side." Rose glanced back toward the road and cleared her throat. "I have some work to do in the office. Things will be busy this week until we get past this party" — she said the word like it tasted bad — "But I'll be by later on to check on you and see how you're getting along."

"That sounds good. Thank you."

Without a goodbye, she turned and walked out the way she had come.

# ELEVEN

Lily's mother was the strongest, most generous woman — person, really — Lily had ever known. Lillian Chapman never turned down anyone who desired a trim, color, or curl-and-set, or even just a chance to sit down and chat in a comfortable place, often working on a bartering system. Women would bring fresh-baked bread or a crate of apples they'd just picked, or they'd offer to wash and fold the towels Lillian used by the basketful. Lily's mother saw her job as more than just cutting and styling hair — it was a way to lighten the load of the women around her, even if the work often increased the load on her own shoulders.

Cutting hair didn't bring in much money, so Lillian cleaned houses on the side. What her mother made — and Lily too, once she started working in the salon full-time — went toward paying bills, putting food on the table, and keeping up the necessary stock of shampoos, dyes, curlers, and combs. Lillian was never one to splurge on anything, other than perhaps a new shampoo when a regular customer mentioned that the scent of lemons always made her happy.

When Lillian died at the age of forty-eight from complications of pneumonia, Lily recovered from the shock as well as she could, then began going through her mother's things with the intention of deciding what to keep for herself and what to donate or give away to customers or neighbors. The last thing she expected to find was money. Jars and tins at the top of her bedroom closet, envelopes slid under the mattress, pouches in her dresser drawers that should have held makeup or toiletries — Lillian had crammed money everywhere, and Lily never had a clue.

Lily checked every possible place her mother might have stashed money, then set it out in piles on the living room floor and counted it. When she wrote down the total, she threw down the pen and put her face in her hands. She knew the house like she knew her own reflection, yet her mother had been able to stash away just under ten thousand dollars, right under Lily's nose.

She and her mother had lived together in

Lily's small childhood home with the peeling blue paint and the sign out front directing customers to park under the hickory tree. All Lily could think about was how her mother had worn the same dresses and pants over and over until they grew soft and threadbare. She never dressed up in anything fancy and had only one pair of "good shoes" she wore to church and the occasional wedding or funeral. Her sole extravagance for herself was buying chocolate ice cream. How could a woman like that manage to put away so much money? And in such a way that Lily had never felt its absence?

Sitting on the floor of their small living room, surrounded by memories, scents, and visions of her mother, she wondered if she had it wrong. Maybe the money wasn't hers, maybe Lillian had stored it away for someone else. Maybe it was all a mistake.

Then, as clear as a blue winter sky, she heard her mother's soft voice. *I did it all for you.*

Maybe Lily imagined it. Any sane person would tell her she conjured her mother's voice out of thin air. Even so, it was a comfort. Lily took the words to heart and saved the money, knowing it was hers, for whatever she needed.

She kept up her mother's work — cleaning houses and running the salon — for as long as she could, but after three years without Lillian's experience and encouragement, Lily ran out of steam. She considered dipping into the money her mom had left her, but she knew she'd run through it quickly keeping the bills paid and the lights on, so she wished her customers well, flipped the Closed sign around for the last time, and put a For Sale sign in the front yard.

When she met Worth, she'd been living in Atlanta for three months, staying in the garage apartment that belonged to a client's niece, and by the time she married him a short while later, she still hadn't touched a dime of Lillian's money. The money she got from the sale of her house in Fox Hill became *their* money — hers and Worth's — but she kept her mother's hard-earned sacrifice a secret from Worth. Ten thousand dollars was a drop in the bucket for a family like the Bishops, but to her it meant much more. It meant love and provision and a mother's selfless gift.

Today, as she pulled out the envelope with the stacks of neatly folded bills inside, she was thankful she'd kept the money close rather than sink it into her and Worth's seemingly bottomless bank account. No reason to call the bank, no messy transfers of money, no need to get Worth involved.

Here she was, years after her mother had hidden away her last secret dollar, finally having a reason to dig into that money. She needed shampoos, conditioners, a supply of foils and dyes, a new curling iron and hair dryer, and an assortment of new brushes, combs, and fluffy towels. She felt good about it, like she was honoring her mom by using her savings to set up a hair salon, even if it was a sudden job in what amounted to a retirement village on the Gulf Coast. She sensed her mother whispering to her, *You could do much worse, my child.* Then, *You can also do better.* And in those last words, she knew Lillian wasn't talking about the village.

Lily spent the rest of the week scrubbing, dusting, scouring, and disinfecting. After purchasing everything she needed to get the salon up and running, she wiped, soaked, and rinsed a little more.

Finally she looked around the salon and realized it was ready. The place sparkled and smelled of lemons and pine. She'd set up a small check-in desk near the front door and hung green-and-white checked café curtains in the windows. She situated the waiting chairs in the sunlight that poured in from the big front window. She'd even cut some vines of clematis from the front porch and stuck them in glass jars she found in the back of the kitchen pantry, scattering them on every flat surface. This salon didn't have the same atmosphere that Lillian's did, with the back room that sweltered in the summer heat, sheltered in the winter, and always overflowed with the warmth of Lillian's smile. Lily used to imagine that the women's conversation and laughter, their joys and sadness, all tangled together and became part of the hazy steam that floated out of the half-propped windows and carried out over the mountain passes.

Lily's salon was different. It was open, airy, the land around it flat, tropical, and tinged with salt and coconut. The hardwood floor was scrubbed to a shine, and the chairs held out their arms for willing customers. Lily turned the ceiling fans on high and relished the breeze that lifted her hair and tickled her cheeks. She smiled, thinking her mom would love the feel of the place.

That evening Lily made her way to the pool for the first time, and just as the sun was going down, as Coach had suggested. As soon as she came out from under the shade of the live oaks that lined Port Place with low-hanging arms, the sky before her exploded in vivid swaths of pink and orange. The cottages she passed all reflected the sky's splendor. A handful of other residents were out for a similar evening excursion. Whether walking or riding in golf carts, all eyes were on the riot of color in the western sky.

As she neared the wooden walkway that led to the pool, a string of folks in bathing suits and wrapped in beach towels was heading out the gate and toward the road. Leading the way was Tiny, the woman in purple she'd met at the grocery store.

"Hello, Lily," Tiny called, wiggling her fingers in a wave. She wore a white swim cap and a terry cloth swimsuit cover-up. "You should have come a little earlier. We just finished water aerobics."

"Oh, it's okay, I'm not wearing my suit. I just came to look around."

"Well." Tiny was breathing hard, as if she'd expended all her energy in underwater leg lifts and squats. "Next time then. Cricket's a doozy of a teacher. She'll whip us all into shape. Even you, Humphrey," she called to a portly man waddling down the steps behind her, clutching a yellow pool noodle under his arm.

When everyone had passed through the gate and she'd said goodbye to Tiny, Lily walked through the gate herself. The wide pool deck and chairs were empty, except for a pair of pink sparkly goggles on the ground next to the diving board and a striped towel folded on the far side of the pool with a pair of flip-flops on top. A single swimmer glided through the water with long, steady strokes. Lily sat in a lounge chair facing the bay as the swimmer, a woman in a turquoise swim cap, finished her last lap and stood in the shallow end.

"Hi there. I didn't see you come in," the woman said, wiping water from her tanned face. "I wanted to get a few laps in before I left. Water aerobics doesn't do quite enough to get my heart pumping like I need it to."

"You must have done something right. I think you got everyone else's hearts racing."

She laughed. "That's good to hear. I bet half of them don't come back next week, though." Instead of using the steps, she hoisted herself onto the side of the pool with fluid grace. Her swimsuit, turquoise like her cap, had straps that crisscrossed in the back. Despite her muscled arms and trim figure, age had taken its toll in the form of lumps and sags in the usual places, but the woman exuded a confidence that didn't have time

171

for embarrassment or shame.

She turned to Lily and pulled off her swim cap, revealing short gray hair threaded with pink streaks that stood in disarray. "You must be our new village hairdresser."

"That's right. I'm Lily."

She nodded. "I'm Cricket. You won't see me in the salon anytime soon." She put a hand up to her hair and ruffled it a bit. "Still trying to grow this out."

"I like the pink," Lily said. "I've always wanted to try a color in my hair."

"You should do it." She tilted her head. "Purple, though. It'd look good with that copper hair."

Cricket looped the towel around her shoulders and waved goodbye before turning away, clad in just her suit and flip-flops for the walk home.

With no one else around, Lily turned her attention back to the sky and the water. She'd checked Google Maps earlier to orient herself, and she now understood that Safe Harbor Village was situated on the sharpest point of a triangle-shaped island that jutted out into Bon Secour Bay. To the north of the island was the narrow Bon Secour River. To the south was the intracoastal waterway, which ran all the way to Florida. Bon Secour Bay, the wide expanse that spread out before her, was tucked into the eastern edge of Mobile Bay, which in turn flowed out into the Gulf of Mexico.

From her vantage point on the lounge chair, with nothing between her and the water except the wooden railing of the pool deck and an expanse of scrubby grass, Lily laid her head back against the chair and closed her eyes. Before she'd left the cottage, she tucked her phone into her pocket, and she felt it now, a slight pressure against her thigh. She did her best to ignore it.

She'd kept busy enough during the week to avoid the temptation of easy online access, but now, with no activity to occupy her mind, the temptation to know what Worth was doing — or at least where he'd disappeared to — grew substantially.

She'd never been very active on social media, but Worth had been. He had hundreds of friends on Facebook, people he saw regularly and others he hadn't seen in years. He was always checking and scrolling, laughing at posts, adding his own two cents.

Lily opened her eyes. She'd checked his page the day he'd disappeared and a couple days after that, but she hadn't looked at it again. Now the possibility that his page could tell her something about where he'd gone was too much to resist. She retrieved the phone from her pocket and typed "Ainsworth Bishop" into the search box on Facebook, but nothing came up. She tried just using Worth, then added the IV after his name, but still nothing. His page was gone. He'd deleted it.

On a hunch, she typed in "Delia Park." When Delia's page loaded, Lily scrolled and scanned the posted articles and essays, mostly about Delia's rise to fame as a movie producer in Hollywood, best known for the strong female leads in her movies and for participating in a recent writers' strike, urging studios to pay their talent fair wages. Lily searched for Worth's name among the comments from friends and fans on Delia's page, but she didn't find anything.

After taking several long moments to remember her password, she opened Instagram and pulled up Delia's page. Her stomach dropped when she saw a photo of Delia and Mertha standing together behind a podium, arms around each other's back. It was dated just three weeks ago. Delia's caption read, "It's an honor to be included in Atlanta's Women Business Leaders' list of Top Tier Women. Accepting the award from my longtime friend Mertha Bishop made it even more special."

Lily inhaled deeply. As she'd told Mertha

on the phone, it didn't matter anymore, but even still, a kernel of anger pushed against the confines of her chest, hard and faintly electric. If she'd never met Worth, she never would have been pulled into the vortex of his family, their business, or their life. And she sure wouldn't have moved to this remote location at the southern tip of Alabama. Because of him, she was a stranger in a strange place, away from everything that was familiar to her.

*But nothing in Atlanta was familiar either.*

She exhaled. Atlanta wasn't the place she loved and missed. It was Fox Hill. It was her mother. And it was everything her mother did to create a home, a sanctuary, a welcome place for others. But her mother was gone. If Lily wanted a home like that again, it was up to her to coax it to life.

Maybe she should be thanking Worth instead for forcing her to stand on her own two feet and build the world she needed.

*Well, let's not get carried away.*

She had an itch to do something impulsive. Jump into the swimming pool fully clothed. Or throw her phone as far as she could into the bay. That one she actually considered. Without it at her fingertips, she'd be less likely to feel the need to check in on Delia again, the woman who had long ago captured her husband's heart, and who very well may still be the keeper of it.

In Worth's absence, she was finding her mind cooler and clearer than ever. Yes, she and Worth had shared an electric handful of months. And yes, a part of her heart had wondered if she'd met "the one." But the strange thing was, even after being married to him for over a year, she readily accepted that she'd never been the keeper of his heart. She'd never had a real grasp of it. And he'd never held hers.

As if coming out of a fog, her eyes focused and she realized the sky had transformed, the oranges and pinks deepening to raspberry, magenta, and violet. The sun was just a blur over the horizon now, though still too intense to look at full on. She'd come here for the sunset and she'd almost missed it. Almost.

A string of seagulls flew in a haphazard line across the highest part of the sky, each one barely flapping its wings, caught up in the breeze. When she lowered her gaze back to the expanse, she noticed a boat approaching the bay from the mouth of the river off to her right. As it drew nearer, Lily could make out the words in swirling cursive along the side — *Miss Stella*. The white of the hull was bright and crisp against the grass-green stripe stretching down its side. Tall poles protruded from the center, and dark green nets hung from some of them, while others were bare, reaching proudly toward the sky. In the wheelhouse, she could just barely make out the shape of a person standing at the window.

As the boat passed in front of Safe Harbor Village and turned out toward the bay, it made a striking presence against the backdrop of the fiery sky. Lily kept her eyes on it until the sky darkened to an artist's palette of purples and blues and the boat was just a smudge on the horizon. The bay was silver, almost velvety, and at the edge down in front of the pool, small waves lapped against the sandy shore in slow licks.

Lily leaned her head back again, the fabric of the chair sun-roughened against her skin. She closed her eyes, this time letting herself imagine someone sitting next to her, someone to share the beauty before her and the tender places of her heart.

# TWELVE

The day of the party began like it was mad. The bay beat its anger against the shoreline during the early morning hours as clouds lunged, low-slung across the sky. Rose was not accustomed to being awake for the day's first stirrings. She'd long ago slipped into the luxurious habit of allowing herself to fall back asleep after her 5 a.m. trip to the bathroom, and she regularly slept until at least seven thirty, Coach's sunrise serenades notwithstanding.

When she was younger, Rose was an early riser, but it wasn't by choice. A sickly child, she usually had a thermometer thrust in her mouth in the wee hours or was woken for a dose of cough syrup or a steamy shower to soothe a bout of croup. Because of that, she was usually awake to see the shrimpers pull into the gravel parking lot of Willett Fisheries, lumber from their trucks to the boats, and prepare the nets for their daily work.

She saw her mother dress and take up her station behind the counter, ready to pour hot coffee for the workers and, later in the morning, ring up customers picking up pints or quarts of shrimp or oysters.

Rose watched her father and Jim, when he was old enough, load their bags for the day on the water. She always wished she could go out on the boats with them, even sometimes packing her own bag and attempting to slip out to the docks without anyone seeing her. But her father would always catch her and lead her away from the docks with a firm grip on her upper arm.

Leonard Willett was a hard man to grow up with. When he was at home, he was never truly at home, always wishing he were back on the water. That's where he came truly alive. He was much more comfortable reading the tides and shrimp habits and thunderstorms than the emotional temperature of the Willett home. Especially the female members. Especially his daughter. Life with him was a delicate dance on eggshells.

Anytime she'd try to slip onto the boat unnoticed, he'd tell her the water was no place for a girl, but that was all she wanted — to work with Jim and the other men, to prove she was strong, that she could do big things, that she could be useful. But he never relented, always choosing to see her as the sick young child she'd been, always disappointed the Lord had seen fit to give him a daughter rather than another son to help with the family business.

Whether he meant all little girls or just her, she wasn't sure. All Rose knew was that her family's work — the work that left them in both plenty and want, that brought them both joy and misery — never seemed to stretch enough to include her in its net. When she was young, that exclusion was a dark bruise she wore, each "no" a firm press on her tender flesh. Once she was a teenager, she'd pushed her affection for the water, the boats, the shrimping lifestyle, and the men who ruled it far out of arm's reach. She made herself give it up. Never getting to experience what a life on the water could be like saddened her, but she told herself to get over it. She began sleeping long enough to miss the early morning buzz of activity, the hopeful expectation of a good haul and a full cash drawer.

Years later when she married Terry, Rose was happy to discover he was a late sleeper too. As a commercial developer, he found no reason to get an early jump on the day, explaining that he never liked to disturb potential clients before their second cup of coffee. As an adult, whether she lived near the water or miles from it, Rose preferred to sleep right through those pastel-brushed morning hours until close to eight, when the boats were gone and the day was already awake.

Yet here she was at five forty-five, lying in her bed, as awake as she'd been when her eyes opened an hour ago, mind racing. The same thing had happened several times in the past week or so, as if something had wormed its way into her brain, causing her synapses to misfire and wake her at the wrong times. She felt expectant, like she was on a moving conveyor belt that was taking her somewhere specific, but she had no way to control where she was going. And Rose didn't like giving up control.

She didn't even know what she was expecting. She never had visitors, wasn't awaiting any packages in the mail beyond her regular mail-order blood pressure medicine, and her birthday wasn't for another seven months. Everything was status quo.

Except it wasn't. She'd received an offer to give up everything she knew here at the village. To hand over her responsibilities and choose for herself what the rest of her days would look like. And her mind had swung between yes and no so many times it nearly made her light-headed.

And in the middle of all this indecision, Lily Bishop had broken into Rose's world, upending it with her fresh beauty, her dogged determination, and her mysterious absent husband.

A nugget of discontent had lodged itself deep down in Rose's innermost being, and Rose guessed this, more than anything, was what was waking her up. Something wasn't cooperating, and she wasn't sure how much longer she could keep insisting everything was just fine.

By late morning, the angry sky had cooled its heels and settled into sunshine and a light breeze. A perfect day for a party, though Rose was always suspicious of seemingly perfect days. Something was usually apt to go wrong when she least expected it.

Rawlins was coming at noon to set up the folding tables and tents and the wooden planks that would serve as a dance floor. A few of the men would come out to help him later in the day, while most of the women would be at home whipping up cheese balls, pigs in a blanket, and barbecue cocktail weenies, and filling pitchers with sweet tea and lemonade. Walking out to check her mailbox, Rose could already smell the sweet, spicy scent of Coach's ribs cooking out in the Big Green Egg behind his cottage on Anchor Lane. He slow-roasted them all day, and by 6 p.m., they were fall-off-the-bone tender. She hated to admit they were the best barbecue ribs she'd ever tasted.

She was placing her sugars, flour, and baking powder back in the cabinet, a coffee cake baking in the oven, when her doorbell rang, followed by the creak of the front door.

"Aunt Rosie!" a little girl's voice squealed.

Amid a pounding of small feet and a blur of red curls, Hazel Willett burst into the kitchen like a summer lightning storm. She pulled out the step stool Rose kept tucked into the crevice beside the fridge and propped it open next to the counter where Rose was working.

"Whatcha making?" she asked, promptly sticking her finger in the bowl of excess crumbled topping.

"Hang on, hang on, there's butter in there," Rose managed before Hazel stuck a piece in her mouth.

"You say that like it's a bad thing." Rawlins entered the kitchen with two duffel bags slung over his shoulder — one pink, one purple.

"Nothing bad about butter, except maybe

a plain chunk of it in your mouth." She grimaced as Hazel ate another piece.

"Okay, little miss. That's enough." Rawlins grabbed a paper towel from the counter and wiped Hazel's greasy fingers. Rose did the same thing to her own hands with a dish towel.

"What brings you two here?" Rose asked, eyebrows raised over Hazel's head so she wouldn't see.

"Tara got a new job," he said, raising his eyebrows back. He lifted the cap on his head and resettled it. "She's working in Destin now, so Hazel and I will be seeing a lot more of each other." He leaned down and kissed the top of her head and picked her up. "Starting with this weekend."

"Daddy's going to let me swim in the pool after he sets up for the party."

"Oh, is he now?"

"Uh-huh. And I'm jumping off the diving board. I brought my bathing suit." She wiggled out of his arms and pulled the pink bag off his shoulder. "I want to put it on." When she finally got the bag free, she ran with it into the bathroom.

While Hazel was gone, singing softly to herself as she changed clothes, Rose set her bowls and measuring cups in the dishwasher, then checked her kitchen timer. "So

Tara has a new job? Again?" Twelve more minutes on the cake.

"Yeah," Rawlins said with a sigh. He dropped the purple bag to the floor and sat on a kitchen stool. "She has a friend who says she makes two hundred dollars a night in tips at this new restaurant on 30A. She's going to give it a shot."

"Hmph." Rose pulled a dozen eggs from the fridge and filled a big pot of water. "That girl's going to give herself whiplash with how quickly she runs from one thing to the next." Setting the pot on the stove, she carefully added the eggs to the water and turned up the heat.

"She loves Hazel." His voice was quiet. "She just . . . I don't know." He rubbed a hand over his face. "But you're right. She's always running."

"Maybe all the running around is her way of trying to replace the good thing she had with you."

"What we had wasn't good. It was young and impulsive and . . . reckless." He released a puff of air from his nose. "The only good that came from those two years is about to pop out of that door in a bathing suit."

As if summoned by their conversation, Hazel burst from the bathroom and ran to the center of the den, hands on her hips,

Wonder Woman–style, little round belly pushing against a yellow-and-white polka-dotted bathing suit. "I'm ready to swim."

"I'm surprised your suit isn't pink, Miss Hazel," Rose said. "Just about everything else you own is."

"My goggles are pink and very sparkly. But I left them at the pool the last time we were here." Her brow furrowed, just a slight dimple in the soft skin between her eyes. "I hope they're still there."

"I haven't seen anyone walking around wearing sparkly swim goggles, so I'd say they're probably right where you left them."

She squealed and jumped up and down a couple times. "Can I go see the roses?" Without waiting for an answer, she darted to the door, threw it open, and raced down the steps.

"Stay away from the road," Rawlins called after her.

"So you'll be keeping Hazel more often now, you say?"

Rawlins nodded, shoved his hands in his pockets. "Tara's taking on as many shifts as she can here at the beginning. I think she's hoping to move up to manager or something. Putting her best foot forward and all that."

"I see." Rose put the lid on the pot of boiling water and turned off the heat, setting another timer for ten minutes. "And how will you manage that with the season just about to kick into high gear? A boat's no place for a little girl." She swallowed hard to dislodge the memories of the last time she'd heard those words.

Rawlins paused, then reached up and scratched the back of his neck. He peered at her.

"Oh no. Don't look at me." She leaned against the counter behind her and crossed her arms. "I don't know the first thing about taking care of kids."

"Sure you do. Hazel loves you. She loves coming here to see you."

"You're always around when she's here. I usually don't keep her for longer than a couple of hours without you."

"You're a girl. She's a girl. You both love cooking and eating and . . . I don't know, flowers? And you know Hazel — she's a great kid. Easy. Happy."

Rose sighed. "You're right. Of course you're right. Hazel is wonderful. I just don't . . . She'd probably get bored with me. And how long are you talking, anyway? Every night? All week?"

"No, of course not. Tara's schedule will fluctuate, and I won't be out on the boat as much as I usually am. Dad is slowly passing some responsibilities to me, finally, so I'll be in the office more than years past. Hazel can come with me on those days. It'll just be here and there that I may need some extra help."

"Well. You try to let me know ahead of time, and I'll see what I can do."

Rawlins grinned. "I'd hate to get in the way of your shuffleboard games."

Rose swiped the dish towel off the counter and threw it at him. "There's no shuffleboard here, thank you very much. Not that I'd play it if there was."

"Oh, that's right," he said in soothing tones meant as a joke, but that only served to raise her hackles. "You don't get involved with the residents. I forgot."

"It's easier that way," she said firmly. "No one wants the manager poking her head into everyone's business."

"It's not poking your head in if you just start a conversation. Or try out the paddleboats. Join a book club."

"For Pete's sake, Rawlins." She worked to keep the irritation out of her voice. "Why do you care if I do any of that? Why does it matter to you so much?"

He stared at her for a moment like he was trying to figure her out, and Rose had such a strong memory of his mother, Stella, that she had to prop a hand against the counter to steady herself. Stella had stared at Rose in that same way the day she found out Terry had proposed to Rose. It was a look that said, *I thought I knew you, but maybe I don't really know you at all.* Finally he looked away, shrugged, and shook his head, and the moment was gone. "I just worry about you sometimes. The way you always keep to yourself. I don't like to think of you as lonely."

"Who said anything about lonely? I've been living here for forty years. Most of those years on my own." She tapped her fingernail on the counter. "I think I've had enough time to figure out how I like to do things. And that's how I do them."

He held up his hands. "Understood. I'm sorry."

"And anyway, I should be the one worrying about you and your loneliness. You're a nice young man, Rawlins. You —"

"I know. I know. I should find myself a nice young woman."

She propped her hands on her hips. "Just because it didn't work out once doesn't mean you're out of chances."

He stood and pushed his stool under the counter and leaned over to where she stood.

"I could say the same thing to you." He kissed her cheek, then pulled away. "I'm going to go find Coach and get the tents and tables from the rec house," he said on his way out the door. "I'll tell Hazel the coffee cake is almost ready."

"Hang on now, we still have —" Rose turned to check the timer, but it dinged as soon as she picked it up.

"It's ready!" Hazel yelled from the front door. She skidded into the kitchen, dirt and grass scattering over Rose's spotless tile floor. "Can I have a big piece?" She grinned. A streak of dirt was smeared straight across her forehead.

"Well, I suppose that wouldn't hurt anything, would it?"

After one Summer Kickoff picnic several years ago that had included music and dancing, the grass was so trampled from feet and soggy from spilled drinks that a large section of sod had to be replaced, taking out a chunk of that year's homeowners' fees Rose had earmarked for new doggy doo trash cans. Ever since, Rose had ordered a temporary dance floor to protect the ground. Everyone thought she was doing it out of the kindness of her heart, to provide a firmer place for everyone to practice their moves, but really it was all in the name of saving the grass.

This year she'd ordered materials to make the dance floor even larger, though when she saw the size of it — taking up about a quarter of the open grassy area next to the pool and overlooking the bay — she almost second-guessed herself. But then she remembered how much space it took for forty senior citizens to line dance to "Y.M.C.A.," and she was glad she'd planned ahead.

Not enjoying the feel of last-minute stress, Rose had planned everything to a T in the days and weeks leading up to the party, and by two o'clock, everything was as ready as it could be. Tables were set out on the grass, waiting for their bounty, white tents spread out against the pale blue sky, and garbage barrels placed at regular intervals to prevent a trash disaster in the morning. The temporary dance floor was opposite the pool with space for the members of Peter Gold's bluegrass band, Old Enough to Know Better, to set up their banjos, mandolins, and Peter's stand-up bass.

In the cottage, Rose and Hazel played three games of Go Fish, almost as many games of Old Maid, consumed half the coffee cake, and sprinkled paprika on the deviled eggs. When they went back outside to check on the men, Coach pronounced them parched.

"I don't know about you all, but I could use one of Roberta's famous Coke floats." He leaned down to Hazel. "Have you ever had a Coke float?"

She shook her head, her eyes wide, taking in his tousled hair, his big grin, his bushy eyebrows that made him look like he was always in on a joke.

"A scoop of ice cream in the bottom of a glass with ice-cold Coca Cola poured on top. Most people use plain old vanilla, but I prefer chocolate chip."

He started walking, leading the way to the café. Hazel whispered to Rawlins, "Can I have chocolate chip too?"

"Maybe. But you have to have some real food first."

A golf cart drew up beside them on the road. The driver, Seymour Eldins — the village's oldest resident, who lived with his much younger live-in nurse — extended his arm out toward Coach, his hand balled up into a fist.

"Seymour!" Coach called with his usual vigor. He bumped his own fist against Seymour's as if that was a normal way to greet acquaintances. "You coming to the party tonight?"

"Sure am," the old man said, his voice strong with only a hint of gravel. It was always surprising to hear such a bold, almost melodic voice coming from a body so wizened with age. Rose had heard that Seymour used to sing with the Baldwin County Choral Singers. "Angie said I can stay until nine."

"That'll give you plenty of time to get a few dances in." Coach shuffled his feet around a few times before glancing at Rose. "Maybe a little do-si-do with Rose?"

"I think not." Rose set her jaw in what she hoped was flippant defiance. "I don't dance."

Coach took a step toward her. "I'm not sure I believe that about you, but I'll let it slide."

The nerve of that man, always acting like he knew her better than she knew herself. She straightened her shirt and took a step back. No need to let any of his sloppiness — what grown man went around wearing wrinkled shirts and flip-flops? — rub off on her.

"Seymour, good to see you." Rose turned to where Rawlins and Hazel stood a few steps away. Rawlins had a sly look on his face. "I think I'll skip lunch. I have plenty to eat at home. I'll see you two when you finish with" — she glanced at Coach — "your float."

"Come on, Rose. No need to run off. I was just kidding about the dancing." Behind him, Seymour zoomed off on his golf cart, likely exceeding the strict fifteen miles per hour policy within the village. "I wouldn't let you dance with him anyway. Word is, he has wandering hands."

"I bet Janelle wouldn't mind that," Rawlins said, prompting a burst of laughter from Coach.

"He's right, Rose. Come on to lunch."

Rose felt Hazel's hand slide into hers. "You can have some of my float."

Rose drew her lips into a thin line and shot a look at her nephew, then looked down at Hazel. Her green eyes were wide and bright. So much innocence in such a small face. "Just for you, Hazel. If it weren't for you, I'd leave these two loonies behind."

Hazel pulled Rose along toward the café, while Coach and Rawlins lagged a few paces behind, talking in low, serious voices about Auburn's chances for a good season in the fall.

When she and Hazel reached the glass door, Lily was just approaching it from the other side. Rose took a step back to allow Lily to exit, but in the process she bumped into Coach, who hadn't realized Rose had stopped.

Coach let out an "Oomph" of surprise as his hand brushed against Rose's lower back, his fingertips gentle points of pressure. He pulled away quickly. "Rose, I'm sorry." His eyebrows pulled together in concern. "Are you okay?"

To her consternation, she still felt the imprint of his hand on the skin of her back. "I'm just fine," she managed. "You?"

"No worse for the wear." He turned to the doorway. "Lily!" Coach boomed. "You're just in time. We're coming in for Coke floats. Can I order you one?"

"Oh no, I . . ." She held up the container in her hands. "I picked up some gumbo to take home." She looked at Rose. "You said her gumbo would be the best I'd ever tasted."

"And it will be. Did you get some crackers?"

Lily held up a white paper bag in her other hand.

Next to her, Hazel hopped from one foot to the other. "Come on!"

Rawlins put a hand on her shoulder. "Patience, Haze," he whispered. When he straightened up, he nodded at Lily. "Good to see you again."

Lily smiled. "You too." She looked down at Hazel again.

"This is my daughter," Rawlins said, sensing Lily's uncertainty. "Hazel."

Lily breathed in deep and her shoulders dropped a little. "Hi, Hazel. I like your swimsuit."

When Hazel didn't answer, Rawlins nudged her. "What do you say?" he whispered.

"Thank you," Hazel said obediently.

"You sure you don't want to stay and eat with us?" Coach asked.

"No, it's okay. I need to . . ." Lily looked across the road toward her cottage. "I should get on back."

"Are you coming to the party?" Hazel was bouncing on the balls of her feet now, yanking Rose's arm each time she launched herself off the ground. "I'm going to jump off the diving board. My daddy's going to catch me."

Lily's eyebrows lifted in surprise and she let out a little laugh. "Is that so?"

"Uh-huh. I was scared to jump off the diving board last summer. But I'm bigger now." She thrust her hand high in the air, still keeping Rose's hand in a firm grip.

"Okay, big girl," Rawlins said, pulling her hand from Rose's and gently tugging her

196

toward the door. "Let's get you inside." He turned to Lily and gave a small, almost apologetic smile as he slipped in the door after Hazel.

Coach grabbed the door. "The offer still stands," he said to Lily. "If you want a ride, I can drive you to the party in style."

Lily smiled. "It's okay. I'll be glad to walk."

When Coach was gone, Rose faced Lily. "You doing okay? Settling in?"

Lily nodded. "I'm good. I have everything ready. For clients, I mean."

"Happy to hear it." Rose waited, but Lily just glanced inside at the rest of the group standing at the counter where Roberta waited to take their orders. Lily had pulled her hair up into a knot at the back of her head. Wavy pieces fell down around her face, and in the sunlight the red shone through the dark brown like copper ribbons. Lily's beauty wasn't common — something in her face was startling, a beauty that sneaked up on you. Her brown eyes were thick-lashed and a little bit weary.

"You're sure you're okay." Rose wasn't usually one to double-check. People were as they said they were. But something about Lily made her feel off balance, like she was on a boat and needed to reach out a hand to keep steady.

"Yeah, yeah. I'm good. Just . . ." She shrugged. "Just getting used to a new place."

"Well." Rose glanced inside to where Rawlins had lifted Hazel up onto a counter stool so she could watch Roberta behind the counter, pouring a bottle of Coke over a parfait glass of ice cream. Chocolate chip. "Let me know if you need anything."

"I will."

Lily walked away, the paper bag under her arm and the Styrofoam container of gumbo in both hands. Watching her from the door, Rose wished she could wrap her arm around Lily. Pull her close. Whisper encouragement and reassurance. Rose wasn't one to hand out good cheer to just anyone, but Lily seemed to be an old soul, someone who'd seen the bottom and was determined to swim her way to the top.

Lily looked both ways, as if a car could be roaring down the gently curving lane, then crossed the street. Her hair gleamed in the sunlight, her movements purposeful and steady.

Rose took a deep breath and stepped inside the café.

# THIRTEEN

Unsure of what to expect at the Summer Kickoff party, Lily dressed with care, skipping her swimsuit, which she found at the bottom of a tote bag, and instead choosing a flowing yellow skirt and plain white tee. She left her hair down, just pinning a lock back to keep it out of her face, and let the afternoon's humidity coax it into loops and waves. Stepping back to look at herself in the bathroom mirror, she marveled at the woman staring back at her. How was it possible to look the same when everything in her life had been turned inside out?

Downstairs she sat gingerly on the couch. All her nerves felt on edge, sparking inside her skin. Something in her craved movement — to stretch herself, to push her limits. She wished she were a swimmer so she could slash through the water with skill and speed. Or a runner, lacing up a pair of running shoes and taking off, burning away her recent memories with pounding feet and pumping arms.

But she wasn't. Wasn't a swimmer, wasn't a runner, was hardly even a wife, though the rings on her left ring finger still sat heavy and tight on her skin. Did Worth still wear his ring? Did he look at it and think about the woman he swept up and away a little over a year ago, only to write her a note and slip away in the night, setting both of them free in the process?

She scanned the room she'd set up with so much care and attention this week. The flowers she'd clipped yesterday still stood tall and crisp, the late afternoon sunlight winking off the glass jars. White towels were folded and stacked on the counter. Baskets held clips and brushes and combs. The pouch containing her mother's scissors sat on top of the rolling cart, waiting for the first person to sit in the chair, exhale, and wait patiently for her to change their life by cutting their hair.

Lily wondered again if she had the same practiced skill Lillian once had — the ability to do so much more than just cut and style hair. Lily could do that, of course. Whether back in Fox Hill or here where the edge of the land dripped into the bay, she knew how to use a pair of scissors to achieve a desired result. But Lillian had gone so much further. She offered her customers a moment of respite, a slice out of time where their burdens slipped to the floor, strand by strand. It was more than the scissors, more than the hair dryers and curling irons. It was *in her* — in her fingers, her laughter, her manner, her very presence. She saw through her customers' words to what they really needed, and she gave it to them.

Lily could fluff her towels all day, set out flowers in every vase she could find, and clean every floorboard and windowsill in the entire cottage, but none of it would matter if her mother's gift didn't flow through Lily's veins too. Lillian had said Lily had the gift — that she'd been born with it. Lily could only hope, for both her sake and that of the villagers, that it was true.

Outside, a couple walked past her cottage, heading toward the big grassy space next to the pool where the party was set up. Even from inside, Lily could hear faint music — something plucky and light. Someone was singing too, though she was too far away to make out any words.

The couple walked slowly, in no hurry to reach the festivities. Lily saw the man's lips moving, and then the woman laughed, head back, smile wide. The evening light was slanted, filtering through the crepe myrtle and magnolia leaves and casting the couple's faces, the shop fronts, even the air, with an orange glow.

Lily stood, unsure of what to do. She could easily kick off her sandals and go back upstairs. Or she could put one foot in front of the other, walk out into the fading sunlight, and go to a party.

When she opened the front door, she half expected to see Coach Beaumont waiting in his golf cart to drive her the short distance to the gathering, but the front porch was empty, as was the street beyond it. Before she could change her mind, Lily walked down the steps, out into the yard, and down the street.

Lily figured she'd met about fifteen people since she'd arrived at the village. Maybe twenty. But there must have been a hundred people at the party. Most were under the tents piling their plates with food, while others sat at long tables set up in the grass. A few danced on the makeshift dance floor set up in front of the band. A tall man with electric white hair and a matching mustache leaned down toward the microphone and sang about love and mountains and something about an old truck. As he crooned, his fingers danced across the strings of a stand-up bass as tall as him. Behind him, two men strummed on banjos while a woman with gray hair shot through with streaks of hot pink played a violin. It took Lily a moment, but she recognized her as Cricket, the woman from the pool the other night at sunset.

Lily scanned the crowd, trying to find Rose or Coach or one of the neighbors who had brought her food, but not a single face looked familiar. People had spilled over onto the pool deck — sitting in the lounge chairs, plates of food balanced on their knees, feet tapping and heads bobbing to the peppy beat of the music. A handful of folks had migrated to the pool itself, some sitting on the top step, their feet in the water, and a few others all the way in.

She had just decided to take a quick walk through the food tent to see if she could spot Rose — not that Rose was particularly warm, but at least she was familiar — when she saw a little girl pull herself up onto the edge of the pool and run for the diving board. Lily recognized her by her hair. Even wet, the red curls were unmistakable. Hazel climbed the steps and walked out to the edge, the board underneath her bouncing with each timid footstep. Her pink goggles were perched on her forehead, just above her eyes.

She hadn't noticed before, but now she saw that one of the people in the pool was Rawlins. He was in the deep end, treading water a few feet away from the diving board. Without his hat and with such an open, cheerful look on his face, she almost didn't recognize him.

From up on the board, Hazel peered down at her dad, her curls wet and sticking to her cheeks and forehead. She pulled the goggles down over her eyes and took the last step forward, so that her toes hung over the end of the board.

Lily stood at the edge of the pool deck now, one hand on the gate, watching. From the water, Rawlins waved up at Hazel.

"Don't jump with your goggles," he called. "They'll hurt your face when you hit the water."

She pulled them off and tossed them to her dad, who caught them with an outstretched hand. "All right, little bug. Let's see you jump."

Instead of jumping, Hazel took a step back. She looked down at the water, as if calculating how far it was to the surface and how far she'd have to drop before she reached it.

"I'm right here," Rawlins said.

Hazel held up both hands, palms toward him. "Don't move."

Lily smiled at the seriousness in her voice. In the water Rawlins was struggling to keep a straight face. "I promise. Not going anywhere. But you can do this. You know it."

Hazel fixed the strap of her bathing suit where it had fallen off her shoulder and took a small step back up to the edge. With a quick glance to the crowd of people watching her from the edge of the pool deck, she counted to three, loudly, and jumped. Her big splash belied her small size, and she came up spluttering and wiping water off her face. Her cheeks stretched into a giddy smile.

Rawlins pulled himself through the water with two quick strokes until he was next to her. "Told you," he said. She laughed and dropped back under the water and swam to the side. She hauled herself out and ran back to the board.

"No running," Rawlins called. "And you've got this, Haze. I'm going to sit on the side."

Watching this scene play out from her spot by the gate, Lily all of a sudden felt as if she'd been peering into a peephole, getting an inside look at something that wasn't hers to watch. Something so tender it made her want to smile and cry at the same time.

When Rawlins climbed the steps out of the shallow end, his eyes met hers. She looked away quickly, but not before she caught the look of surprise on his face.

"Lily." He called her name just as Hazel made another splash down into the water from the diving board.

Caught, she stepped up onto the wooden boards of the pool deck. The gate slammed shut behind her with a metal clang.

"You coming for a swim?" Rawlins pulled a beach towel from a red-and-white striped bag sitting on a chair next to the pool. A yellow snorkel tumbled from the bag with the towel. After shoving it back in the bag, he pressed the towel to his face, then rubbed it over the top of his head.

"No, I was just . . . I just got here." She gestured to the grass where there seemed to be even more people than there were just a few minutes ago. "I didn't see anyone I knew out there, so . . . ."

She shrugged and her gaze slid down. As it did, she noticed a pink scar on his leg that started below his knee and traveled up the side of his thigh. It didn't look like a recent wound, but it was still angry.

He swiftly wrapped his towel around his waist, hiding the scar from her view. She looked back up at him and saw that he was watching her. It was a warm evening, and heat bloomed hotter in her cheeks. She reached up and pulled her hands through her hair, lifting it off her neck for a moment. "I figured it'd be easier to start with one familiar face." She smiled. "Make that two."

He sat and gestured to the adjacent chair for her to do the same. "I'm glad you did. It makes it less obvious that I'm trying to avoid diving into the crowd over there." He nodded his head toward the grass, where a woman in red cowboy boots was dancing with her arms outstretched. "Groups aren't really my thing." Hazel called him, asking him to watch her jump. He watched her, then gave her a thumbs-up. "She's going to be hungry soon, though. Have you eaten?"

Lily shook her head, all of a sudden unable to look at him in the face. Water droplets clinging to his hair and arms glittered in the sunlight, and his skin was a warm honey brown.

"Coach makes good barbecue, if you like that. And there are enough desserts to sink a ship."

"Daddy! When are we gonna eat?" Hazel's voice carried from the middle of the pool, her face full of expectation.

Rawlins chuckled. "Talk about food within fifty feet of that girl and her stomach starts rumbling," he said quietly, then lifted his head and called to her. "How about you jump three more times, and then we'll go eat?"

"How old is she?"

"Five. She'll be six in a few months."

Lily smiled. "She's precious."

He leaned forward and rested his elbows on his knees. "Yeah. She is. She can be a handful too, but I guess that's normal."

"That's what I hear."

He turned back to the pool where Hazel was pulling herself up on the side one more time. "She's a good kid. I'm just glad her mom and I haven't messed her up too much."

"She looks far from messed up."

They watched as she jumped off the diving board in a spin, twirling in the air before splashing down. She came to the surface in a frenzy of splashing and laughter.

He watched his daughter as she paddled to the edge of the pool. "Yeah. Maybe you're right."

Hazel ran up to them, flinging water everywhere, and grabbed her towel. "I'm famished. Let's eat."

Rawlins laughed and his face broke open into a big grin. "Famished, huh? That's a big word for a little girl." He stood and scooped Hazel up into his arms and nuzzled her neck with his face. "I'm famished too, and you look delicious."

Hazel squealed and wiggled. "Your prickles are poking me!"

He set her down on her feet. "Hazel, this is Mrs. . . ." He hesitated. "I just realized I don't know your last name."

"It's —" Lily stopped. *Bishop. Lily Bishop. Worth's wife.* The words usually rolled off her tongue, but today they dissipated into the hot evening air. She leaned down toward Hazel with her hands on her knees. "I'm Lily."

"Like the flower?"

"Yep. Like the flower."

"Aunt Rosie is named after a flower too," Hazel said. "Rose and Lily." She said the words softly, then looked up and smiled. "Like a garden."

Rawlins handed Hazel her flip-flops. "Put these on, kiddo, and we can all go get some food."

Rawlins and Lily followed Hazel around the pool and to the grassy spread where people milled and talked, ate and danced. Rawlins pulled Hazel to the head of the first

209

long table where paper plates were stacked several inches high. As he filled her plate and his, a variety of people came by and greeted him — men pounded on his back or shook his hand, causing him to have to juggle plates and cups, and women air-kissed his cheeks and ruffled Hazel's hair. A few addressed Lily as well, mostly people who'd brought her food when she first moved in.

"Do you live here?" Lily asked as she dolloped potato salad on her plate.

"Me? Live here? No." He shook his head. "No."

"So many people know you. I just assumed."

"No, I live on the other side of the island. I'm just here a lot." He paused, then nodded his head toward a couple sitting a few tables away. "I built the Baxters a bookshelf for their living room last summer. Mona Edberg" — he nodded his head toward the lady in the red cowboy boots who was now tucking into a huge slice of chocolate cake — "has asked me to paint and repaint her bedroom so many times I've lost count. I've installed light fixtures and storm doors. I fix ceiling fans and leaky pipes." He shrugged. "Little bit of everything. It's a good way to make some extra money when I'm not out on the boat. Plus, they usually tip me with food. That makes Hazel happy."

They finally made it to the end of the food line, their plates loaded with spoonfuls of every type of salad and dip imaginable, plus a couple she couldn't identify. A round table in the corner of the tent was stocked with drinks and red Solo cups, and a woman stood next to it holding two ceramic pitchers. "Alabama Slammer or Hurricane?" she asked. "Both guaranteed to help you beat this heat." Her forehead was damp with sweat, though she stood directly in front of a huge box fan set up at the edge of the tent.

Rawlins smiled. "Just water for me, Ms. Baker." He grabbed a juice box and a bottle of water off the table behind her, then nudged Hazel with his hip. "All right, kiddo, let's find a spot to eat."

Hazel trotted out in front of him, searching for an open table or chair. Not wanting to intrude on their dinner together, Lily hung back by the food table. Scanning the crowd, she spotted Coach on the other side of the grass talking to Roberta from the café and a small, trim woman with dark hair styled into a 1950s wave. As the woman spoke to Coach and Roberta, she skipped her feet around as if she were dancing in place.

Lily had almost decided to take her food back to the pool deck when Rawlins waved to her from a spot of grass on a small rise in front of the pool facing the bay. He'd laid his and Hazel's towels on the ground. "Do you want to sit?" he asked when she walked over. "I'm sorry the towels are a little damp, but at least we're out of the way."

Lily sat, tucking her knees to the side and finding a flat spot for her water bottle. Hazel had already started eating, shoveling in fork-fuls of macaroni and cheese.

"Slow down, Haze," Rawlins said. "The food's not going anywhere."

"But it's so good." She chewed thought-fully a moment, then pointed out to the bay. "Is that one of Papa's boats?"

Rawlins turned his head toward the water where a shrimp boat was slowly making its way out into the bay. It had two black masts and a yellow flag at the top of the tallest one. "Nope, not one of ours." He studied the boat as it slowly chugged farther out, leaving silver lines in the water behind it. Seagulls flew around the back of the boat, diving and swooping.

"Do they feed the birds from back there?" Lily asked.

"Nah. But when they're sorting the catch, the birds know it. They come from miles away, looking for a meal."

Hazel slurped the last bit of juice from her juice box, then popped up off the towel. When she started off toward the band, Rawlins called to her.

"I want to dance," she said, her face holding such anguish that Rawlins laughed.

"Just don't go too far."

"I won't!" Then she ran straight across the grass, not stopping until she stood directly in front of the tall man playing the bass. She spun in circles and jumped to the beat. Next to her a table full of ladies clapped and cheered at her arrival.

Behind them in the bay, the boat with the yellow flag moved steadily away from shore. "I think I saw you yesterday," Lily said. "Or at least your boat. It's the *Miss Stella,* right? Green stripe?"

"That's right." He shifted on the towel. "I repainted it last week."

She nodded. "I was out here at sunset yesterday. Someone was standing at the wheel, but I didn't know if it was you or not."

"It was me. I wasn't planning to go out last night, but . . . . sometimes the water calls me. It's nice to be out at the end of the day."

He stared out at the bay, slowly lapping the shore in front of them. "It's the best way to forget your troubles."

She gave a small laugh. "Well, maybe I need to be out on a boat then."

He studied her a moment, then pulled his plate closer to him. "All right, it's time." He pulled apart the ribs on his plate. "You ready?"

She raised her eyebrows. "Ready for what?"

He gestured to the barbecue on her plate. "You have to taste the ribs."

She picked one up and held it gingerly between two fingers.

"You can't be delicate. You have to just go for it." He leaned down and took a big bite. Lily hesitated, then gave up her attempt to be ladylike. She took a bite, pulling the meat with her teeth. Her mouth filled with the tangy sweet sauce and smoky heat. Looking around for a napkin, she found none, so she licked her lips and did the same to her fingertips.

"Look at you." He grinned. "You're a pro."

Out of the corner of her eye, Lily saw Coach walking toward them with a woman on his arm, the same one who'd sat next to him on the golf cart a few days ago. Janelle had tucked a pink hibiscus behind one ear, and on her feet she wore pink rhinestone-studded kitten heels that caused her to walk unsteadily on the grass. Judging from how she clung to Coach's arm for balance, Lily suspected Janelle wore them for that specific reason.

"Roberta said she saw you two going through the food line, but then you disappeared," Coach said.

"We didn't disappear," Rawlins said with a half smile. "We're just keeping out of the way."

"Smart move." Coach gestured to where the band members were setting down their instruments. "They take a break and everyone makes a beeline for the drink table. That's how I broke my finger last year."

"You broke your finger running for the drink table?" Lily laughed. "Sorry, it's not funny."

"Well, it would be if that's how I broke it. But no, Tiny Collins broke it when she stepped on my finger, trying to get to the last of the Hurricane punch."

Rawlins shook his head. "Good thing Peter used to be a doctor."

"Yep. He set it with a tongue depressor, wrapped it in gauze, and I was back in time for the last dance."

Next to him, Janelle patted his arm. "And

now look at you. You're in tip-top form."

"That's me, tip-top." Lily caught an edge of weariness in his voice, and over Janelle's head, Coach's eyes scanned the crowd.

Janelle leaned down to Lily. "When do you open up shop, dear?"

"Monday, I think."

"Perfect. I'll need an appointment in the morning, around ten o'clock. How do I go about scheduling that?"

"Um . . . Well, I guess you just did. I'll plan to see you at ten."

"Wonderful. And I'll be your first customer! I'm looking forward to it. My friend Patsy and I always get our hair cut together. Can you pencil her in as well? She'd be here to ask you herself but . . ." She swiveled her head side to side and cut her voice to a whisper. "Her hemorrhoids are acting up again."

Lily bit her lip and nodded. "Tell Patsy that's just fine."

A moment later Coach took a small, almost unnoticeable step away from Janelle, and a slow smile spread across his face. Lily followed his gaze. Rose walked toward them, weaving through the grass around tables and blankets. Her mouth was set in a grim line, which Lily had decided must be her default setting.

"If it isn't the lovely Rose." Coach's smile grew even wider.

Janelle slipped her arm from Coach's elbow. "I think I'm due for another fruity drink. Need anything?" She looked up at Coach from under a fringe of dark lashes. When he shook his head, she leaned in close to him. "I've asked them to play a certain Shania Twain song for me. When it comes on, I'll be looking for you." She winked, then sauntered toward the drink table.

In her wake, Rose snorted. She looked at Coach. "Lucky you."

"Lucky me nothing. I'm nervous is what I am."

"You're late, Aunt Rose," Rawlins said. "Where have you been?" He had a smudge of sauce on his bottom lip, and for a flash of a second Lily thought of reaching over and wiping it with her thumb.

"I had to take care of some things at the office. Just took me a bit to finish it all up."

"Couldn't it have waited until tomorrow?" Coach asked. "I was looking for you earlier. I wanted to see if you'd tasted my barbecue."

"Well, I think you found the right person to taste your barbecue. And anyway, I'm not very hungry."

Janelle was just stepping away from the

drink table, headed back toward their small knot of people. She held a slim silver can in her manicured hand.

"Quick, Rose," Coach whispered, a touch of panic in his voice. "Come dance with me."

"What? Are you crazy?"

"No, I'm serious. Come out on the dance floor with me and you'll save me from whatever Janelle has in store."

Rose laughed, then nipped it quickly. "It is not my job to save you. And I told you, I don't dance. You'll have to find someone else."

Just then Hazel ran up to the group and Coach leaned down. "Miss Hazel, may I take you for a spin on the dance floor?"

"Yes!"

He followed her across the grass toward the band.

"That man is incorrigible," Rose muttered. She turned to Rawlins. "He's using your daughter to get himself out of an uncomfortable situation. Though he certainly didn't look uncomfortable when he was walking around with her earlier."

Rawlins chuckled. "Cut him some slack. And anyway, how did you see them walking around together? I thought you just got here."

Rose crossed her arms.

"Have you eaten?" Lily asked her. "The barbecue ribs really are good."

She sighed and glanced toward the tents. "I suppose I should go check the food tables. Make sure we're not running low on anything."

Once Rose took off for the food tent, Lily and Rawlins sat in comfortable silence. Out on the dance floor, Coach twirled Hazel, then clapped to the beat. The music played, a light breeze blew off the bay and out toward the horizon, and the sky was the color of ripe peach skin.

Next to her, Rawlins moved his plate to the side and leaned back on his elbows, his legs stretched out in front of him, the long scar she'd seen at the pool just barely visible. It was funny — Lily didn't know him or Hazel any better than she knew anyone else in the village, but seeing the two of them at the pool when she first arrived had felt a little like an exhale. Relaxed on the grass, she was glad she'd come to the party rather than sit inside her cottage alone.

Across the grass, Hazel tapped a woman on the leg. When she looked down, Hazel said something that made her jump back and brush her hands quickly over the sides of her pants. Lily heard her yelp, and then

Hazel knelt down in the grass and scooped up something.

Rawlins shook his head and chuckled.

"What does she have?"

"It's probably some kind of bug. She loves them."

They watched Hazel run to the edge of the grass where the people thinned out, her hands still cupped around whatever critter she'd picked up. She looked around a moment, then leaned down in a patch of grass where the sunlight was still shining. She opened her hands, then sat completely still, watching. The light filtering through her hair lit it up with a golden glow, and the breeze blew the wispy red curls into disarray. She was so alive, so full of breath and spirit and energy, it almost hurt to look at her.

Lily had dreamed of being a mother since she was a young girl. When everyone else was deciding on veterinarian or teacher or nurse as their future career, all Lily could come up with was that she wanted to have children, and lots of them. As she grew older, the feeling never went away, though she did cut back on how many children she once thought she wanted. She'd be happy with any number, but one or two would be perfect.

She and Worth hadn't talked about kids before they married, his proposal coming so soon after the first night they met. After the wedding, once they'd gotten home from the honeymoon and began settling into the life that was now theirs, she brought it up to him. He'd laughed.

"Maybe, one day, yeah," he'd said. "It's a little soon to be talking about it, though, don't you think?"

Considering how things had worked out, she was relieved they hadn't brought a child into their world, though Lily's yearning to be a mother hadn't lessened a bit.

Watching Hazel, who was now sprawled on the grass with her chin propped in her hands, Lily fought the urge to go to her, to touch her soft hair and smooth cheeks. Instead, she tucked her chin into her shoulder for a quick moment and inhaled, the scents of barbecue and grass and lingering sunscreen mixing into an intoxicating blend.

Rawlins sat up and propped his elbows on his knees. Hazel caught his movement and turned to look at him. She grinned and kicked her legs back and forth. Rawlins waved at her, then lifted his chin toward the sky. "Red sky at night."

Lily watched him a moment, waiting to hear the next part of the rhyme — *red sky at night, sailor's delight* — but he was quiet. "Is there any truth in that?" she asked. "The red sky thing?"

He shrugged. "The colors at sunset have a lot to do with molecules in the air and how light hits them, but typically a red sky at sunset usually means high pressure's coming in from the west."

When she didn't respond, he smiled. "That means the next day will usually be clear."

"Ah. And the next part? Red sky at morning?"

"Yep. Sailors take warning. If the sky is red early, it means the high pressure has already passed and a low-pressure system could be on its way. That means stormy weather."

"I bet you got good grades in science when you were a kid."

He laughed through his nose. "I did, actually. But that's not where I learned about weather. That came from the job. Aside from the tides and where the shrimp are biting, weather's the most important thing a shrimper has to know about. You've got to know what storms are coming and when."

"Do storms ever hit you out of the blue, or are you always prepared?"

He was quiet a moment. "I'm hit out of

the blue all the time. All the forecasting and radars and weather wisdom can only get you so far." He shrugged again. "Sometimes you have to just go with what your gut's telling you — and that can be perfectly right or dead wrong. Depending on the day."

Hazel ran up to him then, throwing herself in his lap and situating her legs on top of his. He ruffled her hair and pointed out toward the horizon. "Those colors, though? That means something good is coming." He nuzzled Hazel's cheek, making her laugh. "Mark my words."

# THE VILLAGE VINE

*Your Source for Neighborhood News*

June 6, 2018
Compiled by Shirley Ferrill

## GOOD DAY, SAFE HARBOR VILLAGE!

### WEATHER

This week we should see mostly sunny skies with occasional rain showers. Expect afternoon highs to hit the mid- to upper 80s, with morning lows in the low 70s. In short, your average, garden-variety, early June weather. If you plan to take advantage of outdoor activities, don't forget your sunscreen!

### MARINE LIFE

More manatees! Four have now been spotted, and it's possible there's a fifth, though it could also be the rogue crab trap that fell off the back of Kitty's pontoon last month. The Dauphin Island Sea Lab is asking residents and boaters to report any manatee sightings. With increased summertime water traffic, there's a concern that the creatures could be harmed by boat motors. Thank goodness Coach decided to go with paddleboats instead of Jet Skis.

As if the manatees aren't enough water

excitement, Ruth Beckett says she spotted an alligator in the marina. As of this printing, no one else has seen it, but regardless, please exercise caution on your docks and when entering and exiting your boats. I'm sure no one has forgotten the Hamp Hill incident of three years ago.

(For the newcomers, Hamp was out fishing early one morning when he spotted what he said was a ten-foot gator. For reasons still unknown to us, he proceeded to cast his fishing pole toward the alligator with such vigor that he threw himself right in the water. Thankfully it was high tide and he was able to scramble back up on the dock, but not without scraping his leg on a barnacled piling, resulting in eighteen stitches and two rounds of antibiotics. Let Hamp be a cautionary tale to take care when near the marina!)

## MISCELLANEOUS

- Janelle Blackmon lost a shoe at the Summer Kickoff party. She thinks it happened on the dance floor, possibly during Shania Twain's "I Feel Like a Woman." If you happened to bring home a pink peep-toe kitten heel that isn't yours, please return it to her ASAP.
- The first meeting of the Beachy Book Babes will be Tuesday, June 12, at Beach Reads. Rosé will be provided, but

please bring an appetizer to share.
- To the jokester who scattered pink plastic pelicans around the flagpole at the end of Port Place, please do us all a favor and pick them up. More than one canine villager has used them as toilets, and we don't need to encourage that kind of improper animal behavior. (Please refer to rule 4.2 in the *Safe Harbor Village Handbook*.)

## REMINDERS FROM MANAGEMENT
- When calling Rawlins Willett for help or repairs, please keep in mind that the shrimping season has begun, which limits his time considerably. If you can find a way to hang those picture frames yourself or hold off on any unnecessary painting jobs, I'm sure he will appreciate it. (Note from Shirley: I'd like to point out that I've been holding off on asking him to build a dog shed for Louis the Sixteenth, so when he has available time, I've got dibs on his first slot.)

# FOURTEEN

Dear Stella,

It appears I will be helping Rawlins with babysitting duties, although I don't think it can be called babysitting when it's your own family. Especially not when it's someone like Hazel. Sometimes I think she's an adult trapped in a child's body, but then she does something so outlandish, I think, *Nope, she's all kid.* She's a treasure. It should be you taking care of her, though, not me.

I don't say that because I don't want to spend time with her, because I do. I have no experience caring for a child, and he probably should have asked someone else, but I'm honored that he did ask. No, I say that because you would be the ultimate grandmother. The grandma who'd let a child run free on a beach and not get onto her for making a mess of your clean floors with her sandy feet. You'd let her play in your makeup drawer. You'd probably even let her eat ice cream before dinner. That's why you should be taking care of Hazel when Rawlins is on the boat, not Rose Carrigan, old maid, childless woman of spotless floors, Ice Queen of her own one-person kingdom.

I always wanted children. Did you know that? Even though I worried I'd pass on my weak genes — genes that made me spend countless hours in pediatrician waiting rooms and on the wrong end of a finger-pricker — I still wanted them. I imagined them to be healthy, rambunctious little rascals, full of vim and vigor and sugar and spice.

It was Terry who didn't want them. He said he had too much he wanted to accomplish and that children would only hold him back — hold *us* back. I figured I'd wait, bide my time, and eventually the paternal instinct would kick in. Thankfully (or not, depending on how you look at it), I didn't have to wait long. He was gone and I'd lost my chance.

Should I have pushed harder? Worked with him to hash out our conflicting desires? Maybe. But then again, who wants to have children with a man who didn't want them in the first place?

Because of the genuine kindness in your heart, you'd probably never say out loud that I got what I deserved. You might have thought it, though. And you'd be right. I deserve all that's come my way — the solitude. The loneliness. The inescapable sense of homesickness, though I only live a hop and a skip from where I began. I have many regrets from the course of my life — choices that served as a black stain rather than the defiant but entirely justified actions I thought they were at the time.

The one thing I don't regret is how everything turned out with us. You, me, Terry, Jim. I'm thankful it happened just as it did. Why? Because if you had been the one to marry Terry, you would have been the one without the children, and I know how badly you wanted kids. You admitted it much more freely than I did. You were born to have children, to have a family, to nurture them through the ups and downs of life, and you had that chance because you married Jim — a man born of love and thoughtful devotion — instead of Terry, who was Jim's opposite. So even though our friendship was forever ruined, even though the close relationship Jim and I once had was irrevocably broken, I'm grateful God allowed you to have the family you so desired. You deserved it.

As always,
Love,
Rose

# FIFTEEN

On Sunday afternoon Lily was hosing off the patio furniture when someone called her name. Glancing around, she spotted a cluster of women peering over her side gate, all wearing huge sunglasses and straw hats that jostled against one other.

"Hi. Hang on a sec." Lily turned off the spigot and dried her hands on the sides of her shorts. She walked to the gate and unlatched it.

Tiny took a step forward. "Hello, Lily. Seeing as you're officially a villager now, we'd like to invite you to Sunday afternoon cocktails at the café."

"That's so nice of you, but . . ." Lily looked down at her damp legs. "Right now?"

"Yes, ma'am. No need to change clothes. There's no dress code at the Sunrise."

Lily cocked an eyebrow as she took in the group of women dressed head to toe in pastel Lilly Pulitzer. A tiny dog poked its head through a pair of legs, its eyes wide and its body quivering.

"Really." Tiny grabbed Lily's hand and gave a gentle tug. "We just want to get to know you a little." She looked back at the other ladies. "We're a fun bunch, aren't we, ladies?"

Amid a chorus of agreement, Tiny smiled. "What do you say?"

It was a hot afternoon and Lily's pale skin was ready for a break. "Okay. Let me just grab my wallet."

Tiny shook her head. "Oh no, hon, your drink is on us."

Ten minutes later Lily sat among the handful of women at a table at the back of the Sunrise Café overlooking the water. The bay sparkled in the afternoon sunshine, with only a few high streaks of white clouds interrupting the wide open blue. One of the women leaned down and set a cup of water on the floor below the table, and the tiny dog drank with delicate laps. Even without the yellow rain slicker, Lily recognized it as the same little dog she'd seen the night she sat on her front porch in the rain.

"How cute," Lily said politely to the woman coiling the leash up in her hand.

"Thank you. That's my Prissy."

"How old is she?"

"*He* is three. He's a teacup Chihuahua."

Lily glanced down again at the dog. She noticed that his toenails were painted pink. Lily looked back up at his owner, Kitty, who shrugged. "I thought he was a girl for the first year of his life. Figured it was easier to finish the way we started."

With introductions out of the way, the ladies ordered drinks — Watermelon Bellinis and Strawberry Sundays — and began a rapid-fire exchange of information, mostly centered on the whos, whats, wheres, and whys of the Summer Kickoff party.

"Did any of you try Donna's pimiento cheese dip?" Shirley Ferrill asked to a murmur of yeses. "I was up all that night with a stomachache, and I'm blaming the cheese." She wrinkled her nose and rubbed a hand over her belly. "It's still a little iffy."

"I'd say blame it on that third slice of fudge pie I saw you hiding in a napkin at the end of the night!"

"What about Janelle Blackmon?" Edna Blanchett asked, prompting groans from around the table.

"That blouse was tight as a tick across her chest," Kitty said. "I'm surprised the seams held together."

"I thought she looked nice," Tiny said with a firm nod of her head. "If I had a chest like that, I'd want to show it off too."

"Tiny, if you had a chest like that, you'd topple clean over," Kitty said.

As the ladies were laughing, a young man stopped at the edge of the table with a tray full of colorful drinks.

"Thank you, Elijah," Edna cooed.

"No problem, ladies." He smiled as he set the drinks on the table. His hair stuck up in tiny black braids all over his head. "Y'all enjoy."

Edna watched him walk away until Shirley nudged her. "That boy is at least fifty years younger than you."

"I am well aware of that, but it doesn't mean I can't appreciate the Lord's handiwork."

Laughter followed as Lily tried her drink, something called a Lemon Sparkler. It tasted like pleasantly fizzy lemonade. "Do you all do this every Sunday?"

"Oh yes." Tiny looked around the group. "We're going on what, ten years? It started as a book club, but we finally acknowledged that we weren't enjoying the book discussions half as much as we enjoyed the gossip and laughter."

"And the cocktails!"

"Yes, and those. So we quit the books — most of us are members of other, more serious book clubs anyway — and now we just enjoy the chitchat."

"Is it always just the five of you?"

"Others come in and out, but we're the core group."

"What about Rose — does she ever come?" Lily sipped her drink as the ladies exchanged glances.

"Rose doesn't do very much with other people."

Lily looked from face to face. "Why not?"

Tiny shrugged. "She just doesn't get involved. I used to ask her to come, but she said no so often I guess I just stopped asking." She twisted the umbrella in her Bellini.

Kitty snorted. "Y'all just need to call it what it is. Rose hates people. She thinks she's too good for everyone else. Like she's the high and mighty manager of all us common folk. When she's not barking out orders from the clubhouse, she holes up inside her cottage, isolated from everyone else like a dang hermit crab."

Kitty took a deep breath, then put her lips to her straw and sipped. Only then did she glance around at the other ladies staring at her. "Y'all know I'm telling the truth."

"Kitty, you're being harsh," Tiny admonished, but then she fell quiet.

Rose did seem a little detached, but Lily

felt like something was missing in Kitty's explanation. If Rose hated people, why would she have hired Lily practically on a whim? Not only that, but Rose had agreed to let her live above the salon basically for free. Sure, Lily was doing a service for the village, but Rose had thrown her a lifeline when she needed it. No one who hated people would have been that generous.

"Well," Shirley said brightly. "Lily, why don't you tell us about you?" She leaned forward, hand over her heart. "Now, we all know about your husband. Such a shame, my dear. And you so young. How did it happen?"

"Shirley!" Tiny said. "You can't ask her that."

"Well, why not? She's going to find out everything about us as soon as we sit down in her chair." Shirley patted Lily's hand. "Was it cancer?"

"What? No. But . . . what did you hear?"

"That he's no longer with us, you poor thing." The ladies around the table clucked like hens.

"He didn't die," she said to a collective gasp. "He just left." She glanced around the table at the wide eyes and slack mouths. "He walked out."

Tiny collapsed against her seat back, and

Edna reached into her handbag and handed Lily a tissue.

"What happened?" Shirley whispered. "Where did he go?"

Tiny sighed and rolled her eyes. "I'm sorry," she mouthed to Lily.

"It's okay. You can ask. He just . . ." She paused. There were so many layers and specifics she could mention — all the tiny details that added up to a marriage that had crashed before it had even gotten off the ground — but she decided simple was best. "One day he was there, the next day there was a note."

"A note? Where?"

"On the kitchen counter."

"What did it say?" Kitty's heavily penciled eyebrows arched.

"That he was sorry and that he couldn't do it anymore. He'd already filed for divorce. The papers were next to the note."

Shirley let out a small cry. "That . . . dirtbag." She clapped a hand over her mouth.

"There are a few other, more specific words I think we could use here," Kitty said. "But dirtbag will suffice. Tell me, how long were you married?" Kitty steepled her fingers together and rested her chin on top.

The other ladies stared, their faces a mix of pity and suspicion. Lily hated being on the receiving end of either one. "Just a little over a year. I know this sounds crazy, but I'm mostly okay."

Shirley retrieved the unused tissue Lily had balled up on the table and dabbed it to her own eyes. "How can you say that?"

"Lily," Kitty said loudly, cutting off Shirley's tears. "A disruption like this in a significant relationship can lead to some difficult consequences if you're not prepared. What is your support system like? Family? Friends? Who do you have lined up to step in with help as necessary?"

The table was quiet until Tiny spoke up. "Kitty used to be a psychiatrist. If you can't tell."

"Well, I don't really have family, and I'm definitely not going back to Worth's family, so . . . for now I'm here and I'm going to fix your hair. And who knows" — she nodded her head toward the window — "maybe the water will fix me."

"You make a joke, but there's some truth there. We have evidence that water can be healing to both body and mind. In fact, a former colleague recently sent me an article —"

"But aren't you lonely?" Shirley broke in. Her voice quivered and her eyes swam with tears yet again.

In the face of Shirley's sympathy grief, Lily wished for Rose — the stern set of her jaw, the stubbornness that was almost charming in its refusal to be emotional. Thankfully, the waiter returned then, asking about a second round.

"None for me," Kitty replied, holding a hand over her glass. "We need to be clear-headed to help Lily figure this out."

"It's okay," Lily said. "I . . . I'm figuring things out. On my own." The need to escape tickled her spine. The ladies meant well, but she had a suspicion that as soon as she walked away, they'd spend the next hour gossiping and discussing her future. Best to leave now and let them get to it. She stood, her chair scraping against the old wooden floor. "Thank you for the drink. And the conversation."

"Lily." Tiny reached out and took Lily's hand. Tiny's was small and warm. "You can stay if you want. We won't talk about it anymore."

Lily smiled. "I'm fine. You enjoy your drinks. Maybe I'll see you ladies in the salon soon?"

She gently pulled her hand from Tiny's and made her way out of the café and into the sunshine. Across the street her cottage beckoned with its shaded porch and turquoise front door. It wasn't home yet, but even still, opening the door and walking inside the cool interior felt a little like a hug from someone she trusted.

# SIXTEEN

Rose Carrigan prided herself on her ability to stick to her fixed daily schedule, veering from it only when absolutely necessary. Therefore, every morning, Monday through Friday, Rose unlocked the door to her office at precisely nine o'clock. Clubs and meetings scheduled at the clubhouse didn't start until at least ten, so she had an hour every morning to begin her work without laughter and conversation interrupting her focus.

On Monday, however, the back tire of her bicycle was low on air. She spent fifteen sweaty minutes trying to fit the hose of her bike pump over the nozzle on the tire, which put her walking into the office half an hour late. The first of the Bubbas rolled in a few minutes after to set the coffeepot perking, their conversation muted but still intrusive, and from somewhere outside, a lawn mower whined like a gnat in her ear. She hadn't just lost her rhythm — she'd never grasped it in the first place.

So when the phone rang just as three more Bubbas burst through the office door, ushering in yet more jovial laughter and the scent of glazed doughnuts, Rose answered it with a rather exasperated tone.

"Rose, is that you?" Janelle Blackmon's voice purred through the handset.

"Yes, Janelle. Who else would be answering here in the office?"

"I don't know. You just sounded weird."

*I* feel *weird,* she thought. "How can I help you, Janelle? I have a lot on my plate today."

"I'm here at the hair salon for my ten o'clock appointment with your new girl, but she's not answering the door."

Rose propped her elbow on the desk and rested her forehead in her hand. "Okay, Janelle. Have you tried knocking again? Or louder?" Rose imagined Janelle's kitten heels perched on Lily's front step, her freshly manicured nails softly tapping on Lily's door. "Maybe she didn't hear you."

"I've knocked several times and I even tried the door, but it's locked up tight. Do you think she's run off before she got started?"

"That's ridiculous. She hasn't run anywhere." Of course as Rose said the words, her stomach fluttered with dread. *Surely not . . .*

"I'll try calling," Rose said. "Just . . . keep knocking."

Rose dialed the phone in the cottage, and when she got no answer, she tried Lily's cell, silently fuming that this young woman was further combusting her morning. If Lily was out back and didn't hear the knock at the door, or God forbid, she was still asleep like some teenager, she had some serious attitude adjustment to do if she wanted to make it past her trial period.

The phone rang five times before going to voice mail. Rose stared at the receiver as if it would explain the oddness of the morning. With a sigh, she set down the phone and walked outside to her bike.

As she cruised down Port Place toward the salon, she could see Janelle in her usual cloud of pink, though the woman was doing her best to hide herself on Lily's front porch. On her head was a swirl of pink chiffon.

"Janelle, why are you wearing cotton candy on your head?" Rose asked as she leaned her bike against a palm tree in front of Lily's cottage, noting that Lily's car was in fact parked in the driveway.

"It's my hair-washing morning, and I

243

skipped it today because of my appointment. I thought I'd be able to get in without being seen." She scanned the street with her eyes, straining to spot any stray neighbor before he or she could behold the sight of Janelle's elaborate head covering. At least she was true to who she was, even on a bad hair day.

Rose fished in her pocket for the key to the salon. She was glad she'd stuck to her guns a while back when an HOA member rudely asked her to relinquish the key ring that held a spare key to everyone's cottage. "It's an invasion of privacy," he'd complained.

"Maybe, but it's an invasion you'll be happy to have if you keel over from a heart attack when you're home alone and someone has to kick in your door. Wouldn't you rather I let the paramedics in with a key in a civilized fashion?" The silence in the room told her she'd won that argument.

Inside the salon, all looked shipshape. Towels were folded on the counter, the floor was swept clean, and combs sat in a glass jar ready for the day. Janelle peered over Rose's shoulder, her breath a fog of peppermint. "At least there hasn't been a burglary. And there's her purse." Janelle pointed to the kitchen table at the back of the cottage. "So she probably hasn't run off."

Rose stepped to the side for some air and gestured for Janelle to take a seat in one of the seats under the window. "I'll go see what I can find. Wait here."

Rose walked through the cottage to the back door and peered through the glass. The backyard was empty, the door locked.

Rose sighed and turned toward the staircase. Under the window, Janelle was perched on the edge of her seat, her toe tapping up and down on the hardwood floor.

"Lily?" Rose called as she ascended the staircase. "Are you here? I'm coming up."

No answer.

She peered into the bathroom at the top of the stairs, then the spare bedroom that overlooked the marina. Assured that those rooms were empty, she started for Lily's room, the one that had a view of the bay. The door was cracked, and she reached out to push it open, her heart banging in her chest.

Lily sat on the edge of the bed with her back to the door and her hands tucked under her thighs. It was the same posture she had the day Rose first showed Lily the salon, just before Lily told Rose she needed a job and a home.

"Lily?"

As if coming out of a fog, Lily startled and turned to look over her shoulder.

"Oh, hi, Rose."

"Hi, yourself. What's going on?"

Lily took a deep breath. "Is Janelle here yet?"

"Oh yes. And quite ready for her appointment, I might add." Rose checked her watch. Ten thirty on the nose. "Do you plan to come downstairs anytime soon?"

"I'm sorry. I just needed a minute."

Rose sighed. *So this is how it's going to be.* She hadn't seen a single client and she was already behind schedule. But something about the curve in Lily's back and the way her shoulders were bunched up with tension softened Rose's irritation. She sat on the end of the bed, not too close to Lily, but still within arm's reach.

"Has your life ever felt . . . unraveled?" Lily asked.

"I'm familiar with that feeling, yes."

"Really?" Lily turned to look at Rose, her brown eyes earnest and searching.

Rose nodded. "More than you know." She swallowed, unaccustomed to saying much about her own life, much less asking someone else about hers. "Is that how your life feels?"

Lily exhaled. "A little. It's like my mom's death pulled a string loose and the years just keep . . . stretching it farther out."

"It's hard to tuck a string back in once it's out — especially if it's from a death."

Lily sniffed, nodded.

"And your husband? I bet he gave that string a good yank."

Lily gave a quiet laugh. "He did, but you know what? It was a mercy. I think he only married me to get over another woman. But I wasn't much better. Worth came along at a time when I was completely adrift. We just used each other as life rafts." She looked at Rose and lifted the corner of her mouth into a sad smile. "Not a promising way to start a marriage."

Beginning a marriage as a way to serve a wholly unrelated purpose? Rose was well acquainted with that particular kind of disaster.

"Is that why you're up here?"

Lily laughed, louder this time. "Actually, no. Worth isn't the cause today, thank goodness." She tipped her head back and closed her eyes for a brief moment. Downstairs a door opened and Rose heard Janelle greet Patsy Martin.

"I'm starting over in a salon, just like my mom did after my dad died. And I felt so confident as I was cleaning this place out. Setting out all my brushes and towels and bottles, as if the perfect arrangement of everything could cover up the fact that I'm completely alone."

Both women were quiet as a flock of cackling seagulls soared past the window. When Rose had first stepped into Lily's bedroom, she'd noticed the absence of any photos except for a single silver picture frame next to her bed. Rose glanced at it now. The photo showed a lovely young woman with dark hair, red lips, bobby pins pinched between her lips, and a hairbrush in hand. Her eyes were bright and a little mischievous.

"You know Kitty?" Lily asked.

*Oh, here we go.* "Yes, I know Kitty."

"She said I need a support system. People who know me well who can step in and help. But I don't have that."

"I will grant that Kitty Cooper knows a few things about how the mind works, but she can also run her mouth just for the sake of hearing her own intelligence."

"She did sound smart."

"Yes, well, she succeeded then. And I may not be a fancy doctor, but I do know this: you can't control Worth, you can't control the curveballs life throws at you, but you do have say over what happens next. From this minute forward. That's under *your* control." She hesitated, then reached forward and squeezed Lily's elbow. "And you're not alone. You have a village full of people, and they're all pretty nice. Well, most of them at least. You've landed in a good place here. I think you'll like it." Even as she said the words, she thought of Terry's email and his offer. She could almost hear the ticking clock in her mind, counting down the minutes until she'd need to give him her decision.

Lily's shoulders dropped an inch and she rested her hands in her lap. "Rawlins said the same thing. That I'd like it here."

"Did he? Of course he did. He's a smart boy."

"Thank you again for letting me stay in the cottage."

"You're welcome, but I'm not finished. You have a place to live, and you also have two customers sitting downstairs waiting for haircuts." She raised her eyebrows pointedly.

Lily took a deep breath and stood, then straightened her clothes — a loose black-and-white top and denim shorts. Her hair was pinned up halfway with a clip, and soft waves fell around her face. She squared her shoulders and looked at the door but didn't make a move.

"Do you remember what I told you on the phone the morning you moved here?" Rose asked. "Sometimes the hardest step is the first one. After that it gets easier."

Lily nodded, then said, "It sounds like you've done this before."

"I have a few decades on you. A lot can happen in that much time."

Rose followed Lily down the stairs, where Janelle and Patsy were flipping through magazines, deep in conversation. When Janelle saw Lily, she slapped her magazine closed. "My stars, am I glad to see you. My head's getting hot under all this chiffon." She picked at the edge of her pink turban with a long fingernail.

"I'm sorry I'm late," Lily said. "These first haircuts are on the house."

Patsy's eyes lit up as they always did when she thought she was getting something for free, or close to it — she was the one who turned up her nose at anything at the thrift store that cost more than fifty cents, then complained about it for days — but Janelle swatted Lily's shoulder with her manicured hand. "We won't hear of it. Things happen. But a piece of advice, business owner to business owner? Try to get your ducks in a row before you book any more appointments."

Lily nodded and cast a quick glance back to where Rose stood in the kitchen. "I agree. I think the ducks are in order now."

"I'm glad to hear it." Janelle pointed to her head. "Now about this hair."

Lily grinned. "Yes, ma'am. Why don't we start with a wash." She held out the smock and Janelle took it, slid it over her head, and sat in the chair in front of the deep, white basin sink. She cast a furtive look around the salon — did she think paparazzi were hiding in the corners? — before unwinding the chiffon from her hair, which was indeed in need of a good wash.

Once settled, she closed her eyes. "Don't be afraid to crank up the heat. I like it scalding." Just as Lily was about to wet down her hair, Janelle opened her eyes again. "Oh, and that's my friend Patsy. She's the one with the hemorrhoids I was telling you about at the party."

Patsy shifted in her seat with a squeak, exposing the edge of a light blue doughnut pillow. "They're better today."

The laughter that burst from Lily's mouth sounded like relief. Like gratitude. The kind of laugh Rose knew felt good, though it'd been a while since she'd laughed like that.

With another glance at her watch, Rose turned to leave. She had a job ahead of her, cleaning the doughnut sugar from the top of the clubhouse tables once the Bubbas had vacated the building. At the doorway, she paused.

"Lily, do you know why this place is called Safe Harbor?"

Lily paused in her shampooing of Janelle's hair and glanced back at Rose. She shook her head. "No idea."

"The bay is named *Bon Secour*. Strictly translated from the French, it means 'good help,' but somewhere along the way, the meaning shifted to 'safe harbor.'"

"Huh." Lily resumed her washing, not yet understanding the words, so Rose pressed on.

"For centuries this area has been a safe harbor to boats and ships out in the gulf. The way the land is scooped out here, captains found this was a good spot to wait out squalls and bad weather." She paused. "It offered shelter from unexpected storms."

Lily looked back at Rose and gave a nod only discernible to the two of them. As Rose turned to leave, Lily called to her, "Let me know when you want to make that appointment, Rose. My schedule is pretty open."

Just then Tiny Collins popped her head in

the doorway. "Looks like I'm just in time for the party!" She entered the salon and noticed the clipboard on the desk by the door. After signing in, she picked up a *People* magazine and plopped down in the seat next to Patsy, who shifted again on her doughnut.

On her way out the door, Rose called behind her, "I don't think your schedule will be open for long. And my hair is just fine."

After scraping glazed sugar off the card tables in the clubhouse — how was it that these men couldn't see the mess they left behind each week? Did they all need new prescriptions in their glasses? — Rose settled down at her desk to begin the day's work. A potential new resident had submitted his paperwork, and his background check had returned a misdemeanor. It appeared the fellow had been charged with breaking obscenity laws during a protest for women's rights back in the seventies.

"Well," Rose muttered to herself. "There are definitely worse things to be accused of than righteous indignation over inequality for women." She closed the folder and pulled her email up on the computer. She scanned her inbox for the man's initial email to her — best to make sure he'd been a protestor for the women rather than against — but all thoughts of misdemeanors and obscenity laws dissolved when she saw the email from Terry.

She still hadn't responded to him, though he'd sent the email well over a month ago. She read it again now, her eyes lingering over the phrases *sell Safe Harbor Village . . . new ownership . . . The world is your oyster.*

When her phone rang a few moments later, she shook her head to clear the fog before answering. "Safe Harbor Village, this is Rose."

"Hi, Rose. How are you?"

It had been a long time since she'd heard Terry's voice on the phone. In most cases, if they needed to discuss anything pertaining to the village, they'd email, as he'd done when he sent the news about the interested buyer. Though she'd made nearly all the decisions regarding the village since he'd left with Joan in the spring of 1982 (she could probably come up with the exact date if given a moment to pull it from the recesses of her mind), Terry remained a mostly silent co-owner. If forced to be honest, Rose would have to admit it'd been helpful to have him available over the years if a situation popped up that she couldn't work out on her own. Terry owned several villages like this one across the country and therefore was knowledgeable about all matters regarding property ownership and management.

The occasions when speaking on the phone was necessary were few and far between, but when they did talk, she was always surprised by the rasp in his voice, that he sounded like the seventy-year-old man he was today, not the young, fresh-faced kid he was when they first met.

"I'm fine, Terry. And you?"

"Oh, you know. Good as gold." He paused, and when she didn't respond, he continued. "Anyway, I haven't gotten a response from you, so I just wanted to make sure you received my email."

"I did. I was actually just reading through it now." No need to let on that it was at least the tenth time she'd read it.

"Good, good. I've already sold three of my properties, so only four to go. Two in California, one on the coast in Texas, and ours in Safe Harbor. So if you're ready —"

"Actually, Terry, I'm still making up my mind."

"What do you mean? This is what we talked about from the very beginning. Building the properties, then selling them off . . ."

"That was your plan. It hasn't had a thing to do with me for . . . well, almost forty years."

Terry exhaled deeply. "Be that as it may, it's still my plan, but seeing as we're both named owners, we need to be on the same page about this."

"I understand that."

"If you're interested in buying me out, I'd definitely be willing to listen to your terms."

"It's not that, it's . . ."

When Terry spoke again, his voice was softer. "You've been in that place for so long, Rose. Haven't you ever wondered what else is out there for you? I know you were so insistent I buy that piece of land —"

"It's not like I had to work that hard to convince you," Rose spit out.

"Go easy, Rose. I didn't call to argue with you."

Her breathing was coming faster now. *Why are you so mad?* she asked herself. *He's giving you an out. It's what you've wanted, right?* But something felt different these days, though whether it had to do with her or the village itself, she wasn't sure. Either way, she wasn't sure it was the right time to let the place go.

And yet she couldn't deny the number of times she'd considered leaving, letting the space behind her fill in like she'd never been there at all. Would it be foolish to turn down this chance to set down her responsibilities and move on? He'd said the offer was "a pretty penny," and while her decision was in no way fueled by money, having some extra in her bank account would help pad her new future, wherever it may be.

Terry sighed. "The amount of money they've offered us tells me they're eager to buy. I can probably convince them to wait a bit. But, Rose, I'll need to give them an answer at least by the end of the summer, if not sooner."

She nodded her head firmly, though he couldn't see her. "I'll let you know my decision then."

# SEVENTEEN

Early Wednesday evening Hazel stood on her pink stool at Rose's counter, gently pressing the bottom of a juice glass onto balls of snickerdoodle dough lined up on a cookie sheet. As this was the second night in a row that Hazel would be spending the night at Rose's cottage, Rose had depleted her mental stockpile of child-appropriate activities — swimming, coloring, picking weeds, making paper dolls, folding clothes — and was now moving on to other, less-tested methods of keeping her grandniece entertained.

As Rawlins had predicted, his ex-wife, Tara, began working as many shifts as possible in her new job, and Rose for one was glad for the shift in care. She knew Rawlins was too. Rose could tell he was never entirely comfortable after Tara picked up Hazel for their days together.

So really, her job change was a blessing,

though her timing couldn't have been worse. The beginning of the shrimping season was always the busiest, and with Tara working almost all dinner shifts at the restaurant and many lunches as well, Hazel would be a more frequent presence around the village. And seeing how Rose was her de facto babysitter, Hazel would also be the newest — and youngest — neighbor.

"I love baking," Hazel pronounced as she smashed the glass onto the last ball of dough. "These smell so good."

"You think so?" Rose slid the sheet into the oven, holding an arm out to keep Hazel from coming too close to the heat. "Wait until they finish baking. They'll smell even better. They can be our after-dinner treat." Rose set the timer for sixteen minutes, then led Hazel out the back door. She needed a little breathing room after standing shoulder to shoulder — more like shoulder to elbow — with Hazel for the last half hour. She loved the girl, but Rose's personal bubble was growing smaller and smaller.

Rose pushed open the door and inhaled as she walked out into the evening air. The sun was making its slow descent over the bay, casting the water in a sparkling glow. Clouds pushed in from the south, dark purple-blue over the horizon. Rose hoped

Hazel was okay sleeping during thunderstorms.

Rose sat in one of the Adirondack chairs and set her timer on the table next to her, then stretched her legs out in front. Hazel ran ahead to the grass, hopping through it like a bunny. She investigated each of Rose's three bird feeders hanging from the scrubby oak tree in the side yard. After a few minutes she plopped down in the chair next to Rose.

"Do alligators ever come out of that water?" she asked, one finger pointing to the bay.

"I've never seen one here," she said. "But other places on the island, yes."

"You mean like in the swamp?"

"There, yes. Also in the nature preserve." A few years ago the National Wildlife Service had designated two miles of walking trail through the island's scrubby forest as part of its nature preserve, an honor that ensured developers couldn't sweep in and take land for nefarious purposes. "Have you ever seen an alligator?"

Hazel shook her head. "Papa told me about them, though. About how they live in the swamps."

"Did he?"

She nodded and swiveled in her chair so she faced Rose. "He said you used to go

260

looking for them, and one time he had to save you."

"That's right." Rose nodded slowly. Jim had been talking about her? That she was on his mind at all caused a surprising flutter in her chest. "He did."

She and Jim were born only eleven months apart, and as kids, with their similar white-blond hair and pale eyelashes, not to mention how much time they spent together when Jim wasn't out on their father's boat, many people who didn't know otherwise assumed they were twins. And they might as well have been. Jim was Rose's best friend — her only friend for a while — and she was pretty sure she was his as well.

As soon as school was over for the day, Rose and Jim would hop on their bikes and go exploring, even though they knew almost every inch of the island. Three miles long and populated mostly by fishermen and their families in scattered rural neighborhoods, not much was a surprise on Safe Harbor Island.

But one day there was one. It was early October, a month before Lily turned eleven. Jim had been asked to help an employee untangle a net back in the warehouse after school. He told Rose he'd be done by five and for her to wait for him before setting out on her bike, but she got impatient and left without him. When she was on her own, she usually stuck to the road, winding her way around the island, maybe grabbing a frosty bottle of Coca-Cola from the deep icebox on old Mr. Cox's front porch.

This particular afternoon, though, she felt brave. She was tired of dodging the near-constant resentment and disappointment that peeled off her father in sheets. Tired of the expectation that she'd do nothing more than help in the office or prepare meals with her mother. Tired of no one asking her to do any "real" work. On that afternoon, she was done with it all and determined to show them . . . something.

*I can do hard things,* Rose thought as she pedaled faster toward the entrance to the swamp. Her heartbeat quickened as she approached the space between the trees where kids' bikes had beaten down the tall grass and weeds covering the ground. The flattened brush only went so far, though — most kids turned back after venturing only a few yards into the swampy areas. It was a well-known fact around the island that alligators prowled the swamp, looking for small animals to drag back into the water. Parents always told their kids that to an alligator a small child was no different from a dog or a possum.

Rose hopped off her bike and walked beside it, her eyes scanning the ground for anything that might be moving around, but the only movement was her own. She kept pushing, even when fear told her to turn around and go back to the road. Before she knew it, she was back where she started, having walked her bike clear around the entire swamp. She looked around, half expecting to see someone else there — someone who would have seen her daring feat, someone who would see her pump her fists in the air — but she was alone. She pumped her fists anyway, then resumed pushing her bike toward the space between the trees.

She'd only gone a few feet farther when everything seemed to happen at once. A strange noise came from the swamp behind her — something like leaves rustling, but also like a disturbance in the water. Just as she turned, from somewhere far away she heard the *plink-plink-plink* of playing cards flicking against bicycle spokes — the tires spinning fast — and she knew it was Jim.

Behind her, an enormous alligator had emerged from the water and had three of its four feet on the boggy shore. She watched in awe as it pulled its back foot out of the muddy water with a slurp and stepped forward, its body moving toward her in slow but sure increments.

"Rose!" Jim's voice pitched higher than usual. "Move!"

Terror filled her arms and legs with concrete. She tried to jump on her bike but fell. With a leg finally half-swung over the center bar of her bike, she hopped along the ground on one foot as fast as she could, too scared to look back. If the alligator was approaching with its mouth wide open, she didn't want to know, though the continued commotion behind her told her the gator was definitely not retreating to the water.

After an eternity Jim burst through the trees. He jumped off his bike and threw it to the ground in one fluid movement. Before she knew what was happening, Jim hurled himself forward and grabbed something off the ground. When he straightened back up, he was holding a rock the size of his head. He reared his arm back and flung the rock with a strength and fury she didn't know her brother possessed.

The rock landed with a wet thud several feet in front of the alligator. It shouldn't have made a difference to the animal — even if Jim had landed a bull's-eye hit, it probably would've felt like nothing more than a gentle bump on its thick hide — but for some reason the alligator slowed its forward motion. It paused, and as Rose again tried to set her clumsy foot on the pedal, the gator began to retreat, not taking its eyes off her but backtracking until its long reptilian body was once more under the water.

Both kids were silent on the way home, the only sound the wind in their ears and the rhythmic ticking of Jim's playing cards threaded between his spokes. It wasn't until they propped their bikes up against a tree in the front yard that Jim turned on her.

"What were you thinking, going into the swamp by yourself? Or at all!"

Rose was shocked to see his eyes fill with angry tears.

"I . . . I don't know," she stammered. "I just wanted to do something big. Something boys can do."

"Boys don't go into the swamp! It could have gotten you killed."

"I didn't die, though. You saved me."

He scoffed. "I did not. I threw a rock. You got lucky. *We* got lucky."

Tears of shame burned hot on her cheeks. "You looked like an angel." Rose's words were quiet. "If you hadn't been there . . ." She shook her head to erase the image in her mind of an alligator swallowing a deer in one gulp, something she'd seen in her set of encyclopedias.

He shrugged. "You're my sister." The way he said it — like it was a foregone conclusion that he'd protect her, that there was no question about it — made her heart surge with a flood of love. She reached for Jim and hugged him, hard and quick. He squeezed her back, then pushed her away.

"Come on," he said gruffly, wiping at his eyes with the back of his wrist. "Mama's frying hushpuppies."

On the table next to Rose, the timer dinged, startling her so badly, she jerked her arm and caught her funny bone on the edge of the armrest. She groaned and rubbed her elbow, then grabbed the timer.

"Are the cookies ready?" Out in the yard, Hazel popped up from where she'd been sitting in the grass. Rose had been so lost in her memories, she hadn't even noticed Hazel get out of her chair.

Rose took a deep breath — warm end-of-day air tinged with salt and grass — and stood, smoothing her hands down the sides of her shorts. Memories were such funny things. They could seem so far away, lost forever in the years, and then someone said one little thing and everything flooded back.

She felt unsteady, as if the alligator memory — something she hadn't thought about in who knew how long — had unhinged something inside her. Or turned something on.

*I miss Jim.* The thought came unbidden. Not unwelcome, but unexpected. *I miss my brother.*

She knew she could pick up the phone and call him anytime. But then again, so could he. Communication went two ways, and she hadn't heard hide nor hair from him in a very long time. Not that she expected to. It was foolish to think — to hope — he'd call and offer forgiveness, unprompted and out of the blue.

But he'd talked about her. Rose let that surprising bit of information roll around in her head, but she still wasn't altogether sure what to do with it. He'd talked about her to both Hazel and Rawlins. Did he ever plan to talk to her or just about her?

Other than Rawlins and Hazel, Jim was Rose's only living family, but it was remarkable how often Rose felt alone in a swamp. Like a little girl with a bike, looking around for her brother, worried he might never show up.

After rescuing the snickerdoodles mere seconds before they transitioned from toasty brown to burned, Rose decided to usher Hazel down the street to the Sunrise for a quick dinner. She gave in and let Hazel take a cookie to go, even though it'd ruin her appetite, and Hazel munched on it slowly as they walked the short distance down Port Place.

As they approached the café — smiling faces in the windows and Roberta's form filling up the bulk of the space behind the counter — the door opened and Coach walked out.

"Good evening, ladies," he said, his smile lengthening the corners of his eyes. He lingered on Rose a beat too long, heating her cheeks. Then he looked away, stooping to talk to Hazel.

"What's that you're munching on, little one? I smell cinnamon."

As Hazel gave Coach a rundown of their baking afternoon, Rose did a mental sweep of her appearance. Her white shorts bore a stain on the front from a blob of dough that had fallen off Hazel's spoon, and she was wearing her awful plastic flip-flops, the pair she kept by the front door for the sole purpose of wearing to get *The Village Vine* from her mailbox on Wednesday mornings. Hazel had been trying on Rose's shoes earlier before the baking started, and when it was time to get ready to walk to the café, she couldn't locate a single pair of shoes except these — yellow, rubber, squeaky.

She ran her hands quickly over her hair, noting the flyaway strands all around her face. She tucked what she could behind her ears and tightened a few bobby pins at the back of her head. Coach had straightened up by then and was watching her, a loose grin on his face, but it quickly fell away. He took a step closer to her. "Everything okay, Rose?"

"Of course," she said, hitching up her purse strap on her shoulder. "Why do you ask?"

"You just . . ." He shrugged. "I don't know. I was watching you walk up, and you just seem a little . . . out of sorts."

She took a quick breath, then blew it out of her nose. "You were watching us?"

"Now, don't get all huffy on me. I was just waiting to pay my bill, and I saw the two of you heading over here. Figured if I dragged my feet a little, I'd get a chance to say hello. To you."

"Well. Hello."

"Hello." He smiled, and this time he didn't look goofy as he did it. "You look nice tonight. Relaxed."

She reached up to tuck another stray lock

of hair behind her ear but stopped when he shook his head. "What is it?"

"I like it when you're not all put together. Makes it seem like you're almost human."

Hazel tugged on Rose's hand then. "Aunt Rosie, can we eat now?"

Rose narrowed her eyes as she watched Coach for another second before breaking away. "Yes, ma'am. Let's get you some dinner."

Coach opened the door for them, and as Rose walked past him into the café, she heard him murmur, "Good to see you, Rosie."

Hazel's bedtime was set at seven thirty, as dictated by Rawlins, who, Rose was happy to note, had developed into a very conscientious father. Having no parenting history of her own, Rose had no experience with bedtimes, early or late, but she was sure she would have been the type of parent who enforced a similar strict bedtime schedule.

That being said, Hazel was a very persuasive little girl. Each night she stayed with Rose, Hazel came up with a new reason why she couldn't go to bed at the appropriate time, and each night Rose practically broke a sweat trying every which way to get her to agree to go to bed. But this evening Hazel wasn't having it.

"I'm not tired! I promise. I'll just lie there and lie there and lie there, and then I'll get lonely."

"You won't be lonely," Rose reasoned. "I'll be right downstairs."

"But can I just stay with you for a little bit longer?"

Rose checked the clock on the mantel: 8:12. She sighed. How was this small five-year-old wide-awake when Rose was exhausted?

"Can you turn some music on?"

"Music?" Rose almost laughed. *Music at this hour?* She sighed. "I'll tell you what." She stood and crossed the room to where her little radio sat on the kitchen counter. "I'll play you a song. Then you go to bed. Deal?"

"Deal!"

Rose turned on the radio and set it to the local station, Sunny 102.8. Most music these days made Rose's toes curl, but Sunny 102 played old Motown favorites, music she'd grown up with and would never, ever tire of.

A commercial ended and the next song started — "Heat Wave," one of her favorites. The minute that toe-tapping beat began, Rose was back in her childhood bedroom, only a mile or so from where she stood right now. She was sixteen years old, practicing her dance moves in front of her mirror, her desk chair pushed up under the doorknob to keep her brother from bursting in and catching her mid-dance. She'd just seen Martha and the Vandellas on *American Bandstand,* and visions of those short sequined dresses glimmered in her mind.

Rose heard a noise behind her and turned. Hazel was standing next to her smiling.

"What is it?"

"You were dancing!"

"No, I wasn't. I was just setting up the radio."

"Yes, you were. You were doing this." And Hazel started swiveling her hips like a little dashboard Hawaiian dancer.

"Let's go, little miss." Rose took Hazel's hand and led her to the open space behind the couch. "Now, here's how we used to do it." Rose pinched her nose and did the Swim. "This one's called the Mashed Potato." Hazel laughed and copied the move. "Then there was the Twist." She held her arms out and twisted her hips, lifting one heel, then the other.

Rose showed Hazel everything she knew, and by the time the song was over, they were both laughing and out of breath.

"Okay, fancy pants. Upstairs with you."

After using the potty and climbing into bed in Rose's spare bedroom, Hazel flopped back on her pillow. Freckles had popped out on the bridge of her nose and across her cheeks like little flecks of cinnamon. Her red curls fanned out on the pillow. She yawned, then settled farther into the quilt. "Aunt Rosie, you said a lie."

"I did?"

She nodded. "You told Mr. Coach you're not a dancer, but you are."

"Oh, honey, I'm not really a dancer. I just . . . well, I just really like that song."

"But you're a good dancer. Maybe you should be one."

Rose smiled and kissed Hazel on the forehead. "I think I'll reserve my dancing for you."

By the time Rose made it back downstairs, it was almost nine o'clock. After picking up a few stray cups and napkins in the kitchen and turning on her dishwasher, she eyed the radio that sat on the counter acting all innocent, like it hadn't just unleashed Rose's shoulders and hips and knees in alarming ways. In fact, she hadn't felt so unleashed in a good long while.

Without so much deciding as giving in, Rose turned the radio back on. This time it

273

was Smokey Robinson and the Miracles, "You Really Got a Hold on Me." She let her feet guide her back to the den, where now only a single lamp illuminated the room. The curtains covering her back windows were wide open, but it didn't matter — nothing was watching her but the wide blue water and the inky dark sky.

She closed her eyes and exhaled, long and slow, and let her mind travel back to that pink-walled bedroom with the gauzy curtains and the four-poster bed. The old transistor radio on the windowsill, diary open on her bed, and her heart aching as only a sixteen-year-old girl's heart can ache. Unless you're sixty-eight and your heart still aches just as much, only now it's tuned to a different pitch.

It started with her head gently swaying side to side, then her shoulders, her hips, her arms held outstretched. Rose's bare feet slid across the cool floor, moving her through the space like a puff of air. She wasn't thinking of anything but the lilting music, the soul-stirring words, the yearning in the voices. But after a few moments, her mind's eye filled with image after image, and she danced for them all.

For her brother and his once-fierce protection of her and her shining adoration of him . . .

For her friend she'd never see again, the woman Rose lost when Rose chose her man, thereby severing much of what was good in her life . . .

For the land she'd forsaken, and her remaining family with it . . .

For Coach Beaumont and the peculiar way he made her stomach tie itself up in knots despite her best efforts to stop it . . .

But mostly Rose danced for the little girl she used to be, the one with the bold heart who was told again and again to stay in her place, safe on the shore. She danced for the young woman standing in her bedroom holding all her hopes and dreams in shaky hands. She danced for the old woman she was now and the woman she'd be going forward, for as long as she had breath to live.

When the music ended and the station went off the air for the long overnight hours, Rose kept dancing, her eyes closed, her face to the wide water and endless sky on the other side of the windows. She imagined all manner of faces pressed against the glass, watching her, ghosts of her past peering in to see what she had made of herself. But when she opened her eyes, all she saw was her own reflection. A woman swaying alone to an audience of none.

When she stopped swaying, her face and neck were warm and flushed. She put a cool palm to her cheek, then cleared her throat as if to assure herself she was still in control of all her faculties, though she felt as dazed and loose-limbed as if she'd had two glasses of Toots Baker's Alabama Slammer.

In the kitchen she turned off the radio, twisting the dial harder than necessary to make sure it wouldn't surprise her in the morning when the station kicked back on again. She turned off the single lamp in the den, darkening the memory of that restless dancing, of her flushed cheeks and racing heart, and tiptoed up the stairs, careful not to awaken her grandniece, sleeping peacefully in the spare bedroom.

# EIGHTEEN

Back in Fox Hill Lily had her own pair of scissors for cutting hair. It was impractical for her and her mom to share a pair, so when she graduated from washing and sweeping hair to actually cutting it, she used some of her tip money to buy her own. They never felt right in her hands, though. They made her fingers cramp, and she always felt like she was holding them incorrectly.

After her mother's death it felt almost disrespectful to use Lillian's scissors, as if by doing so she was assuming her mother's role in the salon and in Fox Hill, which everyone knew was impossible. There was only one Lillian Chapman, and Lily couldn't be her, even if they did share a name. But she had to admit, her mother's scissors felt good in her hand. They fit her fingers, didn't pinch her skin, and generally let her do her work effortlessly.

She may not have been able to take her

mother's place in Fox Hill, but this village was a new place. A new beginning. And pulling her mother's scissors out of the red velvet case where they'd spent the majority of the last year and a half felt like bringing her mom along with her.

As Rose had predicted, Lily's schedule didn't stay open for long. It turned out that the residents of Safe Harbor Village had very needy hair — hair that had to be washed, trimmed, dyed, fluffed, combed, and styled on a regular basis. And some even more than that.

Janelle was one of her clients who came faithfully every week; twice a week, in fact. It was hard not to laugh with Janelle, if only for the outlandishly scandalous things that escaped her lips when she was draped in a smock and preening in front of a mirror, and Lily was grateful for her shapely appearance in the doorway again this morning.

Janelle always requested Lily's first appointment of the day — "Before your arms get tired" — but today Ida Gold was up first. Her husband, Peter, had called the day before to schedule an appointment for her, and Janelle had, after much urging on Lily's part, agreed to be seen second, a demotion that was only partly assuaged by the glass of passion fruit La Croix Lily poured for her as soon as she walked in. That and the chocolate muffin Peter brought on a plastic-wrapped plate. She had still come in at ten, though her appointment was now at eleven.

"Peter, honey, you're about the only person who could convince me to give up my slot in that chair," she said, pointing to the black swivel chair that Ida now occupied. "You're lucky you're such a handsome devil." She took a bite of the muffin, groaning in bliss as she chewed.

Peter laughed. "I appreciate you taking one for the team, Janelle. Ida likes to be home by the time her shows start."

He caught Lily's gaze in the mirror and raised his eyebrows just a hair, and Lily nodded to show she understood. Peter had explained on the phone the day before that Ida grew agitated if she got off her schedule. That schedule included specific daytime TV shows that began at eleven. Lily had promised to have her out of the salon well before any agitation set in.

"And don't do anything wild and crazy with her hair," he'd said. "Lord knows what that would do. She's had the same hairstyle for too many years to count."

Lily stood behind Ida, combing her wet hair, trying to ascertain where her natural part was. She bent down to study the ends of Ida's hair, how they fell against her neck and across her forehead. Each time she'd seen Ida — usually when Ida and Peter would pass by her cottage on their daily fast-walk — she'd noticed Ida's striking dark silver hair. But her cut was severe for such a petite, sweet lady — blunt at the ends and angled down toward her chin. Lily wondered if maybe Ida had kept that style for so long only because no one had tried anything different.

Back home, clients had asked Lillian for the cut they thought they wanted, but she regularly sent them out the door with the cut or style they *needed,* the one that made them feel even more like the person they wanted to be, or the person they felt like on the inside. Lily never tried that particular trick of her mother's, mostly because she didn't have the confidence. So far, Lily had done exactly what each client had asked as they settled down into her chair. But maybe now was the time to try a little of her mother's magic.

With a glance at Peter, who was flipping idly through a back issue of *Ladies' Home Journal,* Lily swiveled Ida's chair and stood in front of her.

"Ida, would it be okay with you if I tried

something a little different today?" she asked quietly.

"How different?"

"Just a little. I'll . . . well, I'll need you to trust me." She hoped she wasn't pushing too far.

Ida hesitated, then sat up a little straighter in her chair and nodded.

Lily's mother's scissors were light as air and so sharp she barely needed to apply any pressure as she cut. Small clumps of silver hair fell across the smock and slid to the floor. Lily didn't need to cut much — she just needed to cut thoughtfully. She softened the ends, changing the lines so the hair didn't angle so sharply, and created some layers around Ida's face.

Ida didn't say a word, but she kept her eyes on the mirror, watching Lily's every move and turn. A few minutes later Lily set down her scissors and picked up a round brush and the hair dryer. Ida closed her eyes. When Lily finished drying Ida's hair, she held the dryer out to the side, its warmth still seeping into her hand. "You can look now, Ida," she said quietly.

After a small hesitation, Ida opened her eyes, but then she froze, her eyebrows arched, her lips pulled into a thin line. Lily smoothed the hair around Ida's face, finger-combing it a little, trying in vain to figure out what specifically had so alarmed her client.

*What was I thinking?* She'd tried to channel her mother, but instead she'd upset a sweet woman who didn't need to be distressed about her hair, of all things.

"Oh dear," Ida murmured.

"What is it, Ida?" Ever attuned to his wife's emotional state, Peter hopped up from his chair and walked over. "Oh," he managed, his brow furrowed. "That's not quite what we talked about."

But now a smile danced on Ida's lips. She turned her head to one side, then the other, then reached up and felt the ends of her hair between her fingers. "How do you like it, Peter?" Her smile was wide, the apples of her cheeks pink and round.

Peter looked at his wife — really looked at her. He walked around the chair and stood in front of her, taking in the style, the way her hair lay softly against her neck and framed her face.

"I think you look lovely. Pretty as a picture."

Ida turned in her chair and peered up at Lily. "Thank you," she whispered. She reached and took Lily's hand, squeezing it with strong fingers. "You made me look so pretty."

"You are pretty, Ida," Lily said. "The haircut didn't do that."

Over Ida's head, Peter's smile was both sad and grateful. After helping his wife out of the chair and paying Lily — tipping her generously — Peter found Lily's hand and gave it a squeeze before bustling out of the salon. "Thank you for making her so happy."

Lily watched as they ambled down the front walkway, Peter's hand on Ida's lower back, Ida reaching up to feel her hair. Lily could tell she was smiling even though she couldn't see her face.

When she turned around, Janelle was already across the room, draping herself with a smock. "I hope your arms aren't too tired," she called as she perched in the chair in front of the sink. "My Summer Surprise Sale begins tomorrow and I need to look perfect." She settled into the chair and rested her head on the lip of the sink. "If customers find me looking unkempt, it reflects poorly on my business."

Lily had yet to step inside Janelle's business, the Pink Pearl. Honestly, she doubted she'd find anything that suited her tastes, if Janelle's clothing choices were any indication of the type of clothes she kept in stock at the Pearl. But a handful of women in the village frequented the shop anytime they needed a little retail therapy, as did many "outsiders" who drove from as far away as Perdido and Robertsdale to find "Sensible yet Sensual Attire for Seasoned Southern Women," as Janelle advertised on the front window.

Today Janelle was wearing a sunshine-yellow top with pressed white capris and white strappy sandals. The outfit was mild compared to the tight pink marvel she'd worn to the Summer Kickoff party, though in keeping with her "sensual" preferences, she'd left the top two buttons on her yellow blouse open.

"I'll make sure your hair does nothing to detract from your business," Lily said. "You have my word."

"Good. Do your thing then."

Lily bit back her smile as she washed and conditioned Janelle's hair. A few minutes later, Janelle sat in the swivel chair with her hair hanging in wet waves down her back.

Last week when she'd washed and styled Janelle's hair, she just barely trimmed the ends to keep the locks "long and luscious," as Janelle specified, and touched up her roots with her preferred shade, Electric Blonde 103. Not wanting to disappoint her very first customer, Lily had done just as Janelle had asked, leading Janelle to book twice-a-week appointments for the foreseeable future. Today, though, Lily felt she'd be doing her client a disservice if she didn't at least suggest something a little mellower.

She brushed Janelle's hair, letting it fall into its natural part, and pulled it down alongside Janelle's cheeks. "May I make a suggestion?"

Janelle arched an eyebrow. "What kind of suggestion?"

"Well . . ." Lily walked around the chair and leaned against the counter in front of Janelle, looking her in the eye. She chose her words carefully. "I think we may be able to find a shade of blonde that suits you better. Would you be up for trying something a little special today?"

"Something special?" Clearly she was skeptical. "My blonde is fine. It's very close to my natural hair color."

"Mm-hmm." Lily reached into a drawer and pulled out a color card, pointing to a shade several levels below Janelle's Electric Blonde. "I think something in this range — a warm caramel or honey — would really highlight your eyes and skin tone."

Janelle tilted her head, and Lily slid to the side so Janelle could better study her reflection. Janelle held the card up to the side of her face, narrowed her eyes, and pursed her lips. After a moment, she handed the card back. "Lily, I have a certain . . . reputation to uphold. A fantasy, if you will."

"But can't you still be a . . . fantasy with warm caramel highlights instead of electric blonde ones?"

Janelle hesitated.

"The caramel and honey are both very luscious," Lily said. "Captivating. Maybe even a little mysterious."

"Mysterious." Janelle drew the word out slowly. "I like that. All right, missy, you win. Let's go with the caramel."

What should have been a quick appointment turned into almost two hours, but Lily didn't mind. Her next appointment wasn't until one o'clock anyway, and going through the whole process of wash, trim, color, set, and style gave her a chance to work through her repertoire of skills. Instead of feeling overwhelmed, she was in her element, her arms and hands and fingers doing exactly what they were meant to do. And the dawning joy on Janelle's face when she first saw her new 'do — all dried and curled and sprayed into place — combined with Ida's earlier delight, was a boost to Lily's confidence. She wasn't her mother, not exactly, but she wasn't the old Lily either. She was a new creation.

As sunlight flooded through the windows of her salon, she relished the zip of energy, of purpose, in her body and her heart. Just a handful of weeks before, she'd been staring at a slip of paper that held words that upended her life. Again. And now, here she stood. Not much had changed — her life was still tangled and a little off course — but a seed of hope had planted itself somewhere inside, and that was good enough for her.

## NINETEEN

It was nearly five o'clock on a hot Friday afternoon when Lily heard a knock at the door. At this point most customers walked right into the salon when they arrived, immediately making themselves at home with a magazine and a glass of whatever Lily had set out in a pitcher on the little table by the waiting chairs. When she heard the knock, she was adjusting the dryer hood over Roberta's curls as Roberta and Shirley carried on an in-depth conversation about the correct way to make deviled eggs.

"If you don't start with Duke's mayonnaise, you've ruined the whole batch," Roberta said, talking over Shirley who was just as vigorously arguing that any mayo would do. "Don't tell me you're a secret Yankee, Shirley Ferrill."

Laughing, Lily peered over her shoulder and was surprised to see Rawlins standing at the door. He smiled and pointed toward the end of her porch. "You can't cheat with Hellmann's, or worse, Kraft," Roberta continued. "It's not the real thing. Lily, please tell me you don't use Miracle Whip when you make your deviled eggs."

"Hmm?" Flustered, Lily straightened up from Roberta's dryer and pushed her own hair away from her face. "I don't . . . I've never actually made deviled eggs."

Roberta stared at her. "But you like them, right?"

"Oh yes. I do. Can you . . . give me just a second?"

Without skipping a beat, Roberta continued her tirade against inferior mayonnaise, much to Shirley's dismay, as Lily opened the front door.

Rawlins stood at the opposite end of the porch, inspecting the clematis that climbed the porch rail and all the way up a post to the eaves. Behind him, Hazel took a running start and jumped up on the porch swing.

"Sorry to bother you," he said. "Rose asked me to stop by and check this vine. She was worried it would damage the gutter up there." He leaned over the rail and peered toward the roof.

"Hi," Hazel chirped from the swing. "I came with my daddy. He took the day off and we've been playing. We had a milkshake *before* lunch."

Lily smiled. "That sounds like a very special day." She glanced back at Rawlins. "Do you need help with anything?"

"No, no. It's fine. It looks pretty good to me, but I may run some fishing line along the ceiling here to reroute some of these newer vines. It'll keep them off the eaves. If that's okay with you."

"Sounds good. Whatever Rose says."

On the swing, Hazel leaned her head back, her orange-red curls splayed against the turquoise-painted wood. Her cheeks were pink with the slightest of sunburns, making the smattering of freckles across her nose pop.

"Looks like you're wiped out," Lily said with a smile. "Must have been a full day."

"It was. We went fishing this morning and I caught four fish, but I threw them back. We had cheeseburgers for lunch, and then I practiced riding my bike." She hopped off the swing and ran to the grassy yard. "I've been practicing my cartwheels too." Planting her hands on the grass, she kicked her legs up in the air, then rolled onto her side. "I've almost got it."

Rawlins rubbed the top of his head. "I'm out of my element with the cartwheels."

Lily called to Hazel, "I might be able to help you with those."

Hazel's eyes lit up. "Right now?"

"Well, I can't right now, but soon. How about that?"

Hazel nodded and tried another cartwheel.

"Sounds like your day off wasn't exactly *off,*" Lily said to Rawlins, her voice quiet so Hazel wouldn't overhear.

He smiled. "Yeah. It's okay, though. Playing around with her is better than sitting at home with my feet kicked up."

"Something tells me you don't spend too much time with your feet kicked up."

"Daddy, watch!" Hazel yelled before hurling herself into another cartwheel.

"Awesome, kiddo," he called to Hazel, then turned back to Lily. "You've got me there. But I like to be busy. Then again, I am pretty beat. I'll take it easy tonight."

A burst of laughter came from inside, reminding Lily she had two customers in various stages of hair disarray.

"Sounds like your clients are happy," he said.

"Lily?" Roberta called just then. "I'm getting a little overcooked under this dryer."

"I need to . . ." She gestured back inside.

"Yep. I won't be long out here. We'll stay

out of your way."

"You're not in my way. When you finish, y'all can come on in. I can get you something cold to drink."

"Maybe we'll do that."

Twenty minutes later, Lily swept loose hair into a pile as Roberta and Shirley pulled their purses from the hooks on the wall. Roberta handed Lily a few bills from her wallet. As Lily took them, Roberta raised her eyebrows and nodded her head toward the doorway, where Rawlins stood with his hands in his pockets.

"He's back," Roberta whispered.

"I can see that."

"He's a handy fella, I'll give him that. Now, I told Shirley I'm going to make a batch of deviled eggs tomorrow. Come on over early and get some before she realizes how much better they are with Duke's and eats every last one."

Shirley patted Lily's arm on her way out. "I was so worked up I could barely sleep the other night after hearing about your . . . well, you know." She lowered her voice to a whisper. "The dirtbag."

Lily held back her laughter. "Thanks, Shirley. I appreciate your concern."

"You've had a rough go of it, dear. It's about time for something good to come your way, if you ask me."

Rawlins had been watching them from the doorway, but at Shirley's words, he dropped his gaze. As the women breezed out of the salon, he stepped back and held the door open for them. "Ladies."

Shirley paused on the porch. "Rawlins, honey, the next time you're here, would you mind stopping by and checking the latch on my back fence? Something's jammed it and I can't get it to close right. Louis the Sixteenth keeps getting out and tinkling on Edna's hibiscus."

"Yes, ma'am. I'll stop by early next week, if that's okay."

"That'll be just fine. Come around midday and I'll have lunch for you."

She shuffled out behind Roberta, who was still patting her curls, as if questioning the hold of her hair spray.

Rawlins waited until they stepped off the porch and waved goodbye to Hazel before he exhaled.

"Sounds like you have a lunch date." Lily smiled toward him, standing the broom up in the corner of the salon.

"I guess so. She always has a table full of food when I come by, and I've run out of excuses for not eating."

"I thought you said you like it when they

pay you with food."

"Some more than others. Shirley has a heavy hand on the salt. I'm up half the night guzzling water after the force-feeding."

Lily laughed. "I won't try to feed you, but I can get you a drink. I have lemonade and I think there's a Sprite around here somewhere."

"Just some water would be great."

As she filled a glass with ice and water, the cottage fell silent, a contrast to the laughter and conversation previously filling the salon. When she walked out of the kitchen with two glasses of water, she found Rawlins in front of the window. Outside, Hazel knelt in the grass next to Kitty's Chihuahua, Prissy. Kitty stood nearby holding on to the end of the rhinestone leash with both hands as if Prissy, all three pounds of him, might take off at any minute.

"Hazel is dying for a puppy," he said. "Playing with that little thing's just going to start up her begging all over again."

She handed him the glass. "You don't like dogs?"

"No, it's not that. It's just . . . I'm in and out a lot, and Hazel goes back and forth between me and her mom. It'd be hard to fit a new puppy into the chaos."

Lily looked out the window to where the

294

clematis vines were now draped across the clear filament line Rawlins had stretched between the porch posts. "The vines look good. Thanks for taking care of them."

"No problem." He straightened the cap on his head and took a sip of his water. "Shirley said you've had a rough time."

The abrupt change of topic caught her off guard. "Yeah, I . . . Well, it's kind of a long story."

"Oh, I didn't mean . . . I'm not asking you to tell me. I just . . ." He chewed the edge of his lip, and it seemed he was trying to decide what to say. Or how to say it. "I'm just sorry it's been rough."

"Thank you." She took a deep breath. "It's been a little crazy lately. But things are looking up."

"I'm glad to hear it." Rawlins set his water glass on an end table and moved toward the door. "Thanks for the drink. I need to get out there and rescue Prissy."

Prissy was currently captured in Hazel's tight embrace. His tiny eyes were open even wider than normal.

At the door, Rawlins paused with a hand on the doorframe. "If you don't have plans tonight, my buddy Canaan's son is playing at the Land around eight."

"What's the Land?"

"It's a . . ." He paused and scratched his head. "A roadhouse? Or maybe a dive bar?" He laughed. "It's been a while since I've tried to explain it to someone. You kind of have to see it for yourself. Elijah's band plays there some and . . . well, he's really good. You may already have plans though . . ."

"Plans? My social calendar's pretty empty these days."

"If you'd like to come" — he shrugged — "I'd love the company."

There were at least a dozen reasons why she shouldn't say yes, but before she could gather her thoughts, she heard herself saying, "I think it sounds like fun."

His face brightened. "Really? Great. Should I come — or should you . . ."

"Why don't I just meet you there?" she said. "You said it starts at eight?"

"Technically. Things never start on time, but I'll be there at eight. I'll look for you."

He stepped out on the porch just as Hazel ran up the steps and flung herself around his leg. "Daddy, can we go swimming? I have a swimsuit at Aunt Rosie's house."

"Sorry, baby. I need to get you home to meet your mom. She'll be there soon to pick you up."

Hazel stuck out her bottom lip. "I don't

want to leave. Can I stay with you?"

Rawlins looked back at Lily, then reached down to pull Hazel's arms from his legs. "Let's get going, Haze."

Lily watched them from the porch as they made their way back to Rawlins's truck. Before he could close Hazel's door, she stuck out her head. "Will you still help me with my cartwheels?"

Lily nodded. "I promise. Next time I see you."

Rawlins crossed to the driver's side and climbed inside, then rolled down his window. "When you head out tonight, take a left at the gate and follow the road around the island. You can't miss the Land. And you'll hear it before you see it."

Lily was dressed and ready before all the reasons she shouldn't go to a bar with Rawlins Willett flooded her mind. Sitting on the edge of the bed with one sandal on, she leaned forward over her thighs and held her left hand out in front of her where her ring glittered on her fourth finger.

*I'm married,* she reminded herself. *At least technically.*

The ring had always been a little loose, and now she twisted it round and round with her thumb until her skin felt raw.

297

The silence of her cottage wrapped itself around her, lifting her, bolstering her courage, and she stilled her worried fidgeting. Worth was off somewhere chasing a dream or fabrication in his mind, doing whatever it was he thought he needed to do to make things better. And so was Lily. The pieces of her life had been scattered, but she was slowly pulling them back together.

A new energy bolted through her body, and before she could second-guess her impulse, she pulled the ring from her finger and set it in the drawer of her nightstand, right next to his note and the divorce papers bearing both their signatures. She hadn't mailed them back to Mertha like she'd said she would, but she would do it. Soon.

Lily put on her other sandal and grabbed her purse, ran downstairs, and locked the door behind her.

The farther away she drove from the village, the darker the road became, snaking through tall pines and swaying moss. Through gaps in the branches, moonlight shimmered on the bay. Or maybe it was the river. With the relative hubbub of the village and the nearby businesses behind her, the dense trees and murky darkness felt secluded, almost thick with mystery. Instead of feeling nervous, she was enchanted. Eager.

Just as Rawlins had said, she heard a cacophony of jangly noise as she rounded a bend and approached what must have been the back side of the island. Lights glowed from a shack along the road ahead, and as she drove closer, the sounds and vision clarified. It was no longer just noise, but a slide guitar, a steady drumbeat, and notes from a harmonica floating high above it all. And instead of a shack, it was several buildings, if they could even be called buildings. They looked more like haphazard structures held in place with wood, scrap metal, and blinking neon signs. Above it all a banner flapped in the breeze, proclaiming it the Land of Milk and Honey.

People milled on both sides of the road, trickling across the street from a dirt parking lot opposite the Land and gathering in small clusters outside the buildings. One of the structures appeared to be someone's home, with a tin roof, a pot of flowers by the door, and an orange cat sitting on a metal chair watching the crowd. Another looked like a garage with its sliding door up, but instead of cars, the space was crammed with beer kegs. The third building — the most ramshackle of the three — was the source of the music. Twinkle lights lined the windows, orange ends of cigarettes glowed from the makeshift patio, and a tangle of folks stood near the door, slowly filing inside.

Lily found a sliver of a parking space and climbed out of her car. Another group of people was just leaving the lot and crossing the road, and she followed them to the door of the bar. As she waited for the man sitting on a stool at the door to shine his flashlight on everyone's ID, she tried to peer through the crowd to spot Rawlins.

"First time here?" the man on the stool asked as she handed him her ID. His name tag said Dizzy.

She nodded. "How could you tell?"

"Most new people walk in here with eyes as big as silver dollars. You have the look." He handed back her license and pointed inside. "Bar's to the left. You'll have to fight your way to the front if you want a drink, although women tend to be served quicker than the men." He pointed to the other side. "Tables are to the right. It looks packed, but a lot of those people are just waiting for the bar. You may get lucky and find an open seat."

She followed his direction and squeezed through the warm, close bodies in front of the bar and made her way to the right. Straight ahead, the band was set up on a short wooden platform — not elevated more than four or five inches, but just enough to make the band members easier to see. The harmonica player was a woman shimmying in a tight red dress. The drummer at the back had wild black hair that tumbled over his shoulders, an old man playing the keyboard sat to the side, and up front stood Elijah, the young man she recognized from the Sunrise. His eyes were closed as the ring finger of his left hand, encased in a glass slide, slid effortlessly up and down the guitar strings.

Finally she broke free of the jumble and spotted the tables Dizzy had mentioned. Rawlins sat at one with his arm draped over the back of the only free chair in the whole place.

She exhaled when she saw him, a familiar face in a sea of strangers. She approached the table and stopped just short of his chair. "The Land of Milk and Honey, huh?"

He turned and tipped his face up. "Hey. You made it."

"I did. Sorry I'm late, though."

He pulled his arm from around the chair. "I thought you might have had second thoughts."

"I did." She paused. "But I'm glad I'm here."

"Me too." He stood as she squeezed past him to the open chair, then hung her bag from the back and sat. She took a deep breath and looked around the room. License plates from all around the country covered most of the walls, and on the other side of a sheet of heavy clear plastic hanging on the far wall, an adjoining room held a few couches and a sagging bookshelf. Two men sat at a card table in the middle playing what appeared to be chess.

"I can see why it was hard to explain. How long has this place been here?"

Rawlins sat back and exhaled. "It's hard to say. The owner lives in the house next door, but before him, it was his mother, Desiree. They were always inviting local bands to come play in the garage out behind the house. When the crowds got too big, they built this thing. Word around the island is that Desiree got Louis Armstrong to play here before he moved up to Chicago."

"Really?"

He shrugged. "It may just be a rumor, but people swear it's true."

"That guy at the door — is he the owner?"

"Dizzy? That's the owner's son. Dilbert's the owner. For now. One day it'll all belong to Dizzy."

A few minutes later, Elijah announced from the stage that the band was getting thirsty. "We'll play one more song, then take a short break. Any requests?"

People shouted out various song titles, and the band picked up with a twangy bluegrass tune that pulled folks from their seats.

Next to her, Rawlins stood and Lily's stomach tightened. She imagined him extending his hand and the feel of his skin against hers as he led her to the dance floor. Sweat prickled at the back of her neck and she took an unsteady breath.

He leaned down. "Can I get you a drink?"

She blinked. "What?"

He hooked his thumb behind him to where a line had already started to form in front of the bar. "If I go now, I'll beat the rush."

"Oh, okay." She swallowed hard. "Thanks. I'll have a beer." She fumbled for her bag, but he waved his hand.

"My treat."

He disappeared into the crowd, and she sat back to wait, taking deep breaths to settle her racing heart and overactive imagination. She shook her head at her own silliness. *Ridiculous, Lily.* Not to mention wrong.

He reappeared less than a minute later, a

glass of beer in one hand and a bottle of Coke in the other.

"That was fast."

He grinned. "It pays to befriend bartenders." He lifted his Coke bottle. "Even if you don't drink what they're serving." He set her drink on the table, then sat and stretched his legs in front of him.

"You don't drink but you come to bars?"

"Not bars plural. Just this one. And it's not really a bar. It's more like a cultural experience."

She reached for her beer — which had been poured into a tall glass with Charlie Brown and Snoopy on the side — and took a sip. The cold felt good slipping down her throat. With all the people clustered together plus the balmy night air, the room was more than warm.

The song ended a moment later, and Rawlins and Lily stayed where they were as the crowd around them moved toward the bar, jostling for places in line. Two familiar faces popped out of the crowd and approached their table — Canaan, minus the floppy Hooker hat, and Elijah. Canaan's arm was looped around Elijah's shoulders.

"My boy did good up there tonight, don't you think?"

Rawlins grinned and reached up to shake

Elijah's hand. "Sure did. Good job, kid."

Elijah's smile was shy, but Lily could tell he appreciated Rawlins's praise almost as much as he did his dad's.

"Good to see you again, Lily," Canaan said. "Not sure how Mr. Willett here talked you into coming out tonight, but I'm glad he did."

Lily glanced at Rawlins. "He didn't have to work too hard to convince me. I wanted to see the place for myself."

"And what do you think?"

"It's . . . I've never seen anything like it."

"It's one of the best-kept secrets in the South. Musical greats have played on that very stage." Canaan patted Elijah's chest. "And you get to see one of them play tonight."

Elijah scoffed and shook his head.

"So it seems you do more than just pour drinks at the café on Sunday afternoons," Lily said with a smile.

Elijah chuckled. "I'll do that as long as Roberta will keep me around. Those women tip like crazy. But this is what I really love."

"I can tell."

Canaan bent down next to Rawlins to be heard over the noise. "I talked to my buddy at Southern Breadworks today when I got back to shore. He said he's in."

Rawlins knocked his knuckles against the tabletop. "That's great. Great news."

Canaan nodded. "You've got all you need. You just gotta talk to your old man."

"I know. Soon. I just want everything lined up first."

Canaan lifted his head when someone called to him from the bar area. He raised a hand in greeting, then turned back to Rawlins. "I'm going to the bar." He tapped Rawlins's bottle. "Can I get you another one?"

"Nah. I'm good."

Canaan looked at Lily and she shook her head. "Okay then. I'll see you two on the flip side." He turned to Elijah. "Go get 'em, son. Maybe play these two something special."

Elijah grinned as his dad walked away. "Anything particular you want to hear?"

Rawlins looked at Lily, but she shook her head. He tipped his head up at Elijah. "Your choice. You're in charge up there."

They watched him as he walked away and joined a knot of young people clamoring for his attention. A moment later he was back onstage, tinkering with his guitar stand and talking with the drummer. The woman in the red dress picked up her harmonica and began to play.

Lily heard a faint buzz, and Rawlins pulled

his phone from his pocket. The screen glowed with an incoming text. He sighed and tapped out a quick response.

"Sorry about that," he said, turning the phone facedown on the table.

"It's fine. Everything okay?"

"Yeah." He paused. "It's just been a weird day."

"What made it weird?"

He tilted his bottle back and forth, the green of the glass catching light from those dangling from the ceiling. "Tara and I — Tara's my ex-wife — we set up a deal a while back that works pretty well for us. Hazel stays a week with her, a week with me. Back and forth, with the handoff Fridays at six. Though it's gotten pretty out of whack recently." He was quiet a moment, then rubbed the back of his neck. "Anyway, it turns out Tara's thinking of moving to Destin to be closer to her new job."

"And how far away is Destin?"

"About two hours."

"Wow. That seems far for the back-and-forth."

"Bingo."

She paused before speaking again. "And now you have to figure out who Hazel will stay with?"

He took a deep breath. "She'll be starting

kindergarten in the fall. She has to be in one place by then, not hopping between parents in two different cities."

"Do you want her to be here?"

He exhaled, his cheeks puffing out air. "Yeah. I really do." He looked at her with an apologetic smile. "Sorry to unload all that on you."

"Don't apologize. It's life. It's actually kind of nice to think about someone else's stuff instead of my own." She smiled to show she was at least partly kidding, and he laughed.

"Glad I can help. I have a lot of stuff."

"Don't we all?"

Up on the stage Elijah stepped up to the microphone. "This one is for my two friends." He looked toward Rawlins and Lily and winked. Rawlins laughed. Bodies pressed close to the table as the band segued into a song with a much slower, more languid tempo. All around them arms slung around necks, hips swayed, and smiles loosened. Elijah began to sing, his voice sliding like syrup, and he crooked his finger at them, motioning them to the dance floor.

Lily felt her cheeks redden as the nervousness crept back into her belly. Rawlins stood and extended his hand. She looked up at him.

"May I have this dance?" A corner of his mouth lifted into a smile. "He'll call us out if we don't get up."

She hesitated only a fraction of a second before sliding her hand into his. She stood and he gently pulled her to a spot at the edge of the dance floor where the lights weren't so bright. He lifted her hand and spun her in a slow circle, and when she came back to face him, he was smiling. "Sorry. I couldn't resist."

He adjusted his hand in hers, and she set her other arm around his back as they began to move with the slow beat. Despite the elbows and shoulders they bumped into as folks around them danced and moved, Lily was very aware of the chaste few inches that separated her and Rawlins. It seemed they both were careful not to step too close, not to cross the invisible barrier between them. But then, as if the air around them was charged with an energy they couldn't see but could only feel, something changed. Slowly, inch by inch, the gap between them closed until the warmth and the music felt like a curtain shielding them from everyone else in the room. The rawness and longing in Elijah's voice echoed everything pulsing in Lily's heart until she thought she would melt right there on the floor.

Rawlins's arm tightened around her back and he pulled her even closer, his head tilted down toward hers, and she knew he felt the change too. She let herself lean forward until her head rested against his shoulder and she breathed in deeply.

All she knew about this man was that he had been kind to her on the day she packed up and left her old life behind. And he loved his little girl. And something about him made something in her settle down, quiet and at rest. But even with that scant bit of knowledge, he felt so solid, so real, so *present* right there in front of her, she wished she could stay where she was, in this safe cocoon created by this particular night and these strong arms wrapped around her.

When the song ended, neither of them moved. It wasn't until the drummer knocked his sticks together and sent the band into a far more energetic song that Lily lifted her head from his shoulder and they untangled their arms from around each other. The absence of his skin against hers felt like too-cool shade after time spent in the warm sun.

As they headed back to their seats, she kept her eyes averted, embarrassment coursing through her. *What in the world just happened?*

He went to the bar and returned with two glasses of water. They were both quiet as the next couple of songs slid by. She was acutely aware of him sitting only a foot away — the angle of his shoulders, the line of his jaw — as if that magnetic pull was still there, tugging on all her nerve endings. She stole a glance at him, only to find he was already watching her. They both smiled and started to speak at the same time.

He laughed. "Go ahead."

"I . . ." She didn't know what she was going to say, so she said the first thing that came to her mind. "You don't drink."

"That's correct." He paused. "Is there a question in there?"

"I guess I'm just . . . curious." She shook her head. "It's maybe too personal, though. I shouldn't have asked."

"It's okay. I actually wanted to ask you about the husband you left back at your old house, but I was avoiding it because I worried *I* was getting too personal. But if you're opening that door . . ."

She smiled. "For better or worse, I think the door's wide open now."

He leaned back in his seat. Physically, he was at ease in a way that made her wish she could reach out and pull him toward her, yet something in his bearing held an almost palpable strain — one with which she was well acquainted.

"Who goes first?" he asked.

"I vote you."

He laughed. "Okay. To answer the question you didn't ask, no, I don't drink. I used to but . . . I let it get out of hand." He shrugged. "It's just easier to avoid it now."

"You're not really avoiding it, though, if you come to places like this, right? Seems like it might be hard to put yourself around it."

He shook his head. "No, it was my choice to quit drinking. No one twisted my arm, so it doesn't feel like something I'm missing out on."

On the stage Elijah picked a few chords on his guitar and the drummer set the beat. An old man stepped up onto the platform and picked up a tambourine from a stool and began to tap it against his leg.

"What made you want to quit?"

"In a nutshell, it was Hazel, though the problem started long before her." He angled his chair toward Lily's so they could talk more easily over the music. He set his arm down on the table so close to hers, she could feel the heat from his skin. "Things went a little sideways for me a while back." He was quiet for a moment, and Lily quelled the urge to question him further. "I started drinking to make things feel better. Then I met Tara, and I guess I thought getting married would help whatever was wrong. You can imagine how well that worked out."

Lily propped her chin in her hand. "Yes. I can imagine pretty clearly."

"Rose invited me over for dinner one night. Hazel was just a baby. Rose spared no words telling me I was making a mess of my life and that Hazel was worth giving up the drinking." He pressed his lips together. "Everything in me wanted to fight back. To tell her to take care of her own business and let me take care of mine."

He shrugged and looked back at Lily. "But she was right. I knew I had to quit — there was no other option. And Rose conveniently kept asking me to dinner once a week. Said she was doing it to make sure I got a good meal every now and then, but I know it was to check up on me." He laughed. "She's tough, but she's smart."

The band was playing a jazzy rendition of "Sweet Home Alabama," but Lily was so absorbed in Rawlins's story — the earnest sincerity on his face — she barely noticed the enthusiasm in the room ramp up.

"And you and Tara?"

He sighed. "Tara and I never should have

been together in the first place. I think we used each other to try to fill holes that should have been filled with something healthier. Together we were just . . . combustible." He sat forward and rested his elbows on his knees. "But we got Hazel out of it. She's . . ." He trailed off, then glanced back at Lily. "Well, you've met her."

Lily nodded. "She's really great." In her mind, Lily saw Hazel's dark strawberry curls in disarray as she practiced her cartwheels in Lily's front yard.

"Yeah. Looking at her little face snapped me back into reality. Well, her face and Rose's persistence. Tara and I figured out the custody thing. I finished school . . . Things got better." He hung his head for a moment, then looked at her again. "Now you know everything there is to know about me."

She raised an eyebrow. "Everything?"

"Yeah, okay. Not everything. But a lot. Much more than I know about you." He paused and leaned deeper into his elbows.

Her heart quickened. He was going to ask her about Worth, she knew it. But the empty space on her ring finger felt as tender as new skin, and her divorce papers were still burning a hole in her bedside table. Was it appropriate for her to offer details of the dissolution of her marriage to someone she hardly knew?

*Appropriate?* She almost laughed out loud. Worth hadn't worried about propriety — why should she? Maybe the better question was, did she *want* to tell him?

Rawlins shifted his seat when someone bumped into him, then turned back to her. "So how long have you been cutting hair?"

It took her a moment to register that he hadn't asked her about Worth at all. She looked at him, his face full of curiosity, and relief flooded through her. She exhaled. "Since I was a teenager."

"Really?"

"You sound shocked. Did you think I'd just decided to take it up when I moved to the village?"

"I guess I hadn't put that much thought into it. But . . . since you were a teenager? Did you do it after school or something?"

She nodded. "My mom had a salon at our house. She taught me everything she knew."

As the people around them danced and swayed, Lily told Rawlins all about her mother, their salon, and the warm, shampoo-scented haven in the woods of Fox Hill. As she spoke, he leaned toward her, listening intently. His smile was easy and his gaze on her never faltered. Opening up to someone had never been easier.

"So here you are now, bringing your hair-cutting skills to Safe Harbor Village. How's it been so far?"

"It's . . . Well, everyone's been very welcoming, just like you said. A few feisty folks."

He laughed. "Ten bucks says I can tell you exactly who you're referring to. But I'm glad the transition has been easy. Or at least not terrible."

"No, definitely not terrible."

Their conversation continued to flow, bouncing from Coach's latest paddleboat mishaps and Shirley's sneaky attempts to procure juicy gossip, to Hazel's recent determination to learn how to roller-skate.

When they'd had their fill of music and people, they had to push through the crowd of people to make it to the door. They finally reached the screen door and pushed it open, tumbling like pebbles out into the quiet night air.

Lily exhaled and lifted her hair off the back of her neck as they walked toward the lot across the street. "When will you be back out on your boat again? Do you go every day?"

"I don't go out as much as I used to, but we're out at night, not much during the day.

At one point a few years ago, I went out almost every night during the season. Sometimes I'd stay gone for days at a time. I've pulled back lately, though."

"Because of Hazel?"

"Yeah, she's a big part of it. I also have a new project I'm trying to get off the ground. Thankfully, we have other shrimpers working for us who can pick up my slack."

"Does this project have anything to do with the bread thing Canaan mentioned?"

"Yeah, it does, actually." He told her he wanted to open a market at the front of Willett Fisheries, like a small grocery store with prepackaged salads, sandwiches, and fresh bread.

"There's nothing like it on the island," he said as they walked. "People would be able to come in off their boats and grab lunch or swing by to pick up an easy dinner. It'll be heavy on the shrimp, of course, but we'll have other things too."

"Are you worried your dad won't like it?"

"He'll say no right off the bat, just because it's something different. But the business will be mine in a few years, so he'll at least hear me out."

"Wow. You're taking over the company?"

He nodded. "If we want to keep it going

when my dad decides to retire, it'll be up to me."

Lily slowed as they approached her car. "Well, I don't know your dad or anything about shrimping, but I think it sounds like a great idea."

"Thanks." He stood in front of her now, hands in his pockets, his eyes on her. The same heat that had flooded her cheeks as they danced returned, making her mouth dry and her hands clammy. She shifted her bag on her shoulder. The only light was from the moon, high and clear in the sky, and the faint glow of the neon signs behind them.

"I understand you having second thoughts about coming out tonight. But I'm really glad you came anyway."

"I am too."

"And this is probably too forward, but right now I'm sorry I didn't push harder to come pick you up."

She smiled. "It's okay. I don't have far to drive."

"I know. I just wish I could keep talking to you. I feel like there's more to your story than just moving to a retirement village and cutting everyone's hair."

"There's a bit more, but it's much less exciting."

"Because cutting hair is exciting?"

She laughed. "Sometimes, thank you very much. Especially now that Janelle is a client."

"Well, you let me know when you're ready to tell me the rest of your story. I'd love to hear it, regardless of how boring it is."

"Thanks."

He grinned. "You're welcome." He kept his gaze on her for a beat, and in the span of the moment she knew she wanted to tell him the rest — about Worth, about the note that had capsized her world, and about how she could feel alone one minute and thrilled by new possibilities in the next. She had a hunch he'd understand.

They said their goodbyes, and Lily watched him a moment as he walked toward his truck. When she settled in her own car, she cranked the engine and adjusted the vents so the chilled air blew straight toward her face. Loose hair brushed against her cheeks as she inhaled, exhaled.

Tonight had been *good.* The music and the crowd, the laughter and conversation. She rubbed the skin around her left ring finger, the empty space where her wedding ring had been. The memory of dancing with Rawlins flooded her mind, and her stomach clenched. She knew she shouldn't be dwell-

ing on it, but she couldn't push the thoughts
away.

# TWENTY

"Lily, honey, you've been here, what — a few months now?"

Lily smiled as she smoothed a lock of Tiny's damp hair between her fingers. "A little less than that. Just since the beginning of the summer."

"That's all? I could have sworn you'd been here longer. It feels that way, don't you think?"

"I suppose," Lily said, though it was only partly true. If Tiny had asked her the same question yesterday, she would have answered an honest yes. The truth was, the village was beginning to feel like a new sort of home to her. She'd come to appreciate the neighbors' various personalities and quirks, the laughter that floated across the street from the café, the way the afternoon light slanted in through the salon's big front window. She loved the trees and the seagulls, the pervasive sea breeze and scent of coconut oil. The ebb and flow of life on this postage-stamp spot on the coast had both charmed and accepted her.

But the buzz from her phone early this morning had yanked her right back in her place, feet firmly planted in reality.

She'd just woken up, stretched, and pulled herself from her bed. She'd left her phone plugged in downstairs last night, and as she descended the steps to the coffeepot, it buzzed as a text came through. And as it did anytime her phone buzzed or rang in the months since Worth disappeared, her stomach shrank into a small, hard knot.

The text was from Worth, but there were no words. Not even any emojis, though he wasn't one to use them. It was just a bubble, an empty space where words should have been. She stood staring at the screen, wondering what to do. Should she text him back? If she did, what would she say?

She sighed as she slid her mother's scissors — *her* scissors — through Tiny's fine gray hair. Even now, in the morning's golden sunshine, she was as befuddled as she'd been a few hours ago. What did it mean? If he'd wanted to say something but thought better of it, why hit Send at all? Was it just a simple accident?

Lily nudged the chair to the right so she

could better cut the hair over Tiny's ears.

"Not too short now," Tiny murmured, her eyes on the reflection of Lily's hands in the mirror. "Everything okay with you today? You're quiet."

"I'm always quiet while I work."

"Yes, but today your worry lines are showing."

Lily laughed and nudged the chair back the other way. "I'll have to do a better job of keeping those things hidden."

Conversation swelled behind her, and she tried to put Worth's text out of her mind. The three ladies filling the chairs — Shirley, Kitty, and Janelle — had developed a habit over the summer of coming well before their appointment time so they could catch up on gossip and dish about their favorite shows. Janelle leaned clear over Kitty's lap to peer at a page in the magazine Shirley was holding up. Kitty pulled back as Janelle's ample bosom pressed against her knees.

"Janelle, please. You're all over me."

"I'm sorry, honey. But look." She pointed a pink fingernail at the magazine spread featuring Dolly Parton. "She's just as gorgeous as she was in *9 to 5*. Doesn't look a day older."

Kitty wrinkled her nose. "No offense to

Dolly, but aging happens to the best of us."

"What about Roberta?" Tiny piped up, peeking around a lock of hair that had fallen over her eyes to where Roberta sat under the dryer hood, her hair wrapped around curlers. "Roberta, you look as young as you did when you started working here fifteen years ago."

Roberta smirked and patted her cheeks. "You can blame my mama for that. She gave me the good genes."

Janelle sniffed. "All my mama gave me was high blood pressure."

"What about . . ." Tiny pointed at Janelle's chest. "Those."

"Oh, Dr. Fleming gave me these."

Roberta hooted and Tiny giggled.

Lily moved to stand in front of Tiny, pulling strands of hair down on either side of her face to make sure the cut was even. As she did, Tiny's earrings — the same tiny silver airplanes Lily had noticed when she first met Tiny in the grocery store — caught the light. "Tell me about these earrings," she said. "It feels like every time I see you, you're wearing them."

"Oh, my Catalinas?" She touched one of the planes with the tip of her finger. "I wear them every day. Just to remember."

Lily waited but Tiny didn't elaborate. "To

remember what?"

"I used to be in the women's air force." She sat up a little straighter in the chair, pride shining in her eyes. "I did mostly clerical work, but I served."

"Wow, Tiny. That's amazing. So the earrings are to remember the pilots."

"In a way. I actually was a pilot myself, though I didn't fly for the air force. I learned to fly planes from my daddy. We had a big field behind our house that he used as a runway. He taught me to fly when I was ten years old. Of course, I wasn't allowed to fly by myself until I was much older."

"Where would you fly?"

"Oh, around. I picked up a boyfriend once for a date in my daddy's crop duster."

"You didn't!" Kitty said.

"I did too! I was seventeen. I still remember how googly-eyed he was when he saw me land the plane in their pasture. I also remember how airsick he got on the way home that night."

"How old were you when you joined the air force?" Lily asked. She set down her scissors and picked up a small round brush and the hair dryer to blow-dry Tiny's hair.

"I was nineteen, and my sister was twenty," Tiny explained. She raised her voice to speak over the noise of the dryer.

"Louise and I joined together. And the earrings are for one certain night when we had to rescue three pilots who'd crashed on an island off the coast of South Carolina."

"Tiny Collins, you are making all this up," Kitty said, exasperated.

"I am telling you the gold-plated truth, Kitty Cooper. I heard the SOS call come in to the radio operator, and to keep the boys from getting into trouble for borrowing a plane to take their dates to Myrtle Beach, Louise and I rescued them."

Kitty narrowed one eye. "And what did the rescue entail?"

"Well, I knew a certain airman named Archie was sweet on me, so I asked him if he could get me a plane. I knew he'd do anything I asked. So Louise and I flew to the island, found the boys' plane bobbing in shallow water, and hauled them into our Catalina. Lord knows how they explained the crash to their superiors the next day, but Louise and I did our part to get them home safely."

Other than the roar of the hair dryer, the room was quiet for a moment as everyone absorbed Tiny's tale, each woman judging its credibility.

"Five years later, Louise married one of those boys." Tiny said it so quietly, Lily turned the dryer off. "They were married for sixty years."

Lily hesitated. "Is your sister . . ."

Tiny put a shaking hand up to her lips as she shook her head. After a moment, she sniffed, then cleared her throat. "She went to meet the Lord early last year. I'll see her again one of these days."

"Hopefully not anytime soon," Roberta said. "We'd rather you stick around here for a while . . . especially if one of us turns up bobbing in shallow water."

A small smile lifted Tiny's cheeks, and Lily clicked the hair dryer on again. A few minutes later Tiny's hair was finished and she stood from the chair. She smoothed her hands over it and ran her fingers through the tips. "Just wonderful, honey. How did you make it look so thick?"

"I just tried something a little different. A little tweak to the cut can make hair look completely fresh."

"Well, you succeeded. My hair hasn't looked this healthy since . . . well, since I was much younger." She turned to Lily. "Thank you, my dear. I'll be back on Friday."

Tiny grabbed her purse off its hook and wrote out a check for Lily, then headed toward the door. At the threshold, she stopped. "Janelle, do you still have any of those long wraps you got in a few weeks ago?"

"The sarongs? I believe I have a few left."

"I'd like to purchase one. I think it'll make a great cover-up for my bathing suit."

"Bathing suit?" Kitty asked, aghast. "I thought you didn't believe in bathing suits."

Tiny cast a lingering glance at herself in the mirror and patted her hair, that same small smile on her face. "Beliefs can change. And anyway, none of us knows how much longer we have. Might as well wear the bathing suit, right?"

Janelle hopped up off her chair, dumping her magazine to the floor. "You took the words right out of my mouth. Let's go, dear. I have a sarong with your name on it, but I also have a new shipment of off-the-shoulder two-pieces I think you'll just adore."

Tiny and Janelle stepped onto the porch and down the steps. The remaining ladies heard Tiny's voice floating back, "Let's not get carried away, now."

Lily lifted the hood of Roberta's dryer and led her to the chair. "Let's get you out of these curlers and back to the café. I'm sure you'll have customers waiting on you for lunch."

"Elijah can take care of things while I'm gone," she said, settling her wide bottom down in the chair. "Of course, he still hasn't learned how to make a good roux, but I can forgive him that. It takes years to perfect the technique."

"I heard him play the other night," Lily said, pulling the pins from Roberta's hair. "He's very talented."

"You went to the Land?" Roberta's eyebrows lifted. "By yourself?"

"No, I went with . . . Well, Rawlins was there, Rose's nephew . . ."

"Yes, angel, I know who he is."

"Right. Anyway, he told me about it. He was going and . . . he made it sound like it wouldn't be my kind of place, but I actually liked it." She rubbed her forehead with the back of her wrist.

Roberta watched her with a measured gaze. "I'm sure you got an eyeful at that place. It's not somewhere I'd imagine you going, but you're right that Elijah is talented. He has a much brighter future than just filling lunch orders at the café." She paused. "I'm also glad you took the time to get to know Rawlins a little bit."

"We're not playing matchmaker, Roberta," Kitty said, her eyes on her magazine but her ears obviously tuned to the current conver-

sation. "That game isn't healthy for anyone."

"Don't get on your high horse, Kitty. I'm
not playing any games. I just think it's good
that two people of similar age can enjoy one
another's company. The poor girl spends all
her time with old folks like us."

Kitty rolled her eyes.

"Roberta, didn't I hear your husband was
in the military?" Lily said quickly, desperate
for a change in subject. "ROTC or something?"

Kitty popped out of her seat and pulled
Roberta's purse off the hook on the wall.
"You're about finished, right? I just realized
I never ate breakfast, and you know how I
get if my blood sugar drops. Roberta, I'm
going to need a sandwich. Maybe one of
your Reubens?"

"Sure thing," Roberta murmured. She
rose steadily from the chair as Lily pulled
the last curler from her hair. She thanked
Lily, left money on the desk, and walked
out of the salon.

Lily, stunned, watched her walk across the
street and disappear inside the café. She
looked at Kitty, who stayed behind. "What
just happened?"

"Don't ask Roberta about her husband,"
Kitty said, shaking her head. "It's an unspo-

ken rule."

"Why? What in the world happened?"

Kitty shrugged. "He died."

"Recently?"

"Fifteen years ago. She moved here a few months later, I'm told."

"But that . . . that doesn't make sense. After all this time, she can't —"

"The heart can be a baffling, unexplainable thing. And I've seen it all." She sighed. "He was her love, and he died. When someone you love leaves you, it changes you, and therapy or work or drink can't ever really fix it." She shouldered her purse and smiled. "But she's tough, and she's still here, which says something. If I had to guess, I'd say this place saved her."

She walked to the door, pausing at the threshold. "But we still don't talk about Bob. When her head gets in a bad place, the food at the café goes to pot and not even Elijah can fix it. Now, I'm going to go have lunch. We'll see you at Sunday cocktails?" She waved and followed Roberta's path to the café.

For the rest of the day — as she washed, cut, swept, and cleaned — Lily couldn't stop thinking about Roberta and the way she'd shut down when Lily had mentioned her husband. And how right Kitty's words were — when someone you love leaves you, you're forever changed, from the inside out. And Tiny's and Roberta's stories had shown the very different ways a person could respond to that tumultuous change. Tiny had lived through the heartbreaking loss of her sister, but she kept on living. On the other hand, though Roberta was still living her life, a simple mention of her husband fifteen years after his death had caused her to go practically comatose. Lily didn't want that kind of millstone around her neck for the rest of her days.

As she slammed the washing machine door after shoving a load of towels in, she paused as a thought struck her. *Roberta shouldn't have to carry that either.*

With her appointments finished for the day, Lily grabbed her wallet and locked the front door behind her. Across the street, the Sunrise was quiet, with only a few early-bird diners seated at tables overlooking the bay.

"Hey, Miss Lily." Elijah was drying glasses behind the counter. "What can I do for you?"

"Is Roberta here? I was hoping to catch her before the dinner rush."

"Yeah, she's around here someplace. Let me see if she's in the back."

A moment later Roberta pushed through the swinging door from the kitchen, wiping her hands on her apron. "Hello. Long time no see. Care for some dinner?"

"I was actually hoping you might be able to sit down and eat with me."

"Eat with you?" Roberta laughed. "I don't eat until I get home at night. It's a rare occasion that I get food in my belly before eight thirty."

"I try," Elijah called from the other end of the counter. "I can never get her to eat anything more than a few crackers while she's working."

"Oh, I eat. I eat plenty." She patted her middle. "I just don't do it when I have customers," she said pointedly as Elijah took a bite of a fish sandwich.

"What about just a quick bite?" Lily asked. "I wanted to talk to you about something."

Roberta looked hard at Lily, then checked her watch. "I just pulled some crab claws out of the fryer. I suppose I could be convinced to eat a few with you."

Lily smiled. "Crab claws sound great."

A couple minutes later Roberta came back from the kitchen with two plates of crab claws and two containers of cocktail sauce.

Lily raised her eyebrows at the plates piled high.

"I guess I was hungrier than I thought," Roberta responded.

Lily took a claw and bit. The meat was warm and tender between her teeth. "This is delicious."

"Thank you." Roberta took one for herself. "Now, what is it you want to talk to me about?"

Lily opened her mouth to speak, but all of a sudden her nerve faded. Lily had known about Roberta's husband for all of an afternoon, but Roberta had lived with the loss for years. Who was she to tell a woman much more acquainted with life how she should respond to it?

"Let me guess. You're wondering why I fled your salon this morning practically with my hair on fire."

"Well . . . yes."

"I'm sorry about that. I'm sure Kitty filled you in."

"She did, a little, but . . . well, I was just wondering if you could tell me a little about him."

Roberta paused, a crab claw poised in her fingers. "About Bob?"

Lily nodded.

Roberta dropped her claw on the plate

and sat back in her seat.

"I'm sorry, I —"

"He was the cutest boy I'd ever laid eyes on, and I never knew why he wanted to marry me." Her voice was soft and her eyes held a faraway gaze. "I was big, not that pretty, and my voice was always a little too loud. But that boy took a shine to me and he never looked back."

Lily smiled as the story of Roberta and Bob's courtship poured out of her. They'd gotten married at eighteen and honeymooned in the Caribbean at the home of one of his aunts who lived in the Bahamas.

"She stayed with a friend so we could have our time, and we spent five glorious days covered in sand and salt and baby oil."

"I bet you ate good food too."

"Like you wouldn't believe." The door chimed as a group of diners came in, but Roberta didn't even notice. "Saltfish, plantains, rice pudding. Things my tongue had never tasted. Made me want to be a chef."

"Really? That's what did it?"

Roberta nodded. "I told Bob, expecting him to laugh, but he told me to go for it. Said he knew I could do whatever I wanted." She closed her eyes and inhaled, and Lily worried Roberta was about to slip away, as she had that morning. But she just smiled and opened her eyes again. "I haven't thought about those early days with Bob in a long time. Those are good memories."

They ate their food in silence a moment before Lily spoke again. "Have you ever thought about making some of those foods here at the café? The Caribbean food?"

Roberta laughed. "Folks around here don't take to change very well. If I take the staples off the menu, I'll be run out of here on a rail."

Lily shrugged. "It was just a thought. Maybe a change wouldn't be so bad." She took her last bite of crab claw. "Not that these aren't delicious enough to eat every day of the week."

When she left the diner a bit later and made her way to her cottage across the street, she thought back over the stories she'd heard that day, real stories of joy, pain, and heartache. Decades lived fully and completely. It was easy to think folks in the village were enjoying a sort of Shangri-La, free from the cares happening in the "real world." But now Lily had the dawning realization that these people had cares — happiness and grief, pain and pleasure — that rivaled, probably even surpassed, what she'd experienced in her brief decades of life.

The empty bubble of Worth's text flashed

again in her mind and she realized she hadn't thought of his limp non-message since that morning. Somehow the act of helping Roberta carry her load had made her own feel not so heavy. She decided then she'd do nothing about Worth's text — not panic, not worry, and not respond.

# THE VILLAGE VINE

*Your Source for Neighborhood News*

July 1, 2018
Compiled by Shirley Ferrill

## GOOD DAY, SAFE HARBOR VILLAGE!

This newsletter is brought to you by Beach Reads. This week all romance paperbacks are half off, and waterproof e-reader cases are 30% off.

### MARINE LIFE

Ruth Beckett says she heard what she swears was the alligator bellowing from the marina. I still haven't found anything to back up her claim that gators can, in fact, bellow, but she implores us villagers to take care anytime we're around the water.

### RECREATION

Anyone hungry for a Cheeseburger in Paradise? Looking for Fins in the marina? Thirsty for a Boat Drink? Well, Coach Beaumont may be just the man to give you what you want!

My apologies. I'm getting ahead of myself. A couple of weeks ago I was taking my usual evening walk along the boardwalk — keeping a watchful eye out for the alligator, of course

— when I heard faint strains of "Pencil Thin Mustache" floating from Coach's sailboat docked in the marina. When I came back the other way, it was "Margaritaville."

I asked him if he had a hankering for Jimmy Buffett tunes, and he got what can only be described as a sneaky twinkle in his eye. He told me he was on a mission, though he couldn't release any information just yet. Of course, when I put the heat on him — as any journalist worth her salt would do — he sang like a canary. He did make me promise to keep his secret mission out of *The Vine* until he gave me the go-ahead, and once I promised, he filled me in.

It turns out Coach has been sending emails to Jimmy Buffett's agent for quite some time now, telling him all about our fair Safe Harbor Village. He even went so far as to extend Mr. Buffett an invitation to our So Long, Summer party. Can you imagine?

And stars above, the agent wrote him back! He said he was intrigued and that he would let Mr. Buffett know about our party, though of course he couldn't in good faith promise that we would receive a response.

I just about had to knit my lips together last week to avoid telling you all about it, but Coach has decided I can spill the beans, so here I am, spilling them in *The Vine.* If you're the praying type, consider praying that the good Lord would lay it on Mr. Buffett's heart to make a trip to Safe Harbor at the end of the summer.

## SUNRISE CAFÉ MENU

### July 2–July 8

Villagers, hold on to your sun hats — Roberta is bringing themed meals to the café! The first theme will be Foods of the Caribbean. If you'd like to make a suggestion for a future theme, please write it down and leave it with Elijah at the bar.

**Foods of the Caribbean**

> Mains: ackee and saltfish, conch fritters, Jamaican jerk chicken
> Veggies: rice and peas, callaloo, plantains
> Desserts: coconut rice pudding, flan, Christmas cake

# TWENTY-ONE

Rose had been enjoying the shade of her front porch, having given up her task of pulling weeds in her flower beds in the morning's heat, when she saw Shirley Ferrill creep slowly up the road in her golf cart, pausing every few feet to stick a *Village Vine* newsletter in a mailbox.

Several years ago, when Shirley first started producing *The Village Vine,* she slapped a magnetic sign onto the back of her cart that read, I Brake For Good Gossip. Truer words had never been uttered, though Shirley loved to say her curiosity was not gossip for gossip's sake but was always for the betterment of Village society.

Shirley finally drew up to Rose's mailbox. She grabbed a rolled-up newsletter and reached her arm out toward the mailbox.

"It's a big news day, Rose," Shirley called. "You won't want to wait before reading this one."

"Is that so?" Rose asked, rising slowly to meet Shirley at the street. "Were your gossip sources particularly forthcoming this week?"

Shirley smiled, the apples of her cheeks rosy with her signature Lancôme blush. "Not sources plural. Just one. One Coach Beaumont, in fact."

Rose cocked an eyebrow. "Coach has news?"

Shirley giggled and tapped the newsletter with one finger. "Read it and see."

Rose took the paper from Shirley's outstretched hand and watched as Shirley turned around at the flagpole at the end of the road and sped back down the street, no doubt to take her favorite corner table at the café and wait for her readers to gather and delight in the latest development, whatever it was.

Rose settled back into the rocking chair on the front porch and opened the newsletter. She skimmed the offensive section once, twice, then a third time. Finally she slapped the pages closed and dropped the whole thing down on the ground next to her feet.

"Jimmy Buffett," she muttered. "As if we need to give folks around here any more reason to act like kids on a sugar high."

She crossed her legs and pushed back and

forth with her foot, then stopped still.

*I own this place,* she thought. If anyone had a plan to invite a major celebrity to the village, they — *he* — should have checked with her first. At the very least, she should have been informed beforehand, not left to find out in the local gossip rag along with everyone else.

She jumped to her feet and, without stopping to check her appearance or quiet her angry breathing, shot down the road to the rec house.

The recreation house, a small one-story cottage built alongside the curve of the road, was Coach's domain, as loath as Rose was to admit it. Once he arrived and more or less placed himself in charge of recreation for the village, it became a storage area for paddleboats, tennis rackets and cans of balls, volleyballs, and croquet sets. A coterie of fishing poles leaned against one wall, along with all manner of tackle boxes and spools of fishing line. A few two-seater bikes were suspended from the ceiling, and the tent poles and wooden planks for the summer parties were stacked up in one corner.

Rose had once entered the rec house in search of a folding card table for a particularly large gathering of Bubbas in the clubhouse. When she finally located the table and gave it a firm tug, a whole shelving unit of pool noodles and rubber kickboards cascaded to the floor at her feet. It took her over an hour to get the things all stacked back up again, and by the time she made it to the clubhouse with the table, the Bubbas were exiting the building.

These days Rose avoided entering the rec house unless absolutely necessary, and today was one of those unavoidable occasions. She slowed when she reached the driveway, taking deep, steady breaths to ease her thumping heart.

*Get a grip, Rose,* she thought, as if her heart betrayed her by beating wildly in the presence of a man as frivolous as Coach Beaumont.

The door to the house sat open, the interior darkened with shade. As she approached, she heard various rustles and thumps coming from inside, along with Coach's humming. If forced to describe it, she'd say it was deep and . . . well, rather pleasant. She sniffed and willed her feet to keep moving until she stood in the doorway.

Peering inside, she squinted until her eyes adjusted to the shady depths. "Coach?" she called, her voice cool and measured. The humming stopped and he stood quickly from where he'd been stooped behind a table.

"Rose," he said with a smile. "What a nice surprise. Are you looking for anything specific?"

"Yes, I suppose I am. I'm looking for an explanation for what I read this morning in *The Vine.*" She forced herself to hold his gaze, although those lively blue eyes made her want to look away.

"Well, that depends. Which part?"

"The part about you inviting Jimmy Buffett to our So Long, Summer party."

He grinned. "It's fantastic, isn't it? Just think — everyone in leis and flowered shirts, daiquiris, inflatable parrots . . . I have so many ideas."

Rose buttoned her lips together and breathed through her nose. "Daiquiris? Parrots?" She swallowed. "Leis?"

Coach gave a small laugh and shook his head. "You're not happy. How can the thought of Jimmy Buffett coming here make you anything but happy?"

"You think he's actually going to come? Why would a celebrity of his caliber come anywhere near here?" Her words came out sharper than she intended.

"Well, I don't know, Rose. Maybe because his sister has a restaurant down the road.

345

Maybe he needs a getaway. Maybe he'd want to do a bunch of old folks a favor. And anyway, I'm just asking. It never hurts to ask for what you want." His eyes were piercing.

She shook her head. "It does if it's something like this. You're crazy for setting your mind — not to mention everyone else's — on a ridiculous goal."

He looked at her with such sadness she wanted to reel her words back in and pour her whole heart out in their place. When he spoke again, his voice was calm. "The truth is, I know it won't happen. Jimmy Buffett is not coming to Safe Harbor. You're right — it's a crazy idea. But you know what? People around here have been through a lot. Tiny's sister — her very best friend — died two years ago. Roberta's son almost died in a car accident four years ago, and that's on top of having lost her husband. Peter's so scared to lose Ida, he cries at the drop of a hat. And all those wild colors in Cricket Thompson's hair? Did you realize that's to distract her from the breast cancer she had five years ago that her doctors told her is likely to come back? She's doing all she can now before she loses her hair again."

Rose froze in place, her breath shallow. If a hurricane had blown up onshore right then, she could quite possibly have ignored it, so shocked was she at the words coming out of Coach's mouth. It wasn't that she didn't know these things about the residents. Of course she did — in a small village, word spread like wildfire. But she'd been so absorbed in her own decades-long griefs and battles, she'd heard about the others' bits of news, swallowed them along with all her own hurts, and moved on. She was ashamed to say she hadn't given her neighbors' tragedies much thought, which was fairly easy to do, considering she didn't spend much time with them.

Coach stood watching her, perhaps perceptive to the volcanoes of realization that erupted inside her. Her cheeks burned under his scrutiny.

"And you, Rose. You have your sore places too, not that you'd share them with me."

"What . . . what about you?" It was painful to speak over the lump in her throat. "I can't see you having sore places. You're too cheerful for that."

"Rose, I have sore spots you can't imagine." He began a slow trek toward her, winding around tabletops and bins of rubber flippers and life jackets. She took a step backward. "But you're right — I try to spread cheer as I can. Help lift spirits." He was standing right in front of her now. "If you'd let go of whatever anger you have buried down deep in there . . ." He reached out a hand and tapped her chest with two fingers — nothing scandalous, but just enough pressure to send sparks through her body, stem to stern. "You just might think differently of me. You may even smile once in a while."

She opened her mouth to speak, but when nothing came, she turned around and walked to the door. Even as she moved, she wished she were staying, wished he would say something to bring her back, but he was quiet.

Then he called her name. She turned slowly, almost afraid of what he'd say.

"Have dinner with me."

"What?"

"It's like I told you — it never hurts to ask for what you want. So I'm asking you — will you have dinner with me?"

"I . . . I . . ." She took a couple slow steps backward, then turned and put one foot in front of the other, over and over, until she reached her cottage.

That night after a long, screaming hot bath, Rose reached over the bathroom counter to wipe a clear spot on the steamy mirror. She set her shoulders in place and lifted her chin, turning her head from one side to the other. Then she took a deep breath and began to slowly unwind her hair from its accustomed spot at the back of her head.

Sometime in the years after Terry left, Rose grew tired of the time and energy required to corral her frizz-prone waves into any semblance of submission. One day, in a fit of frustration, she yanked it back into a docile bun and, content with the result, proceeded to leave it like that for the next thirty years, give or take a year or two. She took it down to wash, of course, but it always went right back up, pinned and smoothed into place.

Her bun had become her armor. When her hair was down, she felt exposed, which was the opposite of how it should have felt. Hair was there to cover, to protect, to add another layer between a woman and the world. Yet for Rose, the softness of her hair falling over her shoulders felt almost too sensual, as if her femininity, all her appeal, had disappeared when Terry left, and it was easier to pull reminders of her womanhood back, away from her face, so she couldn't see them, thereby erasing memories along with the need for an array of hair products.

Tonight, as her hair tumbled over the skin

at the back of her neck and the tops of her arms, she inhaled deeply and let it rest there. Her eyes scanned her reflection — her hair now much more gray than the auburn it used to be, her eyes both weary and wary, her cheeks gently sagging instead of taut and smooth.

It was the look of solitude — of total isolation — that did it. Without warning, a sob broke in her chest and she leaned forward, bracing herself with her hands against the counter. She was sixty-eight years old and utterly alone. And though Terry took the blame for a small part of it, so much of it was on her own shoulders. She'd made the decisions, she'd walked her own path, she'd closed the door.

Rose straightened and glared at herself in the mirror, unflinching. Her grip against the cool tile surface tightened. Both freedom and fear bubbled up from deep inside her, like something that had remained below the surface for far too long. Maybe it was time to open that door.

The next morning Rose hopped on her bicycle at six and pedaled down the quiet streets of the village, the air warm and light on her face. Oak and crepe myrtle limbs curved in gentle arcs over the road, and a line of pelicans soared silently above in single file. Sherbet pastels streaked the sky overhead, all set against a backdrop of the palest blue.

Cottages on either side of the road breezed past her as bursts of color awoke in the sky. Back when the village first opened, Joan Temple made the mistake of telling residents they could paint their cottages any color they wanted. Things went haywire quickly in the form of Atomic Blue, Tangerine Tango, and Pink Peony, but Rose reeled them back in after Joan and Terry left together, hands clasped over Terry's silver gearshift.

Under Rose's jurisdiction, the rule stated that residents could paint the inside of their homes as wild as they wanted — and a few took that to the extreme — but outside color choices had to be approved by the HOA. As such, all the cottages now were painted either white or a pale pastel, though Rose did allow shutters and doors to be painted in bolder colors — from a preapproved list, of course — hence the navy shutters on Kitty's cottage and Janelle's carnation-pink front door.

Rose slowed as she approached one particular cottage. Lemon yellow with a sky-blue porch and shutters and an orange surfboard propped up next to the front door. *Always a rule breaker,* Rose thought, though in the day's new light, it all looked different. Instead of feeling irked by Coach's blatant disregard for the approved paint colors, she saw his home as cheerful and welcoming. Happy. And the cottages adjacent to his seemed, well, lackluster in comparison. In her mind she saw her own cottage — creamy white with the palest hint of green on the shutters. Curtains closed against curious eyes. And those aggravating roses lining her front beds.

After another moment she sat back on her padded seat and headed to the gate at the entrance to the village. At the road she turned left and guided her bike to the path that ran alongside the street. One could veer off that path into the nature preserve along the north side of the island, but Rose kept to the path as it wound through the trees and around the island.

She passed the turnoff to Willett Fisheries without pausing, though her mind swam with memories, some light but mostly dark. She kept pedaling and eventually passed the Land of Milk and Honey. Though these days it was a legendary roadhouse boasting impressive names carved into its heart pine stage floor, she liked to remember it as it used to be — nothing more than a cavern-like garage with an icebox full of Coca-Cola bottles on the front porch and an honesty jar next to it, full of dimes from the pockets of neighborhood kids. An old icebox still sat on the front porch, though now it served as a container for a couple of withered ferns.

She kept riding until she came to the break in the trees that led to the swamp. Rose could still remember the hope and terror that filled her limbs when Jim raised that rock and hurled it toward the alligator, the sound the gator made as it gurgled back into the water, Jim's arms around her shoulders, their gangly frames knocking together with fierce devotion.

Before she had time to second-guess herself, she turned back the way she came, flying past the Land, pausing only as she rounded the corner down Willett Road.

The family business was at the end of the road and Jim's house sat just behind it, built up on stilts to protect it from summer storms. In the yard a wooden swing hung from a jasmine-covered arbor, and the mailbox out front still bore the faded markings of yellow flowers, painted by Stella, Rose's once best friend.

Her gaze slid to the screened porch and she saw him. Her brother was sitting with his legs stretched out in front, a coffee mug on the table next to him. She was too far away to see the scar on his arm caused by an oyster shell when he was twelve. Or the slight bend in his nose, broken in a fight at school when he'd defended Rose from a bully who called her weird. But she knew these details about him, as well as she knew the years that swelled between them now. Was it too late to span the gap?

As if he could hear the questions in her mind, Jim turned his head to where she sat on her bike in the road, one foot on the pedal, one on the ground. His eyebrows lifted in surprise, and then he raised his hand. Not exactly a wave, but a gesture. An acknowledgment. She raised hers in return, and they remained like that for seconds that stretched all the way back to a time before everything fell apart.

He dropped his hand when she did but kept his eyes on her as she resettled herself on her bike. It was a start. She smiled before turning around and pedaling home.

This time when Rose stopped in front of Coach's cottage, he was on the porch, feet bare, water hose in hand. He looked up in surprise, silent as she climbed off her bike and strode right up his driveway. Heedless of her breeze-swept hair and damp forehead, she slowed in front of him.

He stared, water pouring from the hose. After several seconds, he dropped the hose in the bushes and reached down to turn off the spigot. When he faced her in the quiet, she spoke.

"Have you changed your mind about wanting to have dinner with me?"

"No."

"Well, I have. My answer is yes."

He didn't grin like a loon as she thought he would. Instead, he exhaled. "I don't know what changed your mind, but I'm glad it did."

"Well." She nodded once, then turned back for her bike. She stopped when he called her name, her heart not racing but thumping steady and sure.

"Rose? I'll pick you up at six."

The salon was empty when Rose arrived, which made perfect sense considering it was not yet eight o'clock. But Rose couldn't wait. She only had to knock once before Lily appeared at the bottom of the stairs in loose linen pants and an emerald-green top. She crossed the hardwood floor, confusion written on her face.

"Rose?" she asked when she opened the door. "Is everything okay?"

"Everything's fine." Rose was pleased to see Lily was already dressed for the day, face scrubbed, eyes bright. She needed Lily to be up to the task. "I need a favor."

Five minutes later Rose was leaning back, her head propped against the gentle dip in the sink's rounded edge. Lily's hands were in her sudsy hair, and her every nerve ending tingled with anxiety and anticipation.

Once Lily rinsed for the final time and squeezed the water from Rose's long hair, she wrapped a towel around her head and led her to the swivel chair in front of the large mirror. Rose settled herself in the chair and smoothed the smock over her legs.

Lily slowly unwound the towel and began combing out Rose's tangles. Rose was thankful for Lily's silence. Other than a concerned, "Are you sure?" Lily hadn't spoken, as if she felt the magnitude of the undertaking as much as Rose did, understood it was more than a haircut.

Instead of looking at herself in the mirror, which was always vaguely unsettling, Rose watched Lily's hands as they worked. Her hands were quick and certain yet fluid, graceful. She pulled the comb through the length of Rose's hair, examined the ends, deliberated over her part, then put down the comb and leaned against the counter, her arms crossed.

Uncomfortable under the scrutiny, Rose looked in the mirror for the first time. Her hair clung to her scalp and fell halfway down her back. The added moisture made it feel heavy, a burden she couldn't wait to shed. At seeing her own rawness, her vulnerability, tears brimmed in her eyes. She tried to blink them away, but one fell, sliding down her cheek and landing on the smock.

Lily moved to stand behind the chair and Rose locked eyes with her in the mirror.

"I want it gone."

Lily nodded. "I know what to do."

As Lily snipped and Rose's hair fell, layers of years-long grief and regret slipped away. As her hair grew lighter, looser, something in her face changed. She looked less . . . drained. Less parched.

Lily continued to work, her brow knitted together, concentrating on her subject. Rose's hair now just skimmed her shoulders, and Lily stood in front of Rose, trimming the hair around her face. Lily stood so close, Rose could smell the lotion on her skin.

"Lily?"

"Mmm?" Lily's hands didn't slow.

"This is . . ." Rose pulled her lips in, then tried again. "I don't . . ." She couldn't even speak, but instead of making her feel silly,

Lily gave the barest hint of a smile.

A knock sounded at the door, and "Hel-looooo" came Shirley Ferrill's voice. "The girls and I were just on our way to the café, but we saw your light on and thought — Oh. Rose."

In the mirror's reflection, Rose saw Kitty and Tiny climbing the porch steps behind Shirley, almost bumping into her when they realized she'd stopped.

"Shirley, I thought you were going to invite her to — Rose Carrigan!" Kitty almost shouted. "You're getting a haircut?"

Rose gave her head a small but sharp shake as a familiar pang of insecurity flooded her heart and her cheeks. "Lily, could you please ask them to come back later?" she whispered through clenched teeth.

Lily leaned in close. "Maybe you should let them in," she whispered back.

Rose chewed on her lip and glanced back at the mirror where she could see the three women and their handbags crowded into the doorway. Kitty still looked incredulous, Shirley was pensive — probably wondering how she could fit this event into her next newsletter — but Tiny was smiling like the sun piercing through dark clouds. From between Kitty's feet came a small, frustrated yip.

"Hush, Prissy," Kitty said. "This is important."

"Okay." Rose gathered herself. "Let them all in."

It was another twenty minutes before Rose's hair was finished. Lily had turned the chair around so the end result would be a surprise. Finally she smoothed the last hair into place and whisked the smock away, then turned the chair back toward the mirror.

Rose gasped. Her hair — a lighter gray now that the darker ends had been cut off — fell to her shoulders in kicky waves. A long fringe framed her face and softened the edges. She shook her head a few times, savoring the cool brush of hair against her neck.

Behind her, the women stared, aghast at the change, and Lily stood with her hands on her hips. "Well?"

"I think . . ." Rose covered her lips with her fingers. "You've outdone yourself."

Lily shook her head, then stepped forward and set her warm hand on Rose's shoulder. "It's not me, Rose. You did this. You made the decision." She dropped her voice low. "What you do next is under your control.

359

Do you remember telling me that?"

Rose nodded. She couldn't forget the image of Lily sitting alone on the side of her bed, afraid to get up and face her new beginning. So different from the woman standing next to her now.

"It's just beautiful," Tiny chirped. "Rose, you're as pretty as your name."

Rose tried to hold it back, but her smile got the best of her.

"Yes, well, this female bonding is nice and all," Kitty said, tugging on Prissy's leash, "but my head is reminding me I'm in serious need of coffee. Ladies, it's time for the café."

They gathered their things, but only Kitty moved toward the door. Tiny and Shirley hung back, their faces swinging between Kitty and Rose.

Kitty glared at them, then turned to Lily and Rose. "You two care to join us?"

"Thanks," Lily said. "Maybe next time?"

Kitty nodded and gave Prissy's rhinestone leash a final tug before walking out, Shirley and Tiny following, offering smiles and promises of another breakfast date as they left.

With the salon quiet, Rose exhaled.

Lily grabbed the broom and corralled Rose's excess hair into the dustpan. "One step at a time, right?"

"One step at a time," Rose replied. "Though at my age, a leap every now and then probably wouldn't be the worst idea."

# TWENTY-TWO

"Lily?"

She was just coming in the back door from
taking out the trash when she heard Coach's
deep voice carry through her cottage.

"Good morning," she said, closing the
door behind her. "I wasn't sure I'd ever see
you in here."

He ran a hand through his hair and
shrugged. "Even I have to admit it's getting
a little too long. I'm not really going for any
particular look, but ragged definitely isn't
it."

Lily smiled and pulled a smock off the
hook on the wall. "I don't think you look
ragged, but I can shape it up pretty easily. I
won't take off too much."

He allowed her to hook the smock around
his neck, then sat in front of the sink where
she directed him. "I trust you completely,
my dear."

She washed his hair and squeezed the

water out with a towel, then led him to one of the chairs in front of the mirror.

"I'm on display here, aren't I?" He glanced around the shop and out the front window that looked over the street and café across the way. "Anyone could come in and see what's going on."

"Are you nervous, Mr. Beaumont?" Lily asked with a smile.

"Aw, no. Of course not. It's just been a while since I've . . . well, since I've gotten all gussied up."

Lily pumped the chair a couple times and ran a comb through his hair. "I'll just take a little off here and here." She indicated where she intended to cut, and he nodded. "You know," she said as she made her first snip, "Rose was in here this morning."

"Was she now?"

"Yes, sir."

"Did she seem . . . Well, what was her mood? Good or bad?"

"You know Rose. Sometimes it's tough to tell. But I think it was good."

"Good, good. And those are some true words, young lady. Rose Carrigan is a tough woman to figure out." He sighed and fidgeted under the smock. "But I'm banking on her not being tough all the way through."

Lily smiled. "I think your odds are good."

A few minutes later she brushed hair off his shoulders and whisked the smock away. "What do you think?"

He turned his head this way and that, then lifted his chin. "Well, I'm still old." He grinned. "But I think you've made an old man look pretty good. Thank you."

"I think you look quite handsome. And you're welcome. Come back anytime."

"Oh, you won't see me in here for a while." He pulled his wallet out of his back pocket. "Goes against my grain to get primped and polished too often."

At the sound of hurried footsteps up the front steps of the cottage, Coach and Lily turned to the door. Kitty burst in juggling a cell phone, an enormous handbag, Prissy's leash, and an umbrella.

"Waiting for rain, Kitty?" Coach asked, stepping to the side so she could get all the way in the door.

Kitty set her phone and bag down on a side table and gave Prissy's leash a tug when he lifted his tiny leg over Coach's shoe. "The girl on Channel 11 said there was a possibility, and I figured if I'm getting my hair done, might as well not take a chance on a summer storm ruining it."

She crossed the room, sat in front of the sink, and exhaled mightily.

"Kitty, are you okay?" Lily asked. "Do you need some water?"

"I'm just going to . . ." Coach signaled he was leaving. Lily waved as he pointed to Kitty and mouthed, "Good luck."

"I'll take something fizzy if you have it, hon," Kitty replied, her eyes closed and her head tipped back against the lip of the sink.

Lily pulled a can out of the fridge and handed it to Kitty. Kitty popped the top open and took a long sip. Finally she exhaled and peered up at Lily. "Sorry for the histrionics. It's been a long day."

Lily set the can on the counter and turned the water on in the sink. After checking to make sure it wasn't too hot, she rinsed Kitty's hair and began washing it. The firm set to Kitty's mouth told her not to ask any questions. And as it turned out, she didn't have to. As she rinsed Kitty's conditioner and wrapped her hair in a towel, Kitty sighed. "My daughter and I aren't speaking."

"Oh no. I'm sorry."

"Yes, well. She made the choice to shut me out of her life, so it's really out of my hands, isn't it?"

Lily combed Kitty's hair and began dividing it into small sections. "How long has this been going on?"

"Since Tuesday."

"Oh. Okay."

Kitty arched an eyebrow. "We usually talk every day. Four days is a long time."

"Yes, I can see how it would feel that way. Did something happen to —"

"It started thirty years ago when she married Hank. He's always been a little too highbrow for my taste. Always the fancy clothes. The expensive cars. The gadgets. Anything to communicate to his friends that he is a well-heeled, successful man. Clearly a narcissist. And now all his money-grubbing tendencies have pulled my daughter down too."

"So it's money troubles?"

"Money troubles?" Kitty snorted. "The trouble is, they don't have any. But Rebecca — that's my daughter — she's too stubborn to accept the help they so obviously need. I mean, what else are they going to do? Wait for it to pop into their bank account?"

Wrapping each separate section of hair around a curler and pinning it in place, Lily stayed silent.

"Bottom line is, I have money. I have plenty of money, definitely enough to get them out of this hole. But she doesn't want it! That's what started this whole thing four days ago. She told me about the debt, then proceeded to tell me she didn't need anything, that she was just *telling* me about it. But does she actually think I can hear about it and not do anything? What kind of mother would I be if all I did was listen?"

She exhaled forcefully and closed her eyes. Lily pinned another curler in place.

"A good one," Kitty said quietly a few moments later. "A good mother would have done nothing but listen." She gripped the arms of the chair. "Giving them a chunk of money isn't going to fix anything. It would only cover up the problem. And she knows that because she's smart. Here I am doing the very thing I would have counseled someone else not to do." She sighed. "And he's not a narcissist. A big spender, for sure, but not a narcissist."

Kitty rubbed her hands over her face, then sat up straighter in her chair. "I can give advice all day long, but when it comes to my own life, I seem to be clueless."

"I think that's just part of being human, Kitty. We know exactly what someone else should do with her life, but when it comes to our own, we just . . . wing it."

"Amen, sister." With all of Kitty's curls pinned in place, Lily led her to the dryer and settled the hood over her head. As she adjusted the dial, Kitty peered up at her. "I don't usually talk about personal things. It's not comfortable for me. And anyway, most people think the psychiatrist could never have problems of her own. Therefore no one asks, and I usually just let them think all is well. But it feels good to get it out. Thank you."

Lily stepped back. "You don't have to thank me. I didn't do anything."

"Sure you did. You asked and you listened." Kitty smiled and settled back under the dryer. "As soon as I walked in here, I knew it was a safe place to let it all out."

During a lull in the afternoon's appointments, Lily threw on her bathing suit and a cover-up and walked to the pool. Ever since the evening she saw Cricket Thompson swimming laps, gliding through the water with strong yet effortless strokes, Lily felt the urge to do the same. To test her strength in the water.

The first time she tried it — the evening of her first day at work — she'd been surprised by how quickly she became winded. One full lap — down and back — left her gasping for air. At the end of the second lap, she lifted her head to see Cricket on the pool deck, kicking off her flip-flops.

"A few pointers?"

Lily nodded, and Cricket hopped in the water, took Lily's arms, and guided them into smooth arcs. She coached Lily on breathing techniques and cautioned her to just flutter her feet, not kick.

"And no slapping the water with your hands. You'll be calling the dolphins soon," she said, demonstrating how Lily's hands should scoop the water.

When Lily surfaced after another lap, Cricket smiled. "Not perfect, but better. Keep at it. The water is a very forgiving teacher. More so than I am."

Since then Cricket and Lily had swam together a couple more times, and each time Lily's strokes and lung capacity grew stronger. She loved the feeling she had in the water — the sensation of weight dissipating, of all noise fading away except the sound of the water rushing past her face.

Today, with a full hour before her next appointment, she lost herself in the water yet again, propelling herself with arms and legs stronger than they were mere weeks ago. As she swam, she thought of Worth. Of how little he would approve of this place. Senior citizens in brightly colored bathing suits, dancing, escorted by tiny dogs on glittery leashes? Golf carts draped with flowered leis and boozy Sunday afternoons?

Everything about Safe Harbor Village screamed *Not Worth*. Yet the longer she was here, the more she allowed herself to sink into its rhythms and ways, the more she felt like she belonged. She hadn't felt as purposeful and as . . . settled . . . as she had since Fox Hill, when she worked with her mother in the hub of the community.

Bubbles of laughter rose around her as she thought of what her mother would say if she could see her now — on her own but doing work that felt good and right, at home in this waterside community far removed from her old world of too much and never enough.

*This is so much better.*

Lily had just finished up and was resting with her arms propped on the edge of the pool when she heard Hazel's voice. "Lily! Over here!"

She turned to see Rawlins's truck rolling to a stop outside the pool, Hazel's head sticking out of the back window. She waved and climbed out of the pool. By the time she'd squeezed the water from her hair and wrapped herself in her towel, Rawlins was walking toward the pool several steps behind Hazel.

The sight of his smiling face sent a quiver of nervousness through her stomach like tiny butterfly wings. Memories of the night at the Land flooded her mind — their easy conversation, the comfortable silence, the lack of all pretense. His arms around her as they danced.

"Do you remember you said you'd show me how to do a cartwheel?" Hazel stood in front of Lily, face upturned, squinting in the sunlight.

"I remember. And I'll do it."

"Now?"

"Hang on, Haze," Rawlins said as the gate swung closed behind him. He tapped Hazel's shoulder. "We're here to work, remember?"

Hazel turned back to Lily. "We're going to work on your house."

"You are?" Lily looked up at Rawlins, eyebrows lifted.

"I was just up at Rose's and she mentioned something about your AC not working well."

"My AC? It's working fine. But . . . well, I guess it could be blowing a little cooler. Yesterday Janelle said she was beginning to *glow*."

He chuckled. "Anything to keep Janelle happy." He paused a moment. "So Rose has a new hairstyle."

"She does. What do you think?"

"I think she looks great. It's a big change. I've never known her to wear her hair in any way except that knot thing at the back of her head."

"It's called a bun." Lily laughed. "And change can be a good thing, right?"

"I think she looks like a model," Hazel said, stretching her arms out to the sides and wiggling her fingers.

Lily laughed. "Did you tell her that?"

Hazel nodded. "She said I was full of poppycock."

Rawlins glanced back at Lily. "Is it okay if we swing by? I just want to see if it's an easy fix or if I need to call someone to come out."

"No problem. I have an appointment at four, but that's it."

"I'll be out of your hair by then. Can we give you a ride back?"

"Oh . . . well, sure. That'd be great."

Rawlins let Hazel sit up front between him and Lily on the short jaunt up the road to Lily's cottage. Hazel was a blur of movement the whole way, pushing buttons, twisting around to peer behind them, reaching over Lily to roll down her window.

"Easy," Rawlins said when Lily got a knee in the belly.

"It's fine," Lily said. Hazel's curls had

mostly escaped from the brightly colored barrettes pinned here and there on her head. Lily lifted her hand and reached out to touch a curl. It was just as cloud-soft as she expected.

Back at the cottage, Lily ran upstairs to put on clothes and pull up her hair while Rawlins checked the unit in the closet. When she returned, the air filter in his hand nearly sagged under the weight of layers of dust and dirt. "I think I found the culprit."

"Ugh. I'd say so. I guess I need a new one, huh?" She checked her watch: 3:40. Not enough time to get out and buy a new one before Edna showed up for her twice-weekly wash and curl. But Rawlins was already on his way to the front door.

"Don't worry about it. I think I have one in my truck. All these units use the same size."

With the new filter in place, it was only a few minutes before the AC was pumping frigid air.

"That should keep Janelle happy. No more glowing while she's sitting under that helmet." He gestured at the hooded dryer.

"Thank you." Lily stretched her arms out to the side in the cool air. "I didn't realize how warm it had been in here until now. This feels great."

Rawlins shifted, peered out the window to where Hazel sat on the porch swing, then stuck one hand in his pocket and jangled his keys. He didn't make a move to leave, but he wasn't speaking either.

"Everything okay?"

"Yeah, I just have to ask . . . Are you married?"

Her breath caught in her throat. Under normal circumstances there would be only one way to answer that question, but these days circumstances were far from normal. With her divorce papers signed but still residing in her bedside table, she had a foot in two different worlds.

She nodded slowly. "Technically yes."

He took off his hat, then set it back down. "Okay. Well, I was going to see if you wanted to come to the house tonight and have dinner with me and Hazel. As friends. But . . ." His cheeks reddened as he sought the right words. "Honestly, I wasn't sure what the deal was with your . . . husband and . . ." He shrugged. "Hazel keeps on me about you showing her this cartwheel." He smiled, then shook his head. "But if you . . . I mean, I'm not —" He held up his hands.

"I understand," Lily said. "The situation with Worth is . . . unfinished." She paused, evaluating the words she wanted to say. "But what if I told you he's gone? And that it'd be nice to have a friend? Or two," she added when Hazel called to her dad from the porch.

"I'd say meet Hazel in my backyard at six thirty."

# TWENTY-THREE

As soon as she opened the car door that evening, Lily smelled the heady scent of a charcoal grill. Rawlins had written down his address before he left her house, though he could have just said, "Turn left, then another left, then follow your nose." The scent held the memory of childhood summer evenings.

Before Lily could unlatch her seat belt, Hazel was standing by the car, tapping on the window.

"Are you ready?" she asked as soon as Lily opened the door. Hazel wore a purple sundress with white flowers at the neck and hem. Her feet were bare, with each little toenail painted bright pink.

"Ready for dinner?" Lily asked.

"No, silly. Ready for cartwheels!"

Lily laughed. "Sure. Let me just find your dad and tell him I'm here."

Hazel led the way around the side of their house to a brick patio where Rawlins stood in front of the grill, his back to them. Music floated from somewhere, and a breeze off the river blew the scent of fresh, briny water through the trees.

"Daddy, she's here!"

Rawlins turned, a smile already on his face.

"This is . . ." She looked around, taking it all in. "This is so great."

The weathered cedar house was up on stilts, with a screened porch up a set of stairs. Twinkle lights were strung all along the ceiling of the porch. Down below the house, two hammocks and a wooden swing hung from the rafters. On the other side of the patio, grass stretched all the way to the water and a short dock. As she watched, a brown pelican glided to a stop and perched on top of one of the posts. She laughed. "It doesn't get more picturesque than this."

He chuckled. "It's not much, but I guess you did get it on a good night." He closed the lid of the grill. "Can I get you something to drink?"

She shook her head. "I'm fine right now."

Hazel tugged on her hand. "Ready?"

"I'm sorry," he mouthed.

"It's why I'm here."

"Hazel, your hot dog will be ready in a few minutes," he called as Hazel dragged

377

Lily out to the center of the grass.

"Okay, I'm ready," Hazel said, propping her hands on her hips.

Lily waited, but Hazel was clearly waiting for Lily to do something. "Why don't you show me what you know?"

Hazel took a deep breath, then set her hands on the ground in front of her and kicked her feet up in the air like a bucking bronco. When they came back down, she added a forward roll as a finishing touch.

"That's a great start. Let's try this next." Lily showed Hazel how to stand with one leg pointed in front of her, then plant both hands next to each other on the ground.

"Now you just kick both legs around." Lily demonstrated, whirling her legs around, stretching her body its full length and surprising herself with her slow control, before setting her feet back down, one at a time.

Behind her, Rawlins let out a cheer. "Look at you go!"

She laughed. "I haven't done one of those in a very long time."

"Could have fooled me."

She took Hazel's hands and showed her how far apart to place them, then helped her kick her legs over, one at a time. "That's it," Lily encouraged. "Let's try again."

This time Hazel got both legs around and stomped them back down on the ground together.

"You're getting it!" Lily turned to glance back to where Rawlins stood at the grill. "Maybe we should get your dad out here to try one."

"I don't think he can do it because of his bad leg."

"His bad leg?"

"Yeah." She twirled, then pointed her toe, ready for another cartwheel. "From the war."

The casual way she said it made the skin on the back of Lily's neck prickle with heat. She thought of the scar she'd noticed on Rawlins's leg the night of the party, the pink slashes on his tan skin. She wanted to ask more, but Hazel raised her arms and turned back to Lily. "Are you watching?"

After several more attempts and another demonstration by Lily, Rawlins called Hazel upstairs to the porch for her dinner.

"I hope you don't mind," he said as he set Hazel's milk cup next to her plate of hot dog, carrot sticks, and watermelon chunks. "I wanted to go ahead and feed her so she can get to bed. Then you and I can eat."

Lily sat across the pine table from Hazel while Rawlins retreated into the kitchen, appearing a moment later with a plate of hummus and crackers.

He sat and popped a cracker in his mouth, then pointed at Hazel. "You're becoming quite a little gymnast."

She grinned. A spot of ketchup wobbled at the corner of her mouth. Rawlins grabbed a napkin and dabbed it. "Can I do gymnastics?" she asked. "I like the cartwheels."

"Sure, we can talk about it."

As Rawlins and Hazel chatted about gymnastics and how badly she wanted a puppy, Lily listened, acutely aware of the longing rising up in her. She always thought she'd have a child by this point in her life. It was almost an actual pain — like something sharp had wormed its way into the crevices of her heart. But there alongside the pain was a wisp of hope. An acknowledgment that maybe she could still one day experience something like the sweetness between this father and daughter.

When Hazel finished her dinner and a strawberry Popsicle, Rawlins proclaimed it time for bed.

"Wait! Daddy, we forgot the sign!" Hazel hopped up off her seat and ran inside.

Lily looked at Rawlins. "Sign?"

Rawlins chuckled. "Just wait. She's really proud of this."

A moment later Hazel came out of the house with her hands behind her back. "Close your eyes," she directed in a singsong voice.

Lily obeyed, and she felt the weight of something in her lap. She opened her eyes and inhaled. "Oh, Hazel. You did this?"

Hazel stuck her hands on her hips, satisfaction lighting up her face. On a piece of poster board, she'd carefully written the words *Lily's Place* in blue-and-green crayon. Underneath the words she'd drawn all manner of hair salon accessories — curlers, hair dryers, brushes, and shampoo bottles. To one side she'd drawn a picture of a girl with a perky pink bow in her hair standing behind a chair holding a very large pair of scissors.

"Is this you?"

"No, it's you! You're about to cut Aunt Rose's hair."

"Hazel, I love this. My mom had a hair salon too. Do you know what it was called?"

Hazel shook her head.

"It was Lillian's Place." Hazel's eyes widened and Lily laughed. "I don't think you could have picked a better name."

Hazel beamed, and Rawlins stood and scooped her up, holding her upside down until she erupted in giggles. "You forgot to tell her how I helped you," he said in her ear before setting her back down again.

"Oh yeah. He told me how to spell the words."

She glanced at Rawlins. "You did a very good job too."

"Thanks. And the pink bow there in your hair really adds something. Maybe you should try one."

She patted her hair. "Maybe I will."

"Will you hang it in your salon?" Hazel asked.

"I'll do it tonight."

After several goodbye hugs and promises of more cartwheels, Hazel waved to Lily and disappeared into the house. "I'll just be a few minutes," he said to Lily.

"Take your time."

He nodded. "I'll get her settled, then I'll get our dinner going."

"Anything I can do to help?"

"Well . . ." He gestured for her to follow him into the kitchen where several bell peppers and onions sat on a cutting board. "If you don't mind chopping these up, it'll save me some time later. I'm going to skewer them with shrimp and sausage. I hope that's good with you. I should have asked."

"Are you kidding? That sounds wonderful."

He showed her where the knives were, then followed Hazel's path down the hallway, and she got to work, rinsing the vegetables and drying them on a dish towel. Rawlins's kitchen was small but neat, and she got the impression he had cleaned and straightened up before she came. The wood countertop bore the hatches and marks of years of use, and a small terra-cotta pot of rosemary sat on the window ledge over the sink. The fridge was covered in Magic Marker artwork and a few photos and wedding invitations. Next to the door handle was a piece of paper with the words *Where Hazel Sleeps* written at the top. Below was a chart showing which nights she'd be with Rawlins and which ones she'd spend with her mom. Hazel had decorated the edges of the page with hearts and smiley faces.

The kitchen opened to a small living area with a TV, a couch, and a couple chairs. A set of shelves against one wall was full of picture frames and books, some of which spilled over onto the floor and the coffee table in the center of the room.

She finished cutting the vegetables and put them all in a glass bowl he'd set out, then dried her hands. A burst of laughter and a quiet admonishment from a back bedroom told her Miss Hazel was not giving up the day easily.

Lily walked to the bookshelves and turned her head to the side so she could scan the titles. A mix of classics — *The Great Gatsby, Lord of the Flies, 1984* — sat alongside everything from Ken Follett to Cormac McCarthy to Tom Franklin. The bottom two shelves were full of kids' books — Dr. Seuss, Shel Silverstein, and an assortment of thick board books. Lily reached down and pulled a book from the shelf: a well-loved copy of *Pat the Bunny,* the familiar peach-colored cover partially torn. She opened the cover, her fingers finding the page with the cotton-soft bunny, then noticed a small silver picture frame lying on the floor partially under the shelf. Assuming it had fallen over, she picked it up to set it back on a shelf.

As she turned it over to prop it up, she saw that it was a photo of Rawlins in military fatigues. His face was much younger than it was now, his cheeks and chin pale, his hair buzzed extremely short. Just as she peered closer, she heard Rawlins's footsteps behind her. She set the photo on a shelf and turned around. His gaze fell to the photo, then to the book in her hands. *"Pat the Bunny?"*

She turned the book over. "Yeah. I had this when I was little. I still have it. Somewhere."

"It was one of Hazel's favorites when she was younger. She still pulls it out sometimes and runs her finger over the dad's sandpaper sideburns."

Lily smiled and replaced the book, glancing one last time at the military photo he obviously wasn't going to mention.

Back in the kitchen, they threaded shrimp, sausage, and vegetables onto skewers and stacked them up on a small tray before heading downstairs. Rawlins set the kebabs on the grill and closed the lid, motioning for her to take one of the black wrought iron chairs at the patio table. In the center of the table sat a small pot of geraniums. Yellow handprints decorated the outside of the pot.

Lily pulled a chair out and sat. "When we were at the Land and I told you about my mom's salon, did I say anything about it being called Lillian's Place?"

"No, you didn't. And Hazel came up with that name on her own."

"That's . . ." Lily shook her head. "Well, it's pretty special. I'm going to hang it on my door when I get home."

"Does it feel like home to you now?"

"You know, it's starting to." She reached forward and brushed away a clump of dirt from the pot of geraniums and thought of Hazel asleep upstairs. "Will she come out here if she needs something?"

He nodded. "Yeah, but she won't be needing anything. Her eyes were already half closed by the time I shut the door behind me. She plays hard and crashes even harder."

"She's such a funny little girl."

"She really is. She catches me off guard sometimes with the things she comes up with. The other day she told me she was going to stay a child forever so she could always live with me and make sure I don't open the door to strangers."

"She thinks you need some looking after?"

"I guess she does." He stood and rotated the kebabs, then closed the grill again. "She's probably right."

"You mentioned at the bar that you wish she could stay with you. For good. Do you think that could happen?"

Rawlins shrugged. "We haven't figured it out yet. Honestly, I think Tara would be happier if Hazel lived with me. I don't think she ever meant to be tied down. She's kind of a free spirit. So much so that having a child who needs stability cramps her style. But she hasn't given me the green light yet."

"What do you think Hazel will say?"

"I've tried talking to her about it a little. If we do change the custody agreement, I want her to be prepared. But it's hard to talk to a kid about something this heavy, you know? She's so young. It's hard to know what she's taking in."

A few minutes later they brought the finished kebabs back upstairs to the table on the porch. Lily poured glasses of tea while Rawlins cleared off Hazel's plate and cup and a stack of coloring books. Finally they sat down to eat.

The shrimp was seasoned lightly but to perfection, and the sausage had just the right amount of heat. "This is delicious," Lily said.

"Thanks. I'm not much of a chef, but I can cook shrimp pretty much any way you can imagine."

"Do you ever get tired of it?"

"Sometimes. But thankfully Hazel loves it. And it's not a bad thing to have a steady supply of fresh seafood straight from the gulf."

"Have you talked to your dad yet? About the market you were telling me about?"

He nodded and took a sip of water. "He

said no."

"What? Why?"

"Stuck in his ways, mostly. He thinks adding a market is pretentious. That it's straying too far from what 'all the Willett men' — he loves to throw that phrase around — have worked for all these years." He propped his elbow on the table and rubbed his forehead. "I think he's worried about the money we'd have to shell out at the beginning — to add on space for it, plus hire someone to make the food, extra employees to work that part of the business . . ." He paused. "I get it's a hard call to make, but I really think it'd be a boon for us. Something to set us apart from the other guys. And maybe it would help us stay in the black."

"Are you going to talk to him about it again, or . . ."

"Yeah. I'll let him cool off, then try again. I ran some numbers, but he didn't care to see them. The bottom line is we're not doing as well as we used to. Definitely not as well as he thinks we are. I don't want to have to do anything drastic, but . . ."

"What would be drastic?"

"I don't know. If he refuses to let me do anything to help turn things around, I'll have no choice. If it were just me, it'd be one thing, but I have Hazel, and I can't afford to . . ." He sighed. "I have a friend who has this big company. They do environmental work. He's called me a few times over the years, but I've always told him no."

"Are you thinking about it now?"

He shrugged. "Maybe."

They ate in silence for a moment.

"I imagine that'd be a last-resort type of decision."

"Yeah. And a hurt-my-dad kind of decision."

Later, when they'd both finished dinner, Rawlins stood and carried their plates to the kitchen and called back to Lily, "Do you like peach cobbler?"

"Very much," she called back.

He reappeared with scoops of cobbler on two plates with forks. "Rose sent us home with this today." He nodded to the screen door. "Let's take it down by the water."

The sun had just about set over the trees to their left, leaving the sky over the river a splash of coral and pink, with scattered clouds darkening to a deep purple. Two old wooden chairs were set up near the water, and when Lily sat, she immediately slipped off her shoes and dug her toes into the thick, cool grass. He handed her a plate, and she set it on the wide arm of the chair.

He took off his hat and rested his head

against the back of his chair. She did the same and sighed. "Do you sit here every night?"

"Pretty much. It's hard to get tired of this view."

Here at the edge of Rawlins's yard, the river was fully shaded to a dark blue-green, but farther out where it widened, a swath was illuminated by the waning sunlight, setting it ablaze with fiery orange and yellow. The shoreline was dotted here and there by pilings and docks jutting out from the land.

The silence between them was broken only by the gentle lapping of the water and the creaking of a sailboat at the neighbor's dock. As they watched, a huge heron swooped close and landed on the end of Rawlins's dock. It fluttered its wings once, then tucked them in behind him.

"So are you ready to tell me a little more of your story?" Rawlins's voice was quiet.

Lily turned to look at him.

"You don't have to. I'd just like to get to know my friend a little better."

Lily's heart picked up its pace at the mere thought of talking about Worth. Of explaining everything. It felt like an intrusion here in this moment of utter peace. But the way Rawlins was watching her, she saw no judgment, or even pity.

"I think I'm ready. Thanks for being patient."

"Of course. So how did you and your husband meet?"

"You want to know how we met? Lately most people have wanted to know about the end, not the beginning."

He shrugged. "Endings are always ugly. I try not to dwell on the bad stuff anymore."

"Well, we met while I was on a date — a rare date — with someone else."

"You left one guy for another?"

"Kind of, but not exactly. My date got sick and had to leave, and I told him I'd find a way back to my apartment. I met Worth while I was sitting at the bar."

"And you let him take you home?"

"No — I got a ride home with a friend, but Worth and I talked while I was waiting, and . . ." She trailed off, thinking how quickly everything had moved after that one chance meeting.

"And the rest is history."

"Don't they usually say that when things turn out well?"

"I guess you're right."

She took a bite of her dessert as a chorus of tree frogs filled the evening air, their croaks and chirps overlapping to create a wall of noise. Rawlins waited until the frogs

391

quieted down before speaking again. "So what does that history look like?"

She turned to look at him. Even in the falling darkness, she could see the gentleness in his eyes. He wasn't prodding, wasn't demanding. He was just offering her a safe place to rest. And in that rest, she told him the story, from the first night when she wondered if she'd stumbled on *the one,* to the last, when Worth had pressed himself against her, held her close, then disappeared before she awoke. She told Rawlins about the papers and the ring sitting in the drawer of her bedside table. About Mertha and her interference, her hounding and badgering. And about her own mother and how even though she'd been gone five years now, Lily felt her presence with her much more now than she had back in Atlanta.

As she spoke, Rawlins was quiet, only asking for clarification here and there. At one point he rubbed his forehead, and by the end he was leaning forward, elbows on his knees, staring out at the water.

Finally he turned to look back at her. "You are remarkably well adjusted for what you've been through. What he — and his mother — put you through. I think a lot of people would have crumbled. But you didn't."

"You didn't see me the day he left."

"However you handled that was the right way, I'm sure." He paused. "When Canaan and I showed up to move you out of your house, he'd recently left?"

"Just a couple of weeks before."

"And look at you now."

Lily laughed. "I'm no poster child for overcoming adversity. I've had plenty of doubt this summer. I'm swimming in doubt. But . . . I think the tide has turned for me. Or at least it's turning. I'm feeling pretty good."

"I'm glad. You know, it sounds like Worth never had a chance, with a mother like that."

"You're probably right. I do think his problems likely stem from her."

"Not that he's the victim in this." He turned to her, his eyes searching. "But you're not either. Regardless of what Worth's life looks like now, I'd say you're the survivor."

In the deepening dusk, Lily could just see the outline of the heron as it ruffled its feathers and tiptoed down the dock.

Rawlins sat back in his seat and sighed. Then, "My mom died too."

"Really?" Lily breathed.

He nodded. "It was a long time ago. I was only two." He smiled. "I named my boat after her."

"I bet she'd love to know that."

He reached down and rubbed the side of his leg. In the dark, she could barely see the scar.

"When I was out here earlier with Hazel, she . . . said something about your bad leg."

He chuckled. "Did she?"

"She blamed your leg when I said we should ask you to show us your cartwheel."

That got a full laugh from him. "That may be the first time I've been thankful for this thing." His fingers trailed over the line at the side of his knee.

"I saw the photo inside. You in an army uniform."

He nodded slowly. "My dad kept that photo in his Bible, even after I came home. Hazel found it at his house and insisted on me framing it. Now she displays it in unexpected places all over the house."

"What happened?"

He sighed. "I thought I'd do my part for my country. I knew shrimping would always be here waiting for me, so I went off to prove something first." He shook his head and blew air from his nose. "Can't very well do your part with a hole in your leg."

"Were you in combat?" She was reluctant to ask the question, not knowing how he'd

394

react, but he shook his head.

"I was in Iraq in 2004, so we were all in combat to some extent, but this" — he reached down and ran his thumb over the scar — "it was just an ill-timed roadside bomb." He was quiet for a moment. "That's pretty much when the drinking started. I had a long recovery for my leg, and then I started working full-time on the boats, but my head was all over the place. I took some classes but couldn't really focus enough to stick with it." He took a deep breath and rubbed his hands over the tops of his legs, then turned back to her. "After everything happened with Tara, I quit drinking, finished my classes, and actually got a degree. So now I'm here with a five-year-old and some shrimp boats and . . . well, you and me sitting here." He smiled. "And it's a beautiful night for such sad stories."

"Yes, it is." Their eyes met and she lingered on his face, drinking him in in a way she never would have had the nerve to do in sunlight. His mouth lifted in a small smile, and she wanted to reach out and touch it, right there at the corner. She dropped her gaze and swallowed. "So you've been divorced for how many years now?"

"Four."

"Has there been anyone else in that time?

Anyone you've considered . . ."

"There was someone, a little while back. A part of me wishes it had worked out, but . . ." He shook his head. "But now I think it was really more for Hazel. To give her a chance to be around someone more, I don't know, more nurturing than me."

"Don't sell yourself short. I think you're a very nurturing dad. I think you make her happy. And I think . . ."

"You think what?" He reached over to where her hand lay on the armrest. He hesitated, then grazed the back of her hand, his fingertips trailing over her skin. It was such a brief touch, there then gone, but it caused goose bumps to rise on her arms.

Her thoughts scattered and it took her a second to remember what she'd intended to say. "I think . . . if you're going to be with someone, choose someone who makes *you* happy. Hazel will sense that. Your happiness will be good for her."

They sat that way for a long while, their hands close, their eyes out to the water. In the moon-swept dark, their conversation flowed easily, drifting from memories of their mothers to childhood dreams, to future hopes. As they talked, high clouds crossed the inky sky, blotting out the moon, but then its light returned, piercing through the thin cloud cover. Faint glimmers danced on the ripples and swells in the river.

"I should get going," she finally said, though she didn't really want to leave this moment or this place.

He sighed. "I'll walk you out."

She grabbed Hazel's sign from the patio table and tucked it under her arm, then followed him around the side of the house to where her car was parked. She opened the door and set the sign inside, then turned back to him. All of a sudden she felt sixteen again, nervous in front of a cute boy.

"Thank you for coming." A streetlight a few houses away cast a glow in the road, but it faded before it made it to her car. "And thank you for being so sweet with Hazel."

She smiled. "It was my pleasure. Really. And I'm glad I came."

"Would it be okay if I called you sometime?"

"Yes. You can call me."

"Okay. Good. I don't want to keep using the excuse that I need to fix something anytime I want to see you."

She laughed and he took a step closer, making her heart stumble. Then he hesitated and shoved his hands in his pockets. "I'm going to be pretty busy the next few days, but I'd love to see you again. Soon."

She nodded. "I'd like that too."

"Okay then." He stepped back, and she sat and cranked the engine. He closed the door behind her, and she rolled down the window.

"Thanks for dinner. And for the conversation. You're easy to talk to. I appreciate that."

"Likewise." He took another step back, and she drove off, the breeze through the open window cooling her warm cheeks. It felt so good to be alive, to feel the night air and the zip of electricity on her skin. She inhaled deeply as she drove, then let her breath out slowly, pushing away the lingering aches and sore spots in her heart.

# THE VILLAGE VINE

*Your Source for Neighborhood News*

July 25, 2018
Compiled by Shirley Ferrill

## GOOD DAY, SAFE HARBOR VILLAGE!

### WEATHER

We've been lucky with hurricanes this summer, though there is a slight disturbance out in the Gulf that could potentially grow into something worth watching. Keep your eyes on the radar in the coming week.

### MARINE LIFE

The manatees have finally made their way back out to sea. It wasn't due to anything anyone did — they just moseyed out on their own. As far as the alligator, Ruth has neither seen nor heard it again, but she did find what appears to be an alligator tooth on the swimming pool deck. I'm not one for superstition, but it feels like a bad omen to me.

### RECREATION

At the last association meeting, someone brought up the possibility of adding a shuffleboard court on the concrete area to the side of the tennis courts. Who knew something as benign as shuffleboard could divide the village so starkly? Many are excited about the prospect of competitive shuffling, while others feel adding a court would only reinforce the stereotype that seniors do nothing but play shuffleboard all day. It goes without saying that a decision has not yet been made.

Three of Coach's paddleboats now have holes in the hull. He's working to fix them, but for the time being, paddleboat tours are on hold.

## IMPORTANT REMINDER

Friends, I mean no offense by this, but didn't your mothers raise you better? In just the last week, I have seen trash bags outside their receptacles, wet towels hanging over balcony rails, and golf carts parked at haphazard angles. Please remember we must all work together to keep our village looking its best.

## TWENTY-FOUR

Though she'd never been much for vanity, Rose couldn't stop looking at herself in the mirror. Or any reflective surface, really. Anytime she caught a glimpse of her new, swingy hair, she froze and stared. It was so unlike her to do something so drastic. So reckless and impulsive.

But was it really that impulsive — that reckless — if the change had been years in the making? She didn't know, and frankly she didn't care. Her new hair made her feel like she had a new life, and standing in front of the bedroom mirror mere minutes before the first date she'd had in too many years to count, she was determined to shut down any rogue thoughts that threatened to derail what could potentially be the best evening of her life.

Or the worst. It could go either way.

She let her gaze fall from her hair to her clothes. She still couldn't believe she'd darkened the doorway of the Pink Pearl, much less shelled out good money to buy clothes from there. But seeing as she didn't have much in her closet aside from office-appropriate knits and soil-stained capris and tees for everything else — and she was short on time — she had no choice but to patronize Janelle's saccharine-sweet, and yet oddly sensual, boutique.

"Rose? Is everything all right?" Janelle had sputtered as soon as Rose walked in that afternoon.

Rose stopped just inside the doorway and glanced around the shop. "Do you have anything in my size?"

"Well, I . . ." Then something in Janelle clicked into gear. She tilted her head and narrowed one eye, scanning Rose head to toe. Rose willed herself not to squirm. "I think I can scrounge up something. What's the occasion?"

Rose swallowed and lifted her chin. "A date. I have a date."

Janelle's eyes bored into hers, and then she turned on her heel. "Follow me," she said, leaving a trail of perfume behind her.

Rose tried on outfit after outfit as Janelle tossed them over the dressing room door, but everything was too tight, too sheer, or too pink. She thought she'd have to go to dinner with Coach dressed in her gardening clothes until Janelle passed a flowy blouse over the door. It was light as a whisper and blue as a Caribbean sea. When she slipped it on, it fell against her skin like silk. She pulled on a pair of white linen pants that hugged her curves and angles but rose high enough in the waist to keep everything securely in place.

When she opened the dressing room door to check herself in the three-way mirror, Janelle stood completely still. She eyed Rose for a moment, then sighed and took a step back so Rose could walk to the large mirror. Janelle clicked her tongue. "I think Coach will approve."

Rose checked herself in the mirror, then turned to appraise her backside. "I don't know about him, but I approve. I'll take it."

Now, standing in her bedroom and assessing her appearance one last time, nerves rippled through her stomach. She took a deep breath just as the doorbell rang.

Downstairs Coach stood on her doorstep wearing khaki pants and an untucked linen button-down shirt with the sleeves rolled up. His gray hair was in disarray as usual, but it appeared recently trimmed, though still longer than most old men would dare. He'd brushed it off his forehead and tucked the loose ends behind his ears. One lock had escaped, and it fell over his forehead. Without thinking, Rose reached up to smooth it back. As she lifted her hand, he did the same, just barely touching the ends of her hair. His eyes were wide and his lips parted in surprise.

Then, without speaking, he extended his elbow and led her off her porch to the street where a blue four-door sedan was parked at the curb.

"Is this yours?" Rose laughed. "I didn't even know you had a car."

"Did you think I'd pick you up in my golf cart?"

"Well, I . . . I don't know. I guess I just assumed."

He opened the door for her and gently closed it behind her. He waited until he sat down and started the car before speaking. "I had to get out my real car, considering the golf cart is illegal on major roadways."

"Major roadways?" Rose looked at him in confusion as he drove slowly down the road, passing the café on the left. "We're not going to the Sunrise?"

Coach glanced at her, then pulled carefully onto the oyster shell gravel on the side of the road and stopped the car. "Rose, when I asked you to have dinner with me, I intended to take you on a real date. A real date means a real car that takes us away from here. It means a white tablecloth, candles, the whole bit. Now, if that doesn't work for you, or you've changed your —"

"It works just fine."

A glimmer of a smile relaxed his bearded face. "You sure?"

"Positive."

As they pulled out of the gates and drove toward civilization, anticipation replaced the nerves bubbling in her chest. She had assumed they'd be dining at the Sunrise with neighbors' faces all but pressed against the windows, hungry for gossip about their reticent manager and her unlikely date.

But in truth she and Coach would be alone, far from curious glances and prying eyes. She'd be free to test out — cautiously, of course — her newfound boldness without worrying about how she appeared to the rest of the village. The change in the evening's plans — even if the change was only in her mind — was a welcome one.

Instead of questioning him further about their mysterious destination, she enjoyed the suspense and let herself relax. The inside of Coach's car was clean and shined, and when she inhaled she breathed in a blend of musk and mint. The decidedly male scent was both foreign and delicious. Despite the absolute riot that was his golf cart, his car was surprisingly sedate.

She smiled, then turned back to the window.

"What's that smile for?" Coach asked.

"Nothing. You just surprise me."

"The night is young, Rose. There may be more surprises yet."

The restaurant overlooked Terry Cove, which was aglow in the last sun rays of the day. Their table — indeed covered in a white tablecloth and topped with a single candle — sat out on the back deck under a perfectly situated ceiling fan, with a view up into Bayou Saint John. The mouth of Old River was just visible past the boats docked around Robinson's Island.

They ordered drinks from the waitress, then relaxed back into their chairs. They laughed when they both exhaled at the same time.

"We made it," he said.

"We did." She gazed at the full tables around them. "Sometimes I forget other people are out here living lives while we stay behind our gates."

"That just means you and I should get out like this more often." He gave a sly grin and cocked an eyebrow, pulling a laugh from her.

"Something's changed in you, Rose. And not just the hair, though your hair is . . . astounding." Rose's cheeks warmed. "It's something else, isn't it?"

She shrugged. "It is something else, though what that is, I'm not sure I can explain."

"Well, if you want to try, it's a perfect evening for a good story."

The waitress returned with bread and a dish of olive oil sprinkled with black pepper.

"You're not one of those women who avoids bread, are you?"

In answer, Rose picked up a slice, dipped it in the oil, and took a big bite. She closed her eyes for a moment, savoring the peppery smoothness, and when she opened them, he was smiling.

"I guess that's a no."

Out on the water, a long sailboat crept by, its sails crisp against the early evening sky, the wooden rails gleaming.

"I used to sail a boat like that," Coach said when he noticed her watching the boat.

"When?" She didn't remember him ever having a sailboat at the village.

He shook his head. "Long time ago. I bought it after my wife died. Sailed it down to the Bahamas, then sold it and flew home."

"You . . . What? Why?"

"Have you ever been on a boat for four solid days? I was so seasick I could hardly stand up straight. And it was my first time to sail farther than a few dozen miles. Still can't believe I didn't end up in France. Or Canada."

Rose laughed, though her mind was still circling what he'd said about his wife. She'd never heard him mention her. "Why'd you sail to the Bahamas if you hardly knew how to sail?"

"I needed to do something big. Something daring. Something to jar some life back into me. I knew if I didn't, my grief over losing Carol would kill me." He laughed, a quick burst of air from his nose. "Instead, the Atlantic Ocean almost killed me."

Rose was silent, digesting that devastating piece of information. All around them was laughter and conversation, the clinking of silverware, the popping of wine corks, but all Rose could focus on was Coach's face. "What happened to Carol?" she asked after a moment.

He rubbed the edge of his napkin between two fingers. "Short version or long?"

She shrugged. "Your choice."

408

"Okay." He took a deep breath and crossed an ankle over his knee. "I'll shoot for somewhere in the middle. Carol and I had been married for thirty-seven years when we got the diagnosis. Ovarian cancer, advanced stage four."

Rose put her hand to her cheek, then rested her chin in her hand.

"Carol was always the fun-loving one in our marriage. She'd plan vacations, decorate the house for every holiday, even ones I'd never heard of. She was generous to a fault and never had a bad word to say about anyone. I, on the other hand, was an ogre."

Rose smiled, then widened her eyes when she realized he wasn't kidding.

"Nope, I'm serious. I was a stockbroker, always focused on financial reports, tickers, Wall Street ups and downs. I was a hard man and a workaholic. Not much fun to be around. Carol deserved someone much better than me, but for some reason she stuck around. She loved me. And all those years that love never wavered. It held all the way to the very end."

Rose shook her head. "I can't . . . That's —You were a stockbroker?"

He nodded slowly. "After she died and I made that ill-fated sailing journey, I decided I needed to change. That fast-paced, high-stress work just didn't matter to me anymore. And I wanted to honor Carol in some way. The only thing I could think of was to take up her mantle of . . . well, of joy. Of fun and lightheartedness." He held up his hands and shrugged. "So here I am, helping people like you learn to have a little fun. I like this life much better."

A shot of dread shot through her at his words. Was that the whole reason he was here? Was she just a project for him?

He must have seen the worry on her face, because he reached across the table and gently squeezed her hand. "You don't need my help, Rose. I think you're learning to have fun all on your own. And I, for one, am enjoying watching it happen."

"But . . . where did 'Coach' come from?"

"Oh." He laughed. "After the sailing gig, I quit my day job and coached football at an inner-city high school for a few years before finding Safe Harbor. From day one everyone from the kids to the other teachers called me Coach. I guess it stuck."

"So you just . . . went out and got a job coaching football?"

"Yeah. Well, I played in college, so . . ."

Rose laughed and shook her head. "Talk about surprises."

He rubbed his cheek. "So now you know

me. I'm still waiting on you."

The waitress appeared again to take their dinner order and refill their tea glasses. "Are you two celebrating anything special this evening?" she asked as she poured.

"No, not anything . . . ," Rose began.

"We are celebrating, in fact." Coach sat forward and leaned his arms on the table. He picked up his glass and tapped it against Rose's. "To starting over."

He continued to watch her, not looking away even as the waitress spoke.

"Well, if that isn't just the sweetest thing." She stepped back from the table. "I'll have your food out soon."

Rose finally looked away, smoothed the front of her blouse, and tucked her hair behind her ear. When she looked back at him, he was watching her. "I'm still waiting."

Rose sighed and clasped her hands together in her lap. "What do you want to know?"

"What happened to your husband?"

"He ran off with his receptionist." It came right out, blunt as the day it had happened. He stared, uncomprehending, and she lifted a shoulder. "I figured you'd appreciate me getting right to the point."

"I do. Although . . ." He rubbed a hand

across his forehead. "Pardon me for saying so, but you don't seem like a woman to cross. Either your husband was an idiot or . . ."

"Or I let him leave."

He raised his eyebrows. "Is that what happened?"

Rose shrugged. "I don't know. Maybe? Maybe not."

Coach shifted his seat so it angled more toward the water. He leaned an elbow on the arm of his chair and propped his chin in his hand. "That's all you're going to give me, isn't it?"

Rose sighed, and as she did she studied him. Such a rugged face, so handsome in its color and lines. Years of living written in the angles and curves. She was surprised to realize she already knew his face, as if she'd been watching him all these years, taking him in bit by bit. And in a way she supposed she had. Even when she was pushing him away, she'd been preparing to let him in. She hoped he was as sturdy as he seemed.

"It's a long story, and I'll tell you the whole thing if you want to hear it. But not tonight. Tonight I'll just say I married exactly who I deserved, and I ruined friendships in the process. Then having Terry hire Joan, second-guessing what was happening behind closed doors, and watching the whole inevitable thing play out in front of me — it felt almost like . . ."

"Like penance?"

Rose looked up and met his understanding gaze. "Exactly. Penance."

"Is that why you've stayed bottled up all these years? Removed from everyone else, like you deserved to be alone?"

She looked down, no longer able to hold eye contact.

Coach reached across the table unexpectedly and took her hand. His skin was warm and soft against hers. "Rose, I don't know you well, though I hope that after tonight that can change. What I do know of you tells me that no matter how distant or how grumpy you may be" — she raised an eyebrow and he grinned — "regardless of all that, you are not a cruel woman. You would not purposely hurt someone you loved."

"But what if I did?" Her voice was so low, he had to lean across the table to hear her. "What if I did something — something big — even though I knew it was hurtful?" Her voice dropped to a whisper now. "What if I did it *because* it was hurtful?"

Her cheeks burned, but he just shook his head.

"There's more to that story. Whatever it is, there has to be more. And whenever you're ready to tell me, I'll be ready to listen." His fingers tightened on hers and she didn't pull away. "People change, Rose. All the time. Every day." After a moment he smiled, his eyes crinkled at the corners.

"What's that smile for?" Rose asked.

"I've wanted to sit across a candlelit table from you for so long, I just can't believe it's finally happened. That I had the nerve to ask and you actually said yes. Well, come to think of it, you did say no first."

Rose chuckled but shook her head. "I've not been kind to you. I haven't been very kind to anyone, for that matter. But after all this time, why are you still pursuing me?"

He rubbed his thumb softly over the skin on the back of her hand. "I see what others don't. I *see* you." She soaked in his words. "I've always known there was something else hiding underneath your sharp exterior. Something soft." He shrugged a shoulder. "I wanted to be the one to get to the soft part. Call it stubbornness or pride, but I wanted it to be me."

When the waitress arrived with their food, neither of them noticed. Finally she cleared her throat, prompting Rose to pull her hand back from Coach's to make room. As the waitress set down their plates, Rose took a second to collect herself and her scattered thoughts. It was a lot all at once — the focused attention, the intimacy, the revelations. She was only just now learning to let anyone in, not least of all a man she'd known for years but had never thought of as anything but irritatingly upbeat.

But that wasn't the entire truth. The truth was, in the deepest, most honest places of her heart, Coach was already there, with his flip-flops and his messy hair. His wide smile and his big heart.

After bowls of gumbo, plates of redfish and crispy potatoes, and an on-the-house salted bread pudding — "You are celebrating, right?" the waitress had said with a wink — Rose and Coach returned to his car and began the trek back to Safe Harbor Island.

"Do you mind if we make a stop before heading home?"

Rose shook her head. "Not at all. Unless it involves more food. I don't think I could eat another bite if you paid me."

"Nope, it's not food."

She expected him to stop somewhere before they got to the long, dark road that led to the island and the village, but that was the direction he went.

"Weren't we making a stop?" she asked, but Coach didn't answer.

They passed Safe Harbor Village and continued around the island. Rose's heart sped up as they approached the turn to Willett Fisheries and Jim's house, but Coach passed the road and kept going. Finally he slowed at the roadside shack that had been a staple of life on the island for decades, though she hadn't gone farther than the front porch in many years.

"The Land?" she asked. "Surely you don't expect . . ."

"Oh, but I do." He parked and climbed out of his car, then opened her door, extending a hand to help her out. "The Mudbugs are playing tonight, and they're my favorite."

"Do you come here often?"

He laughed. "Does that surprise you?"

"Actually, no. Not at all."

The inside looked remarkably unchanged from its appearance the last time she was there. Same stage, same sticky bar, same card table in the back, possibly even the same men playing chess.

"Can I get you a drink?" Coach had to lean close so Rose could hear him above the music.

She nodded. "Whatever you're having."

He raised his eyebrows. "Really?"

416

"Sure," she said, laughing a little at her own spontaneity.

"You got it."

Through the crowd, Rose could just barely make out the knot of men on the stage producing a happy jumble of sounds from a washboard, two triangles, a stand-up bass, and a banjo. The dance floor was packed full of bodies of all colors, moving and swaying and laughing together.

Coach reappeared and handed her a can of beer.

She took it and popped the can open and took a slow sip. "I don't know what it is, but I like it." Then in a further burst of boldness, she set down her can on the table next to them and took Coach's can from his hand and put it next to hers.

"What . . ."

She tugged his hand, nodding her head toward the dance floor. "Care to dance with me?"

He hesitated for just a second before following her. They found an open space and began to move, letting the twangy, upbeat music move their hips, their knees, their arms. Coach was a good dancer — confident and comfortable — and she was relieved.

He leaned toward her and spoke in her

ear, his voice low. "I thought you didn't dance."

She smiled. "I didn't. But I do now."

An hour and a half later they emerged from the Land sweaty, tired, and full of laughter. The short trip home was mostly silent but the most comfortable silence Rose had ever felt.

Coach drove to her cottage and put the car in park. He'd cranked the AC, and her damp face had cooled, her heart slowing to its normal pace. Though when Coach crossed in front of his car to open her door, it picked right back up again. Once on her doorstep, he opened his mouth, but she spoke first.

"John Beaumont."

"What . . . Where did that come from?"

"I'm in charge of this place. I know everyone's secrets."

"My real name isn't a secret."

"I know. But no one calls you that."

"That's true."

"I thought maybe I'd start using your real name."

He smiled. "I don't mind that at all. In fact, I'd quite like it." He paused. "I'd also quite like to kiss you right now, although I'm a little afraid of your reaction."

She bit her lip, then smiled. "You don't

need to be." She lifted herself up on her toes and placed one hand on his shoulder. When her face came near his, he closed the space between them, pressing his lips to hers, just once. But it was enough.

"I think I've been waiting for you my whole life," she said when she pulled away from him.

"Rose, I've been here for years. I've been right here."

"I know. And it's taken me all this time to see myself so I could really see you."

He leaned forward again and she held her breath, but he moved his head to the side and kissed her cheek, then rested his cheek against hers for a brief moment. "The time doesn't matter, does it? We're here now."

# TWENTY-FIVE

Dear Stella,

It still pains me that you left this world only knowing your side of the story that affected us all so critically. Well, yours and Jim's. I never explained my side, the seed of which was planted long before you, me, Jim, and Terry became our tight-knit group of four. Back even to when I was a little girl, never allowed the freedoms I longed for. I felt smothered in Safe Harbor, and by the time I made it to college, I was looking for any way to never have to return here.

That's where *our* story starts. There are so many reasons why I never told you my side. Maybe I thought it wouldn't matter. Maybe I thought you'd close the door in my face. It's too late now, but I'm going to fill you in on some things.

Once the four of us settled into life

together, it was obvious you liked Terry. More than that, you loved him. Stella, loving him was probably the only mistake you ever made in your life. You were too sweet for him. Too innocent. The two of you would have been like a lion and a lamb, and I couldn't let you be undone by him. Couldn't let you be hardened as I was.

And then there was the fact that my sweet brother was head over heels in love with you. I know you saw it. His heart was so full of love for you, it was impossible to ignore. As a woman, I knew Jim's quiet devotion and kindness were no match for Terry's swagger and charm. But I also sensed that Jim was the man to give you what you really wanted — what you both wanted: stability, children, a family. A good and simple life.

I loved both of you — Lord help me, I loved all three of you. So when Terry decided, for some reason I still don't understand, that he wanted to be with me, I agreed. I thought I was doing you and Jim a favor by taking Terry out of the picture, but part of it was my own selfishness, though I didn't fully realize that until later. I knew Terry was going places and that hitching my wagon to his would keep me away from Safe Harbor. Best of all, he had absolutely nothing to do with shrimping.

Did I meddle too much? It's likely. But I consider myself a darn good judge of character, and you have to admit I pegged us all pretty accurately. Terry got the flashy life, I got the crummy husband, and you got the good, simple life you wanted, plus a good, simple man to go with it.

Whatever my intentions, however pure or impure they may have been, I paid a huge price. I lost you and Jim, the two people most important to me.

If you were sitting in your house down the road reading this letter, you'd probably rip it to shreds and throw it out. Then again, maybe you'd take a deep breath and remember that my betrayal led you to Jim's strong arms, where you found safety and love for the rest of your too-short life.

There's more — there's so much more — but I think there's someone else who needs to hear it more than you. Maybe the exposure will bring some kind of release. For both of us. For all of us.

Love,
Rose

Rose was just pulling a lasagna out of the oven when she heard Rawlins's *tap-tap-tap* on her front door. Her stomach tangled itself in a knot before she took a deep breath and let it out slowly. *It's time,* she reminded herself. *Let come what may.*

"I don't know what it is, but it smells cheesy and delicious," he said as he rounded the corner into the kitchen from the living room.

"It's nothing special, just lasagna. Oh, will you pull the salad out of the fridge?"

"Anything I don't have to cook myself is pretty special." He set the salad bowl on the kitchen table and pulled a pair of tongs from the drawer.

"I'm always happy to cook for you. And thank you for coming over tonight. I know it's not our usual night, but I have something I want to talk to you about." Better to get it out in the open so she couldn't back out.

He glanced at her as he put down the tongs. "That sounds ominous. Let's hear it."

She smiled. "Eat first, then we'll talk."

They chatted as they ate, though conversation was forced. The unspoken hung in the air between them, with curiosity written on her nephew's face and her own heart banging in her chest.

A little while later Rawlins stood and put his and Rose's plates in the sink, then turned back to her. "Please don't make me wait any longer."

She stood and led him into the living room, offering him the couch while she sat in her favorite seat, a blue-and-white pinstriped easy chair she'd found at Mary's Antiques.

"You know Willett Fisheries used to be here, right?" She pointed out the window. "Just a few hundred feet that way."

Rawlins lifted an eyebrow. "You want to talk to me about work?"

"No, not work. I just . . . I need to explain some things to you."

He nodded slowly. "Okay. Yes, I know it used to be somewhere around here. Dad told me someone cheated them out of the land. Bought it out from under them or something. So they rebuilt."

She closed her eyes for a brief moment. "That someone was me."

He stared, glanced away, then looked at her again. "You — But how could . . ." He rubbed his eyes. "I don't understand."

"I don't understand a lot of it either, even now. It all made sense at the time, but time has a way of softening things. Things like pettiness, anger . . ."

"Who were you mad at? My dad?"

"No," she said firmly. "No. Your dad was completely innocent. It was all on me."

"I still don't understand."

"I know. I have to start at the beginning."

She told Rawlins about her father, his coldness and stubbornness. She told him about the four of them — Rose, Terry, Stella, and Jim. About how her friendship with his mother was the one bright shining light in her life, other than the love of her brother, Rawlins's father. How she'd gone to college looking for any way never to have to return to Safe Harbor Island, and how Terry provided her ticket out.

But being away from the island hadn't made her hurt go away. Instead, she became angry. She felt she'd missed out on what her life could have been if her dad had looked at her long enough to see her strength. Her fire. Her determination to *be* good, to *do* good. She was angry with him for what had been taken from her, and she was angry with her mom for being too weak to stand up to him.

"Anger never leads you anywhere good,"

Rawlins said quietly. He regarded her as if he could already see all the way to the bottom of her, but she continued.

"After Terry and I married, he started quickly on his plan to buy properties and build neighborhoods and villages. He'd already broken ground on a couple down in Florida and was looking for his next piece of property to purchase when my father died. We came back for the funeral, of course, and crossing the bridge onto these quiet, moss-shaded roads was the first time I'd been on the island in the two years we'd been married. But instead of feeling welcomed by this place I still knew so well, all that anger bubbled back up. And I wanted to do something with it.

"So I told Terry about our property, the land that had been in our family for generations. Back then the tip of the island, where this village now sits, was mostly empty and had been forever. But Willett Fisheries was close. Much closer than it is now, as you know."

Rawlins sighed and took off his cap. He ran a hand roughly over the top of his head, then sat forward on his knees. If she stopped too long, she wouldn't start again, so she kept going.

"I suggested to Terry that if he offered a

decent amount of money to my mom —
who was now in control of the family's land
— she just might sell.

"To Terry's credit, he did ask me if I was
sure. It was the thing that had surprised me
the most — that he'd been the one to question the plan."

*It's your family's business,* Rose remembered him saying. *I can't take another man's
livelihood from him. Even if he did just die.*

"But I told him it wouldn't hurt to try. I
rationalized it — I said the money we'd be
giving them could allow them to rebuild up
the river. A bigger place, room to grow.
Honestly, it had sounded just as crazy to
me as it did to Terry, but something in me
wanted to tear down, to burn bridges. To
flaunt my newfound freedom, a freedom I
never had while living at home. My dad had
always taken from me. Now I was taking
from him, and in the way that mattered
most."

Rose swallowed hard. "The plan worked,
obviously, and we built the village. Your dad,
who took over the business from your
grandmother, had no choice but to rebuild
up the river. Terry stuck around here for a
few years, and then he and Joan left and I
was alone. Well, alone with that first wave of
residents." And she'd realized with crushing

clarity that everything she'd done had been out of spite. Once her spite and anger were gone, so was everyone else.

One night Rose couldn't take it anymore, and she went to Jim and Stella's house. As soon as she tried to explain herself, Stella — kind Stella who'd never said a harsh word to anyone — stopped her. *You always do the thing that's good for you,* she said. *Always the selfish choice. So don't come in here and try to explain it all away. It's too late now.*

"Your dad had been standing in the corner of their little kitchen, unsure of who to respond to — his sister in tears or his wife with her fists clenched in fury. Finally he moved toward Stella and put his arms around her. He looked at me . . ." Rose looked down at her hands in her lap. "He told me it was time for me to leave, and I did. Your mom got sick a year or so later. She and I never spoke again."

With the story out, Rose's shoulders sagged. The heavy weight of all she'd carried was gone, but in its place was the pain of realizing how much Rawlins would hurt now, knowing the truth about her.

She rubbed a tear from the corner of her eye as Rawlins sat with his elbows propped on his knees.

"Do you know what my dad said to me," he asked, "when I told him you'd asked me to help out around here?"

Rose shook her head.

"He told me he couldn't tell me to stay away from you, but that I should be careful. You and I hadn't spent much time around each other before then — now it makes sense why — but when he said that, it stuck with me. When I first started doing odd jobs around here — fixing stuck windows, painting walls, cutting grass — I kept my distance from you."

"I remember. I figured it just took you some time to warm up to me."

"Well, it did, but it was because of my dad's caution. But the thing was, you didn't seem selfish. Not mean, not rude, not angry — not to me, anyway. I didn't see any reason to stay away."

"Now you see why, though?"

He nodded. He didn't speak for a long moment, and she gave him time to process. To decide if he'd stay in her life or if her past sins were too big, too much, too final. If that was what he decided, she'd accept it. She deserved nothing more and nothing less.

When he finally opened his mouth to speak, her breath evaporated in her lungs.

"Rose . . . you need to talk to my dad." He looked up at her. "Just talk to him. He needs to hear this. Yes, I know," he said, speaking over her protests. "I know he knows how it all went down, but that was so long ago. So much has happened since then. You're both carrying these burdens around alone — why don't you put them down together?"

"What will he say?" she whispered.

"I don't know, but I think he may surprise you. It's worth a shot anyway."

"But you're not . . ." Her voice broke. "You don't hate me?"

He shook his head slowly. "I don't hate you, Aunt Rose. People make mistakes. All of us." He stood and reached out a hand to her. When she took it, he gently pulled her from her chair and hugged her. "Thank you for telling me. A lot of things make sense now. But I'm serious about talking to my dad." He pulled back and looked her in the face. "And you . . . Well, there's something to be said for forgiving yourself. It's okay to do that, you know. Not that you need anyone's permission, but if you do" — he shrugged — "I'm giving it."

Later that night, long after Rawlins had left, after she'd cleaned her kitchen and turned off all the lights, Rose stretched out in bed. The sheets were cool against her tired legs, and the ceiling fan coaxed the air into a soft breeze. She exhaled long and deep, and for what felt like the first time in months, maybe even years, her weight was gone. As her mind settled into slumber, she not so much thought as felt the words in her mind: *My penance is over.*

GOOD DAY, SAFE HARBOR VILLAGE!

## FROM THE CAFÉ

Due to complaints regarding the recent Caribbean food experiment, themed meals will no longer be on the menu. Please see the message below from Roberta:

Dear Villagers,

I'll have you know I received a culinary degree with honors from Johnson and Wales, and I've cooked under everyone from Wolfgang Puck to Emeril Lagasse. My skills and experience tell me I should be able to choose the menu for my own café. However, due to the volume of distraught phone calls I received in the wake of my experiment, I have decided to suspend the themed meals until further notice. Be assured I will keep the meals as plain as possible so as not to upset your delicate sensibilities.

# SUNRISE CAFÉ MENU

## August 16–August 21

Mains: boiled chicken breast, broth and noodle soup, meat loaf

Veggies: three-bean salad, mashed cauliflower, green pea puree

Desserts: vanilla pudding, lemon Jell-O, poached apples

Lily opened her front door to air out the salon — a new village resident had requested a perm, which filled Lily's whole cottage with the odor of sulfur — just in time to hear Prissy's high-pitched yips. She glanced toward the road as the small dog darted away from Kitty, who stood just outside the café, and dashed across the street toward the salon, just barely missing a cruising golf cart.

"Prissy!" Kitty yelled as she bustled across the street after the dog.

Prissy hopped up Lily's porch steps and sat, his tiny body quivering from nose to tail. A second later Kitty scooped him up. "Bad boy, Prissy. You were almost flattened. And by Seymour Eldins, of all people."

Lily stood, pushing the door back and forth to encourage fresh airflow into the salon. "Everything okay there?"

"Oh, we're fine. Prissy's been feeling a

little frisky since I switched his medicine." She lowered her voice to a whisper and put her hand over Prissy's tiny ears. "He has hypoglycemia, but don't let him hear you talk about it. He gets embarrassed." She pulled her hand away and kissed his nose. His eyes were wide as saucers.

"Okay. Well, take good care of him. I need to check Belinda's perm . . ." She stepped back toward the door, but Kitty didn't budge.

"While I have you, I wanted to see if you have plans for Saturday. The ladies and I are taking my pontoon up to Pirate's Cove for lunch. We'd love for you to come with us."

"What's Pirate's Cove?"

Kitty's eyes widened, mimicking Prissy's. "Are you kidding me? You've never been to Pirate's Cove?"

Lily shook her head.

"Well, that settles it. You're coming."

"But . . . well, okay. Who all is coming?"

"Let's see — it's me and Shirley, Edna, and Tiny. And now you."

"Do you mind if Rose comes too?"

"Rose?" Kitty leaned down and set Prissy on the ground. "Riding on a boat and eating a cheeseburger in paradise isn't exactly Rose's scene, you have to admit. Even if she does have a nice new haircut."

Lily shrugged. "What do you say we try anyway?"

Kitty waved her hand. "Suit yourself. You can ask her. Her burger's on me if she says yes. Meet us on my dock at eleven on Saturday." She turned to leave and called over her shoulder, "Wear your suit and bring a towel."

"Whose idea was it to ask me?" Rose asked when Lily called her after her last client of the day on Friday.

"Well, it was mine," Lily answered, collapsing into her soft watermelon-colored chair and tucking her feet under her. "But Kitty said she'd love for you to come."

"Mm-hmm. Sure she did. What'd she really say?"

Lily sighed. "That a boat ride and a cheeseburger isn't your scene."

"That's more like it."

"So give them a good shock. What have you got to lose? One step at a time, right?"

Rose sighed. "You know what? You're right. I'm in."

Lily smiled. "I'll swing by your place, and we can meet the girls at the dock together."

The next morning Lily set her straw beach bag on Rose's doorstep and rang the bell.

In her bag, she'd packed a beach towel, hat, and sunscreen, along with her wallet and phone. She wore her bathing suit and a cover-up she'd picked up at the Pink Pearl. It was sedate for Janelle's taste, but with its big splashes of aqua, yellow, and white, it suited Lily just fine.

A moment later Rose opened the door wearing shorts and a sleeveless blouse.

"Oh. Well, ah . . . Kitty said we're supposed to wear our bathing suits. Did I forget to mention that?"

Rose cocked an eyebrow. "One step at a time doesn't extend to having all my . . . parts . . . flopping around in a bathing suit all afternoon. That's a step for another day."

Lily laughed. "Fair enough."

As they approached Kitty's dock, they could see the other ladies already there, dressed for a day in the sun with skirted swimsuits and floppy straw hats. The heady scent of Coppertone and coconut permeated the air.

"Lily, Rose," Tiny called. "You came!"

Kitty's pontoon boat was huge — it could have easily fit twelve or more people — and the white leather and chrome made it shine in the sun. A couple of coolers sat on the floor, and folding chairs were propped between the two captain's seats.

"Kitty, this is amazing," Lily said.

"It's the Cadillac of pontoon boats," Shirley chirped as she uncapped her lipstick and swiped on another coat of fuchsia. "Kitty likes to ride in style."

"Okay, girls, untie those lines and let's get going."

As if they did this every day, Tiny and Edna loosened the lines that kept the boat tethered to the dock. Rose reached out and grabbed hold of the back of a seat for balance as Kitty kicked it into reverse.

"Rules of the water for you newcomers," Kitty called over the motor as they idled through the marina and toward the waterway. "Number one, no fiddling with the music. That's the captain's choice, and I'm the captain."

Tiny caught Lily's eye and winked.

"Number two, no complaining about the speed. I like to drive fast."

Tiny leaned forward and whispered to Rose and Lily, "Don't worry. It barely goes over twenty miles per hour."

"And number three, hang on to your hats. If it flies off, we're not turning around to get it. Now, are y'all ready?"

After nods all around, Kitty opened the throttle and the pontoon hurtled up the waterway, the sudden wind pulling everyone's hair back. Not wanting to break a rule first thing, Lily put a hand to the brim of her hat to keep it from flying off. Kitty cranked the music through speakers hidden somewhere in the side panels of the boat, and The Band's "Up on Cripple Creek" began to play. To Lily's surprise, everyone on the boat began to sing along. After The Band, it was Van Morrison, then James Taylor, then Bruce Springsteen, and the ladies knew the words to every song.

During a lull in the music, Tiny leaned over to Lily. "We may be a bunch of old women, but we know good tunes when we hear them."

Lily grinned and glanced at Rose sitting at the back of the boat behind Kitty. She motioned to the open seat next to her, but Rose shook her head. "I'm fine," she mouthed.

Lily had been hoping to ask Rose about her evening with Coach, but at that moment another song came on — Bruce's "Born to Run" — and the ladies started up again, singing so loudly it wouldn't have mattered if Rose had been sitting right next to Lily. She wouldn't have been able to hear her anyway.

They rode for what felt like forever, the wind in their faces softening the sun's searing heat. When Lily asked Tiny how long it took to get to Pirate's Cove, Tiny explained how they had to go the length of the intra-coastal waterway until they reached Wolf Bay, then through another bay and hang a left to get to the famed beach dive.

Finally a little brown shack began to distinguish itself from the trees and houses on the opposite side of the water. The closer they got, the clearer the image became: a long pier studded with boats, people and dogs splashing around in the shallow water along the shore, and more people — and more dogs — milling around an outdoor deck.

Kitty deftly guided the pontoon into an open slot at the pier, and Edna and Shirley tied the ropes to the pilings. As they all exited the boat, Lily hung back to wait for Rose, the last to climb out of the boat.

"Were you okay back there?" she asked.

"Oh, just fine," Rose said, tucking her hair back into her visor. "A little windblown, but nothing I can't handle."

Kitty marched inside — her bright red sun hat leading the way — and everyone else fell in line behind her. Inside was dim after the sunshine, and the floor was damp and sandy. As they stood in line, three dogs nosed their way through the screen door on one side, bouncing around the legs of everyone standing in line, then shooting out the door on the other side. No one but Lily and Rose seemed to notice. Rose stared at Lily, her eyes wide, but Lily shrugged. "Just go with it," she whispered.

When Rose made it to the front of the line and asked to see a menu, Kitty leaned forward and spoke to the man behind the register. "Sorry about that," she said. "It's her first time. She'll have a burger and fries and a Bushwacker." Kitty stepped back and patted Lily on the back. "That goes for both of them."

"How do you know that's what I want?" Rose asked.

"Trust me. Oh, and, Rose, your burger's on me."

"I can pay for my own lunch, Kitty."

"I know you can. Now pipe down and let me keep my word."

By the time the three of them made it outside to the deck, Edna and Shirley had already snagged a table overlooking the lagoon and were talking animatedly, but their conversation stopped as soon as the other women approached.

"As usual, they said our food would be twenty minutes," Kitty said.

"Which means we have an hour to kill,"

Edna replied.

"Precisely."

Shirley leaned back in her seat and sighed. "No matter — I could sit here all day people-watching."

The corner table gave them a perfect view of the boats coming in and out, most of them full of jovial vacationers showing off too much skin. Laughter rang out from another table on the deck, but their little table was quiet.

"It's a nice day, isn't it?" Tiny asked, a courageous attempt to start conversation, but the others just nodded in silence. Shirley's eyes darted from Rose to Kitty. Kitty had pulled her sun hat off and was using it to fan her face.

Lily felt a compulsion to help Rose win over these ladies. If what they'd said earlier in the summer was true — that Rose never got involved with any of the people in the village — Lily knew Rose must have a good reason, but she was determined to help her take the next step, which right now meant learning how to befriend the women at this table.

"Rose," Lily asked, "how is the planning going for the end-of-summer party?"

"Oh, it's fine," Rose said. "At this point it pretty much runs like clockwork. Everyone knows their duties and how much food to bring. I just make sure everything's checked off the list."

"It's handy to have a checklist, isn't it?" Kitty said, setting her hat back on her head. "As long as every item is ticked off, you don't really have to get involved in the goings-on."

"Kitty Cooper," Tiny whispered in admonishment.

Rose stood and excused herself to go to the restroom. Before she left, she turned to Lily and motioned for her to come along. As Lily turned to follow her, Tiny leaned forward and pinched Kitty's shoulder. "What is *with* you today?"

Once inside the relative quiet of the restroom, Rose washed her hands and whispered frantically, "I shouldn't have let you talk me into this. This is crazy. No one wants me here."

"That's not true. Tiny was very happy to see you."

"It *is* true, and Tiny's nice to everyone. It's been too long. What was I thinking, that I could waltz into a group of women who've been friends for years and be invited in, just like that? It doesn't work that way."

"They just aren't sure how to take you. You've never been interested in joining them before. They're suspicious, but that doesn't mean they won't widen their arms to include you. Show them you're looking for friendship."

"Who says I even need —"

Lily cocked an eyebrow, and Rose stopped. "You *are* looking for friendship. Now, let's get back out there. Be nice. Make conversation."

When they returned to the table, a waiter was just setting down a tray of Bushwackers. Each lady took a cup and a grateful sip of the cold, frothy drink. Rose took a second sip of hers and cleared her throat. "How much alcohol is in this thing?"

"Just enough to take the edge off, I'd say," Kitty said. "I'm sorry I was touchy earlier, Rose." She shrugged. "It's a personality defect. But I'm glad you came today."

Rose smiled. "I'll be glad too just as soon as I get about half of this drink in me."

The ladies laughed, and Lily felt tension leak away from the table. Tiny took a dainty sip of her drink before setting the cup on the table. "Rose, your hair is just darling."

The others murmured their approval. Shirley patted the back of her hair. "I don't know if I could be as bold. I haven't changed my haircut in decades."

"Maybe it's time, old girl," Kitty said, putting a hand up to her own chic bob. "And the boldness suits you, Rose. You know you can't go backward now, right? Once you get moving, you have to keep pressing forward."

"I intend to do just that."

After a moment Kitty drained her cup and plunked it down on the table. "We have at least half an hour before our food gets here and I'm hot. What do y'all say we take this party to the water?"

A few minutes later they were sitting in Kitty's folding chairs with their feet in the shallow water. All around them, children built sand castles, dogs played chase with the gentle waves lapping the shore, and music floated from radios and speakers all around.

Lily leaned her head against the back of her chair and dug her toes into the cool, wet sand. She let her eyes close and listened to the ladies' conversations next to her, grateful they were including Rose. Then a rustle pulled her eyes open. Rose had risen from her chair and, to the delight of the others, walked purposefully into the water.

"Rose, your clothes!" Tiny called, her voice dissolving into laughter.

But Rose kept walking. As the water grew deeper, creeping up her legs to the bottom of her shorts, she trailed her fingers on the surface. Instead of stopping, she kept going. Kitty shot up out of her chair and followed her, her black one-piece shimmering in the sun. Tiny peeled off her palm-printed sarong and followed Kitty as Shirley and Edna did the same.

A moment later all five of them were chest-deep in the water, their laughter loud and full, their faces alight with joy. Lily focused on Rose, who moved her arms back and forth in the water with no care for her soaking clothes, then leaned her head back and faced the sun, like a flower bending toward the light.

The return trip seemed to take even longer, but it may have been because their bellies were full of food and going against the current of Wolf Bay made the pontoon feel a little like a bumper car.

"It's always worse on the way home," Kitty called out over the wind as the boat bumped over the wake of a large fishing boat. Edna groaned. "Just look at it as an adventure."

Finally they made it to smoother waters. Lily had just grabbed her tube of sunscreen to reapply to her arms and legs when Rose tapped her shoulder. "Your bag is buzzing," she said, motioning toward Lily's bag sitting near Rose's feet. Lily dug her hand around inside until she felt her phone. By the time she pulled it out, the phone had stopped ringing. The screen showed the name of the missed call. It was Worth.

Lily's heart thudded and she held the phone, waiting for the next ding that would alert her to a voice mail, but it never came. Instead, a text appeared.

Hi Lily. Would it be okay if I called you?

She swallowed and reached up to pull away a lock of hair that had blown against her lips. The breeze rushed in her ears along with the blood that pounded in her head. It took a minute to realize Rose was talking to her. She turned to Rose, who sat in the seat behind her.

"Anyone important?" Rose asked.

Lily hesitated. "I . . ."

Rose scrunched her eyebrows and touched Lily's shoulder. "Are you okay?"

Lily nodded. Rose gave her one last lingering glance before returning to her conversation with Tiny and Edna about the latest season of *Dancing with the Stars*. The speakers poured out Bob Marley's "No Woman No Cry," Kitty was showing Shirley how to drive the boat, and the sun continued to blaze, but Lily was stuck in a fog.

What did he want? Other than the divorce

papers, of course. In the end, Lily had decided not to mail them back to Mertha, not to allow her mother-in-law to interfere in any way in what Lily and Worth decided to do with their broken marriage.

But what else would he want? Closure? Forgiveness? The throw pillows Lily took with her when she moved to Safe Harbor? It had been four long months with no word from him. She couldn't imagine talking to him now.

She thought of the way he looked the last night she saw him. The sadness in his eyes, the tension in his body. *I haven't been a very good husband to you.* The scratched-out places on his note. All his unspoken words.

She wondered if his text meant he was ready to speak them.

Was she ready to listen?

As the boat swung around one last curve, the village came into view, its cottages lined up along the marina, sailboats and pontoons tied up to the docks, and someone walking a dog along the boardwalk. There was life here in Safe Harbor Village. *She* had a life here, and no one was more surprised than she was that she'd been the one to build it, piece by piece. Almost without realizing it.

As they pulled into the marina, Lily tapped out a message.

448

I'm busy now. But I can talk later.

Kitty slid the pontoon back into her space, and the ladies unloaded their bags, coolers, books, and hats. Tiny gave Rose a shy hug goodbye, and Rose hugged her back. Kitty nodded and awkwardly patted Rose's shoulder. "Four o'clock Sunday at the Sunrise. We'd be glad to have you."

"Thanks, Kitty," Rose said. "I'll try to make it."

As Lily and Rose walked away, Rose's face bore the faint stirrings of a smile. "Are you glad you came?" Lily asked.

"I suppose so. I could have done without all the choppy water, but that cheeseburger may have been the best I've ever had. Plus it was free." Lily bumped Rose with her shoulder. "Okay, the company was good too. They're not so bad after all." A moment later she added, "You don't have to walk me home, you know. I do know my way back."

Lily smiled. "I know you do. Maybe I'm not quite ready to go back to my quiet house yet."

"Everything okay?"

Lily nodded.

Rose's cottage was just up ahead. As Rose approached the front walkway, she stepped into the grass and stopped in front of her rosebushes. "Have I ever told you that I hate these things?"

"You hate your roses? Why?"

"Terry planted them for me. I think they were a guilt offering after he realized his receptionist was going to be a problem."

"Why don't you get rid of them?"

"These bushes are almost forty years old! It's a miracle they've lasted this long. I can't just get rid of them."

"Why not?"

Rose glared at her.

"You don't like them. They remind you of someone who hurt you. Why are you hanging on?"

Rose shifted her glare from Lily to the bushes. She reached forward, snapped off a leaf, and rubbed it between her fingers. "It would feel really good to see them go."

"Do you have a shovel?"

Rose looked back at Lily, her eyes wide. Lily shrugged. "At the moment I don't have anything better to do. I don't have any appointments scheduled this afternoon, and . . . I understand the need to uproot something."

Without another word Rose pulled a shovel from her storage closet and they borrowed a second one from a neighbor. Together the two women stomped their feet on the shovels, loosened the bushes from the soil around the roots, and forced them out of the ground. Several neighbors stopped by to see what on earth they were doing, and at one point Coach came by on his golf cart. He exited and approached them slowly.

"Is everything okay here?" He looked back and forth between them, his face creased with worry. "You both look like you're taking revenge on these poor bushes."

Rose took a few steps toward him. Lily glanced over her shoulder to watch them, her hand up to block the sun's sharp rays from her eyes. "Just taking care of something I should have done a long time ago," Rose said.

"Okay. As long as you're sure. Do you need any help?"

She shook her head. "I think we'll manage just fine."

Coach reached forward and squeezed Rose's hand before heading back to his golf cart. "You are two remarkable women," he called back before driving off with a wave.

When they finished, a pile of scraggly roots and branches lay in a heap in Rose's driveway, and her flower beds sat empty and lifeless. Rose stood in front of the beds, her arms outstretched. "I have big plans for you," she said. "You won't be empty for long."

"But no more roses?" Lily asked.

Rose laughed. "Nothing even remotely close to roses."

Lily returned the neighbor's shovel, picked up her beach bag, and waved goodbye to Rose.

"Lily," Rose called. "That phone call earlier on the boat. It was something important, wasn't it?"

Lily took a deep breath. "Yeah. Probably so."

Rose nodded. "Whatever it is, don't let it derail you."

"I won't. I promise."

That evening, after dinner and a shower, Lily sat outside on her porch swing. With the ceiling fan on high, the heat was tolerable, especially now that the sun had set. She rocked a few minutes with her phone on the seat next to her before picking it up and resolutely calling Worth's number.

"Lily," he said, the single word an exhale. "Hello."

The distance between them was quiet for a long moment before he sighed. "I wasn't sure if I'd hear from you. I'd already told myself if you hadn't called by eight o'clock

452

I was going to call you again."

"I beat you to it."

"Yeah."

Again, the silence.

"I signed the papers. I guess you're wanting them back."

"Yes." His voice caught a little on the word. "But that's not why I called."

"Why'd you call then?" she asked gently.

He sighed again. "I don't know, Lily. Because I have a mountain of things to say to you, but now that I have you on the phone, I can't get any of it out."

"Well, let's start with this — where are you?"

He exhaled. "I'm here at the house."

"In Atlanta?"

"No, in Foley. I'm packing up what's left of our things."

She tried to make sense of his words, but she couldn't. "You're at our old house? But I thought someone else was moving in."

"That was the plan, from what I understand, but the person Harold hired to replace me had already found a house to buy. They didn't need this place, so all our stuff has just been sitting here. Lily — where did you go?"

Lily chuckled. "I didn't go far. I'm just down the road a bit."

453

"You're — what? I figured you would've gone back to Fox Hill."

Lily shook her head. "There was no one for me to go back to there. Not in Atlanta either. So I . . . well, I found somewhere new. It's called Safe Harbor Village."

"I can't believe I did this to you. I've made a mess of so much. I can't even believe you're talking to me. I figured if I actually got you on the phone, you'd just yell at me."

"Yell? I'm not going to yell at you, Worth. You're an adult — you can make your own decisions. We both can. Why don't . . ." She paused, evaluating the words she was considering. "If we're going to talk, we should do it in person. Why don't you come here?"

Half an hour later he pulled up in front of her cottage. When he emerged from his car, she had to tamp down an urge to bolt, but whether it was a desire to run to him or away from him, she wasn't sure.

She watched him as he made his way up her front walkway. He'd let his hair grow a little, and his cheeks and chin were covered in a several-days-old beard. The T-shirt and shorts he wore were so different from his usual starched and pressed look.

Or maybe this was the real Worth, and what she'd seen in the short year of their marriage had been a lie, an attempt to be someone he wasn't.

She wasn't sure she'd ever know.

He stepped up onto the porch and looked at her. She hesitated, then scooted over, making room on the swing for him. When he sat, he placed his hands carefully on his knees, a comfortable two feet of space between them.

"Hi," he said without looking at her.

"Hi."

He took a deep breath and let it out slowly. She kept her feet on the ground, rocking them gently back and forth. "Where have you been all summer? I haven't talked to your mom in a while, but at least at the beginning it seemed like she had no idea."

He blew a puff of air from his nose. "She didn't. I didn't tell her where I was going. I didn't tell anyone." He glanced sideways at her, then lowered his gaze. "I went to California."

Lily closed her eyes. In her mind's eye she saw the newspaper clipping with Mertha's words written along the side of the photo. *That's our girl.*

"It's not what you think, though." She cocked a skeptical eyebrow in his direction. "Lily, my head was such a mess when we first met. I'd spent years having little pieces chipped off me by my mother. By Delia and our breakup. By all the expectations people had for me that I failed and failed to measure up to. And yes, before you ask, I know how pitiful this sounds. But I can't lie anymore. Not to you, not to myself.

"My mother had this idea of what her son would be like, the kind of life I'd live, the kind of man I'd be, and nothing less than her ideal image was enough. I don't know where it came from — this need for everything to look perfect, to measure up. But it was there, and I was the one who was never perfect enough."

Lily remained quiet as the words poured out of him.

"Even with Delia . . . My mom loved her. She treated her like a daughter-in-law even when we were in high school. It was almost embarrassing how much my mom fawned over her. But I loved Delia too. Like everyone else, I assumed we'd get married.

"When she broke up with me after college, I was crushed, but so was my mother. Not being good enough for Delia was just another way for me to fail. To fail her. I lived with that for a while, worked as hard as I could at the office, and tried to keep her off my back. By the time I met you, my mind was such a firestorm, I was in no place to try to make anyone else happy.

"But you were so sweet and quiet and steady. You were so opposite of everything else in my life. The opposite of my mother and the opposite of Delia. Maybe in some way I thought I'd be getting back at Mom by marrying someone she thought was so wrong for me. But you can't build a marriage trying to get back at your mom, can you?"

Suddenly he rose from the swing and took several steps away. He stuck his hands in his pockets, his back to her, and exhaled hard.

"Did you know she got me my job down here? At Pender Properties. Here I was thinking I was finally leaving the family business, making a fresh start in a new company. Making my own way." His shoulders drooped. "I had no idea she'd called Harold and gotten him to offer me a job. I guess — well, she probably thought I couldn't do it on my own. And maybe she was right. I did screw it all up."

Lily waited a moment before asking, "What happened in California?"

He shook his head. "I had this crazy idea that because I'd failed miserably at being a decent husband to you, that must mean Delia and I really were supposed to be together after all. See? Crazy. So I went out there to see her. To see if there was any chance. Thankfully, she put me in my place quickly."

"She did?"

"Oh yes. She told me she didn't love me anymore, that she hadn't for years, and that I didn't really love her either."

He finally turned around and faced Lily. "She was right. Going to California didn't have anything to do with any remaining feelings for Delia. It was just my way of . . . breathing for a minute, I guess. Which turned into a summer."

"Were you out there the whole time?"

"No." He sat back down next to her, his frame less taut. "I just sort of . . . drove. I went up to Washington, then out to Montana for a while. Down to Colorado. Texas. I've only been back a few days. I stopped in Atlanta, then figured I needed to clean up my mess here. Not that you're the mess. I just . . . It was time for me to face everything I left behind."

"Speaking of . . ." Lily rose and walked inside and up to her bedroom. She took the papers and the ring from the drawer next to her bed and brought them back outside to Worth. She set them on the swing between them.

He sighed and picked up the ring, turning it side to side to catch the glow from the porch light before putting it down again. He stretched his legs out in front of him.

Lily tipped her head back. "You know what? I think we both used each other."

He lifted his gaze and searched hers. "How's that?"

She shrugged. "We were Band-Aids to fix each other's wounds, but we couldn't fix each other. It's too much to expect another person to be able to do that."

He nodded slowly. "I left you those papers as a way to let you off the hook. To keep you from having to spend the rest of your life with someone so . . . unstable."

"Maybe you're not unstable anymore, Worth. Maybe now's the time for you to figure out what *you* want. Who cares what your mom wants?" She lifted the corner of her mouth into a smile, and he smiled back.

Just then a voice called to her from the street. "Hello there, Lily." She turned to face the street. She could barely make out the shape of a woman walking past her cottage.

"Shirley? Is that you?"

"It is. Just getting in my nighttime stroll. I prefer to get my exercise when it's not hot as blue blazes. Oh, excuse me, dear. I didn't realize you had company."

"Oh yes you did," Lily said under her

breath. She turned her head slightly so only Worth could hear her. "This woman doesn't exercise. She probably saw your car in front of my house and wanted to get the scoop."

He laughed quietly.

At the street Shirley was fanning herself with her hand. "Well, if you're sure everything's okay, I'll get on back home. I'll see you tomorrow, though, right? Eleven thirty for a cut and blow-dry."

"Yes, ma'am," Lily called with a wave. "I'll see you then."

They watched until Shirley disappeared around the bend in the road, and then Worth picked up the ring and papers and stood. He stared at the ring a moment before dropping it into his pocket. "I've taken up too much of your night. I need to be getting back. But, Lily . . . I'm really glad to see you again. To know we're not ending everything as ugly as I left it. And I'm happy to see you looking so . . . well, happy, I guess. This place seems to fit you."

Behind him, the Lily's Place sign on the front door fluttered in the breeze from the fan. She inhaled. "I think it does. I don't know what comes next, but for now I think this is where I need to be."

He stood awkwardly in front of her, as if unsure how to wrap things up. She crossed

460

her arms in front of her. "Take care, Worth."

He nodded. "You too."

Then he was gone, driving away from her cottage and down the road. In a minute he'd be passing through the gates of the village, turning back toward the rest of civilization, away from this place of water and salt and second chances. Lily took one last deep breath, then turned off the porch light and stepped inside.

# TWENTY-SEVEN

Lily's phone rang just as her last appointment of the day headed out the door. She checked the screen and smiled at the name she saw there. When she answered, it was so noisy, she could barely hear him.

"Sorry," Rawlins said. "Hang on a sec." After another moment Lily heard a door close and the noise, while not gone, dulled a bit. "I'm sorry. It's been a crazy day."

"Good crazy or bad crazy?" Lily stood the broom up in the corner of the salon and sat, relishing the ease of pressure off her feet.

"A little of both. I called for two reasons. One, I wanted to say hi."

Lily smiled into the phone. "Hi."

"Second, do you have plans tonight?"

"I don't."

"Mind if I swing by for a bit?"

"Not at all."

"It may be late. I have to drive to Pensa-

462

cola this afternoon to see a guy about some nets. It may be dinnertime or a little later."

"I'll be here."

And she was there, until seven forty-five when someone knocked on her door. She opened it to see Coach and Rose standing on her porch.

"We're here to kidnap you," Coach said.

Lily laughed. "I'm sorry?"

"Apparently Ida Gold had a hankering to see a young Robert Redford on the big screen, so Peter did his thing and somehow came up with a screen and a projector. *Barefoot in the Park* starts on the grass in fifteen minutes."

"Oh. Thanks, but I have —"

"You're not working this late, are you?" Coach peered around her into the cottage. "Do you have a visitor?"

"No. Not now, but —"

"Great. Let's go then. A little fresh air will be good for you."

Lily looked helplessly at Rose, who only shrugged. "You might as well come on. When he decides he wants something, he generally doesn't give up until he gets it."

"I . . . Okay. Let me just grab my phone."

Lily perched on the back seat of Coach's golf cart and typed out a quick text to Rawlins.

Slight change of plans. When you get here, come to the grass.

It's village movie night.

Rawlins's reply came quickly.

See you in twenty.

When he arrived, Corie and Paul's quirky attic neighbor had just climbed through their apartment window, sparking laughter from the villagers in attendance on the lawn. Lily was sitting on Coach's extra beach towel, and she scooted over to make room for Rawlins.

When he sat, only a few inches separated them, and Lily inhaled, breathing in his scent of soap and musk. His hair was still damp, and it curled up a little in the back.

"Movie night, huh?" he said, looking around at the couple dozen people scattered around the grass on blankets and folding chairs.

"Coach and Rose picked me up. I had no choice. They were very persuasive."

He smiled, but it didn't quite make it all the way to his eyes.

"Everything go okay today?"

Behind them, someone shushed her. Rawlins lowered his voice to a whisper. "Yeah, it's fine. We're actually catching a lot right now. We're in a good spot for the season, but . . ."

"But what?"

He shook his head. "It's just hard for me to trust it. Who knows if it'll stay like this or if it'll dip back down again." He ran his hand through his hair. "I didn't worry as much before, but . . . I just need to know it's going to be steady. Especially since Dad is still against the market."

"He is?"

Rawlins nodded. "Yeah. He's not budging."

Lily bumped her shoulder gently against his. "I'm sorry."

He looked at her and sighed. "Me too." He looked down, then sat up straighter. "I've got to fill you in on something."

A man behind them leaned forward and tapped Rawlins on the shoulder. "Can you two keep it down? This is a very important part of the movie."

On the screen Jane Fonda was casually leaning against a doorframe wearing her husband's button-down shirt and nothing else. Lily looked back at the man and rolled her eyes.

Rawlins stood and held a hand down to Lily. "Take a walk with me?"

She took his hand and stood, and they walked across the street to the boardwalk that lined the marina. It was a long moment before he started talking.

"Do you remember the friend I told you about, whose company does environmental work in the Gulf?"

"I think so. You made it sound like he was wanting you to join the company."

"That's right. He still does. They do a lot, but mostly they make sure something like the BP oil spill doesn't happen again. Or if it does, they make sure plans are in place to mitigate it. He knows all about Willett, knows we know every inch of these waters." He reached out and took her arm as they stepped around a pile of fishing poles and long, thin spears laid out in the middle of the boardwalk.

"Sorry about the mess," a man called from the deck of a pontoon boat. "We're loading up for some flounder gigging. Interested?"

Rawlins shook his head no, and they continued walking. With the men behind them, he continued. "At first I told him I wasn't interested, that I already have a job and it's the family business. But he kept asking, kept making the deal more and more attractive. And now . . ." Rawlins sighed. "Well, I agreed to interview for the position."

"That's . . . good, right?"

"I don't know. Maybe." He took a deep

breath. "It's a job I think I can do well. My marine science degree would be put to good use. It'd pay well too. And it'd be steady money, not dependent on what we pull out of the water." He stopped walking. "It's based in Louisiana."

Lily swallowed. "Oh."

"Yeah."

They walked on, the lights from the docks casting wobbly glimmers on the water.

"The timing couldn't be worse. I talked to Tara, and she's agreed to give me primary custody of Hazel."

Now it was Lily's turn to stop walking. "Really?" She gave his hand a gentle tug. "That's great. It's just what you wanted."

He nodded. "I didn't think she'd agree to it, but she has this new boyfriend. I think she wants her own fresh start."

"Have you talked to Hazel about it?"

"A little. I asked her if she thinks Pancake would be okay living with me instead of her mom. Pancake is this stuffed rabbit she leaves at Tara's."

"What'd she say?"

"She said Pancake's always wanted to live at my house." After a moment he sighed. "I just feel like I can't ignore this opportunity. I shouldn't ignore it. I've been trying to do what I can to shore up the business, but

467

I'm just not getting anywhere. Then this job comes out of nowhere . . ."

"I agree. It seems like something you should pay attention to."

He nodded. "If this had happened three or four months ago, I would have jumped on it, no problem. Well, except for the small fact that taking another job could spell the eventual end of Willett Fisheries. But . . ."

Lily looked up at him. His face was shadowed, with just his cheekbone and the curve of his jaw highlighted by a light at the end of a dock.

"Things feel a little different now."

Above them, the summer sky was speckled with stars, the moon a thin eyelash. He took a step toward her, and she let herself relax into the circle of his arms, resting her cheek on his shoulder and breathing him in like he was air, sustenance, strength. After a moment she lifted her head and found his face, his eyes. She softly touched her forehead to his and spoke quietly. "I think you should do what's best for you and Hazel."

He remained still for a long moment, then reached up and brushed her cheek with the backs of his fingers. "Let's get you home."

# THE VILLAGE VINE

*Your Source for Neighborhood News*

August 22, 2018
Compiled by Shirley Ferrill

## GOOD DAY, SAFE HARBOR VILLAGE!

### TIDES

Low tides will occur around 8:00 p.m. for the first few days of the week, and the Bubbas tell me that's the best time to try your hand at flounder gigging. They've already been out once this week and brought in quite a haul. If you'd like to participate, meet on the Golds' dock at 8:15 p.m. Bring your own gig and a headlamp or lantern if you have one.

### WEATHER

Thankfully the disturbance in the gulf has fizzled and we're back to plain old summertime H&H. We've been lucky in the hurricane department, though let's not say that out loud. No reason to jinx ourselves, right?

Mosquito index remains high. Fran Metzger at the Masthead reports that she can't restock her supply of calamine lotion fast enough. Just this morning I popped in for a bottle, but she was wiped clean. Please consider sharing with your neighbors, though it's probably best to use your own cotton balls.

## RECREATION

With the paddleboat tours still on hold, Coach has invited everyone to try their hand at beach volleyball. He has staked a net up in the grass by the swimming pool, so it's more grass than beach volleyball, but no matter. We appreciate his dedication to our recreation and exercise.

## MISCELLANEOUS

- The So Long, Summer party has been scheduled for Friday, August 31. If you have an extra cooler to contribute, please let Toots Baker know.
- I know everyone is on pins and needles wondering whether Jimmy Buffett will be making an appearance at the aforementioned So Long, Summer party. Regardless of the outcome, let's all agree that the mere possibility of it (however remote it may be) is more than we could ask for. In honor of Mr. Buffett, Elijah has added a new drink to the bar menu at the café. It's called a Five O'Clock Somewhere, and it is delicious.

# SUNRISE CAFÉ MENU

## August 23–August 29

I know I speak for everyone when I say we are thoroughly enjoying the café now that the menu has returned to normal. Personally, I enjoyed the Jell-O, but it's hard to deny the perfection of Roberta's bread pudding.

Mains: chicken-fried steak, gumbo with
    lump crabmeat, fried catfish
Sides: collards, field peas, coleslaw, mac-
    aroni & cheese
Desserts: bourbon bread pudding, chess
    pie, key lime pie

# TWENTY-EIGHT

The higher Rose's age climbed, the quicker time seemed to speed by. It felt as though they'd just put away the wooden dance floor, white tents, and trash barrels, yet here they were dusting them off again, getting ready to close up another summer.

And this particular one had been a summer like no other. So many changes, so many adventures she never thought possible. She reached up and ran her fingers through the ends of her hair, already grown out a bit from her initial cut a few weeks ago. She'd be due for a trim soon.

Rose had just pulled out a couple of the big coolers they used to store drinks and was washing them out in her front yard when she heard ladies chatting. As she rinsed, her back to the street, the voices approached.

"Rose?"

She turned to see two villagers walking

toward her. Melba Lane held a clipboard in her hand, and Carlene Cobb wore her trademark yellow sunglasses. Rose turned off the spigot and shaded her eyes with her hand just as Carlene tipped her glasses down to better see Rose's empty flower beds.

"I heard you pulled up your rosebushes," she said.

*Well, they sure didn't get up and walk away,* Rose thought, then almost immediately bit her own tongue. *Kindness . . . friendship,* she told herself. "I did."

"Hmm. It does give you a blank slate now, doesn't it?" Carlene placed her glasses back on her nose.

Melba tapped a pen against the surface of her clipboard. "As you know, the Romance Readers meet on the third Thursday of every month. We wanted to invite you to our upcoming meeting, which is next week."

"We're reading the third book in the Outlander series," Carlene said, her eyebrows raised. "Have you read them?"

Rose shook her head, and Carlene fanned her face with her hand. "Prepare yourself."

"Can you make it?" Melba asked.

"Well, I . . . I suppose I can. Thank you for asking. How long are the first two books?

Will I have time to catch up before next week?"

"Depends on your appetite for scandal," Carlene said.

Melba elbowed her. "What she means to say is it depends on how fast you read." She scanned her clipboard. "Looks like we're good on fruit and cheese — how do you feel about firecrackers?"

Rose hesitated. "At the book club?"

"She means the actual crackers," Carlene explained. "You know, saltines, canola oil, spices . . ."

"Oh . . . I've heard of them, yes."

"Great, so I'll just mark you down to bring those." Melba made a distinct check mark on her list. "Don't worry, I'll send you the recipe. Kitty Cooper is very particular about the seasonings." She tucked her clipboard under her arm. "We'll see you Thursday at eleven then."

As the two ladies turned to leave, Carlene looked back and called out, "It's good to see you out and about more, Rose. Keep it up and people may stop calling you the Ice Queen."

Rose watched them a moment as they walked, realizing her long-held nickname — no one had ever said it to her face, but she heard the whispers nonetheless — no longer held any power over her. She was a new Rose.

Just as she was about to turn the spigot back on, Coach's golf cart rounded the curve toward her cottage. She felt her cheeks lift involuntarily. *How does he do that?* Her defenses had been up, iron-clad, for years, and yet he'd still found a way in. And she was so glad he did.

As he popped one wheel up on the curb and climbed out, the evening's sun rays casting an orange glow over everything, Rose was still smiling.

"That's a happy face," he said, taking her hand.

She exhaled and felt her shoulders drop, grateful for the release. "It's a good day, I think."

"I have to agree with you. I managed to repair the holes in the paddleboats so we can resume our river tours. And I get to end the day with you. Can I buy you dinner?"

Coach extended his elbow, but instead of taking it, she stood on her tiptoes and kissed his cheek.

"Now, Rose." Coach feigned looking over both shoulders. "You have to understand I'm not one for PDA." He grinned, then pulled her toward him and kissed her full on the mouth.

Her heart fluttered, and when he took a step back, she swatted his shoulder. "Shame on you."

"I feel no shame at all. But does that mean you can't have dinner with me?"

"It does. I have to go see someone. Okay if I take a rain check?"

"As long as you cash it in tomorrow."

Rose slowed as she turned down Willett Drive. By the time she made it to her brother's house, the car was barely creeping. Her stomach crawled with nerves, but at the same time a new and unwavering hope carried her feet down the driveway and up the steps to his back porch.

Jim was seated at the kitchen table with his back to the glass door. A plate of fried fish, green beans, and corn bread sat in front of him, and next to his plate was the newspaper. Knowing Jim, it was the sports section.

It was strange to look at him and see an old man when she half expected him to still look like the twelve-year-old who hurled the rock or the eighteen-year-old who fell in love with a girl named Stella.

She watched him as long as she could, and then she took a step forward and tapped on the door. He put his finger on the page to mark his place, then turned slowly, not in any hurry. When he saw it was Rose, he turned farther, propping his arm on the back of his chair to get a better look.

They remained like that for a long moment — brother and sister through the glass, separated by so many lost years. Finally he turned back around in his seat, causing her breath to catch in her throat. But he picked up his newspaper and set it to the side. Then he stretched out his leg and nudged the chair next to him back a little, to make room for her.

She took a deep breath and opened the door. The kitchen smelled like heaven — like good food and Stella, and memories, and their childhood.

"Come on and have a seat," he said. "You hungry?"

Rose shook her head, not trusting herself to speak. She sat down and clasped her hands in her lap. Next to her, Jim took off his glasses and massaged the bridge of his nose. He replaced his glasses and peered at her, as if making sure it was really his sister sitting there.

"Jim, I —"

"It was a long time ago," he said quietly. "There were a lot of hurts then. On all sides."

"I know, but I owe you an apology. Many apologies."

He propped his chin in his hand. "Can we just let it go? I have my business, you have your village. Life goes on. No need to dig everything back up and air it all out." He paused. "I'm *tired.* And I miss you." Then he smiled. "Took you long enough to make it here."

Rose's eyebrows rose. "You wanted to talk to me? Why didn't you call?"

He shrugged. "Stubborn, I guess."

Rose laughed, a quick burst. "You and me both."

"Well, I guess that's one thing we have in common." He reached and covered her hands with his big one. It was sun spotted and rough, the hand of someone who'd worked all his life and made an honest living.

"You can move past it all?" she asked, her voice low. "Just like that?"

He shook his head. "No. Not just like that. It took a long time. But I forgave you a long time ago. I've just been waiting for you to show back up." He pulled his hand away and stood. "Now, you look like you could use some meat on your bones. Let me fix you a plate."

## TWENTY-NINE

Just like the party at the beginning of the summer, the day of the So Long, Summer party broke with a thunderstorm that tore open the sky. All of Lily's customers canceled their appointments. Even Janelle wouldn't brave the elements to make it to the salon for her ten o'clock.

"The partygoers will have to make do with my gray roots," she told Lily on the phone. "And anyway, I'm thinking of going back to Electric Blonde. The caramel may be mysterious, but Seymour told me he liked it better when it was lighter."

The rain finally slacked in the late afternoon, just in time to get ready for the party. Lily dressed comfortably in a pale green linen dress and sandals, though they'd be covered in mud in minutes. She knew she wouldn't see Rawlins, as he'd called the evening before to tell her he'd miss the party.

"They called to set up an interview," he'd said. "The catch is, they want to see me tomorrow. Their timeline is bumped up, and they need someone to start quickly."

"Wow. Well, that could be good for you. You won't have to wait as long, wondering."

"Yeah." He hesitated. "They're only interviewing one other candidate. They're talking to him today, me tomorrow."

"Will you miss the party?"

He sighed. "I don't think I'll be back in time. The interview's not until four, and it's more than three hours away."

Lily nodded, though Rawlins couldn't see her.

"I'm sorry to miss it. Can I call you this weekend? Let you know how the interview goes?"

"Of course," she'd said.

She glanced at the clock on her phone. By now he probably knew whether he got the job.

Just before leaving her cottage, she paused in the doorway. She could already hear the music — Peter's bass and Cricket's high, lonesome violin. She took a deep, satisfying breath. This place, these people, this time in her life — this was her second chance. Her do-over. Her reclaimed life. She shook the hair back from her face and stepped out into the balmy evening.

The party was in full swing by the time she arrived, the food tables half-empty, and Toots Baker's pitcher of Alabama Slammer almost drained. She wasn't hungry anyway, or thirsty for that matter. Without stopping to chat with anyone, Lily walked along the perimeter of the crowd down the grass to the shoreline where the bay — so still it looked almost solid — just barely made a ripple on the sandy shore.

She slipped off her sandals and walked all the way to the water, not stopping until her feet were fully submerged. The water was bath-warm and soft as silk. Beneath her toes she felt tiny shards of shells, broken by the currents and tides. The moon, on its slow way back to full, was a pale glimmer in the otherwise purple sky.

As Lily stared out at the water, her mind trapped somewhere between Georgia and Louisiana, she saw a tiny disturbance in the water, not much more than an odd ripple, several feet from the shore. She watched the spot carefully, trying to see clearly in the twilight, and as she did, something surfaced. She saw sleek gray skin, a rounded head, and a whiskered muzzle like a hippo's.

She almost laughed out loud, though after a summer of such unexpected surprises and beauty, it made perfect sense that she'd spot this creature returning again to the shores of the village.

"Lily, is that you?" Rose's voice carried through the music and to Lily's ears. She turned. Rose stood a ways back with Tiny and Kitty.

"What are you doing, standing out there like a statue all alone?" Kitty called. "Are you going to come dance with us or what?"

Lily checked the water again, but the manatee was gone. She watched a moment, willing its bulbous body to surface again, but the bay was calm and unbroken. She took a deep breath and turned back.

"How about that dance?" Rose asked, one eyebrow raised.

"One dance," Lily said, making her way toward her friends.

"If we make it a good one, that's all we need," Kitty said, running ahead to whisper something in Peter's ear.

A moment later they began "Brown Eyed Girl," and every able body on the grass jumped up to dance. Even Seymour Eldins danced, though he remained seated on his motorized scooter. Standing next to him, Janelle swiveled her hips.

Coach found his way to the group and, with a smile of apology, twirled a laughing Rose and whispered something in her ear. Lily closed her eyes and let the music carry her away. She focused only on the feel of her feet in the grass, the air on her cheeks, the merry laughter around her. Her heart beat steadily in her chest, reminding her she was still wholly and doggedly alive.

When the song ended, Coach pulled away from Rose and ran up to the makeshift stage. "If I can just have a second," he said to the band members. When Peter nodded, Coach tapped the microphone a few times and grinned. "I've always wanted to do that." He cleared his throat. "Many of you have asked if we will be treated to an appearance by Jimmy Buffett at tonight's party."

A buzz of chatter began and spread quickly through the grass. Lily looked at Rose, who only shrugged.

"I'm sorry to say he is not coming." Coach held up a hand to quiet the murmur of disappointment. "But if you can believe it, he sent me an email today." The buzz picked back up. "If you'd let me, I'd like to read it to you all."

He slid a pair of wire-rimmed glasses onto his nose, then peered at his phone and began to read.

" 'Dear Safe Harbor Village, I'm sorry I can't be there to help you bring the summer to a close, but I have a feeling you'll do just fine on your own. It makes me smile knowing there's a village on the Alabama coast, all of you learning and loving and laughing together and enjoying life to the fullest. You're an inspiring bunch of old coots, and my hat's off to you! I hear you've got a swinging band playing there tonight, so do me a favor and tell them Jimmy is asking if they know a song called "Changes in Latitudes, Changes in Attitudes." If they do, this one's from me.' "

As the band took their cue from Mr. Buffett himself, Coach took off his glasses and pocketed his phone, and cheers erupted all over the grass.

Lily's dancing lasted for much longer than the single dance she'd promised, but finally she said it was time for her to turn in.

"Never thought I'd see the day," Rose said. "Me out here dancing in my bare feet while someone forty years younger than me goes home to bed."

Lily smiled. "Wonders never cease." She reached out and hugged Rose. "Thank you. For everything."

She turned to go, but Rose called her. "I think it's safe to say you've survived your trial period."

Lily laughed. "You think so? I'd almost forgotten about that."

"I didn't. And I could use some help in the office, if you're interested."

"Really?"

Rose nodded. "I was going to hire someone anyway, but then you came along. I figured if you made it past the trial period, I'd bring you in, show you the ropes in the clubhouse."

"Well, Rose, I'm glad I made it."

"Me too."

Rose turned back to the music and her friends, and Lily headed home. At her cottage she propped open the door so she could still hear the music, then left her dirty sandals on the front porch. She walked across the cool floor and sat on the couch, relishing the chilled air after the thick heat outside. After a moment she leaned her head back and closed her eyes.

When she heard the tap on the door, she almost thought she'd imagined it. But when she sat up and looked back, Rawlins stood just outside her open door, his eyes lit with the glow from the single lamp on inside. She stood and they stared at each other for a long moment, the scent of salt and comfort mingling in the air.

"I thought you weren't going to make it tonight."

"I didn't think I would either."

She hesitated, unsure of what to say. "How did it go?" she finally asked.

"I turned around at the Louisiana line."

"You . . . what?"

"I canceled the interview." He held up his arms, then let them drop. "I realized I had what I wanted back at home. My family. Hazel finally with me. I'd be an idiot to uproot her again. She loves it here." He took a step forward. "And then there's you. I've only just found you. I don't want to be the one to walk away."

"But . . . what about your dad? And the business?"

He chuckled, rubbed a hand over his cheek. "He called me on the road. I'd almost made it back to Mobile. He said he wants to talk about my ideas. That I have some good ones, and that we're long overdue for making decisions together."

Lily opened her mouth to speak, but no words came. She smiled and bit her lip.

"Lily, I . . . ," he began. "I don't know where things stand with you and Worth. I would never want to get in the way of something that still had a chance at life. At giving *you* life. But I also . . ." His brow furrowed and he paused. "I just want to make you happy. Whatever that looks like. And I want to be here for you, however much you need — or want — me to be."

He stopped when she crossed the room toward him — two feet away, one, now only inches. She took his hand and wrapped her fingers around his. She looked up at him, and her heart felt light, freer than it had in months, years. A lifetime.

She gave his hand a gentle tug and led him outside. Music from the party floated down Port Place from the grass to the porch swing where she and Rawlins sat, side by side, legs pressed against each other. She leaned her head on his shoulder, and he wrapped his arm around her, pulling her close.

After a moment she lifted her head and laced her fingers through the back of his hair. "My offer for a haircut still stands, you know."

He grinned and pulled her close again. "I think I'm just about ready."

# THIRTY

Dear Stella,

Do you think it's ever too late to change? To be someone new? Or maybe not someone entirely new, but a new version of yourself? Can you shed the old version like skin that's grown too tight?

I certainly hope the answer is yes, because it feels like that's what's happening to me — the old me is falling away, and in her place is this new woman. I barely recognize her, but at the same time, I feel like I'm saying hello to an old friend who's been away for a very long time. I'm learning to like the feeling a lot.

Do you remember that young lady I mentioned a while back? The hairdresser? It turns out she has captured your son's heart. And he just may have captured hers as well. Don't you worry — I've already done all the checking and sniffing out. She's a good one.

And it appears we're all going to be sticking around here for a while longer. I called Terry tonight and told him I was staying put. That the village is staying just as it is. After all, we have Jimmy Buffett's blessing. Can't argue with that.

And, Stella, Jim and I are okay. Not perfect, not like it once was, but it's good. And I have to think that somehow, now that my flawed but steadfast heart and my intentions all those years ago have been laid bare, you'd be okay with me too.

You used to love to say, "Life is beautiful." I always thought it was just you spilling spoonfuls of sugar and sunshine everywhere you went. But, my dear friend, I think you were right. This life is a beautiful thing — it's precious and fleeting, and we'd all be crazy not to reach out and grab it with both hands and hang on tight.

Thank you for showing me that. It took me a while, but I see it now. And I intend to do it.

All my love, as always,
Rose

# ACKNOWLEDGMENTS

Thank you to everyone at Thomas Nelson, especially my editor, Kim Carlton. Thank you, Kim, for encouraging me to dig deeper to make this story and these characters shine as much as they do. You're a whiz and I'm thankful you're my editor! Thank you to Amanda Bostic for your continued faith in me as an author. I may have written this book, but there are so many smart, enthusiastic people who had a hand in bringing *The Summer House* to life and helping it find its audience, especially Paul Fisher, Jodi Hughes, Matt Bray, Becky Monds, Savannah Summers, Kerri Potts, and Julie Breihan. (Thank you, Julie, for saving readers from all that brightness!) Thank you to the sales team for your dedication to getting my books into the hands of readers. Thank you also to the creative cover designers — I'm batting a thousand on covers. Thank you for another stunner.

491

Thank you to my agent, Karen Solem. I always come away from our conversations feeling stronger and ready to go out and write the book that needs to be written.

Thank you to my sweet family — Matt, Kate, and Sela — especially toward the end of writing this book when I spent a lot of time holed up in that back bedroom. I love you and thank you for being excited for me and for supporting this "job" of mine. And, Matt, keep the ideas coming. One day I'll write one of those books! To my bigger family, including all the Kofflers and Dentons, thank you for your love, guidance, and support for oh-so-many years.

The further I get in this journey, the more writer friends I meet along the way who help in so many ways — from listening to me gripe or vent, to offering much-needed advice, to commiserating about the ups and downs. Thank you especially to my dear friends Anna Gresham and Holly Mackle for being on the receiving end of many of those gripes and venting sessions and for cheering me on, especially when this particular book hit bumps in the road. Thank you also to Holly for the eagle-eye edits and for keeping my characters from bumping into each other so much! Thank you, Anna, for letting me borrow the phrase on Canaan's hat! Thank you to the ladies of Tea and Empathy, and to author Rachel Linden for creating such a warm and inviting space to ask questions, receive feedback, and learn and laugh together. Maybe one day we can all get together IRL!

Thank you to my dear friend Amanda Lane for many years of solving problems one afternoon at a time. I'm thankful for our friendship, forged over Halloween traditions and backyard Popsicles.

Thank you to Jaye and Doug Plash and Molly Stone for helpful tidbits of information on the shrimping industry. Thank you to my friend Nancy Meigs Mills, who should win an award for buying the most books from an author. I will always sign another copy for you, Nancy! Thank you to the delightful followers of my Facebook page (Lauren K. Denton, Author) who helped me figure out what those stand-up hair dryers are actually called!

As always, thank you to the Bookstagrammers and book bloggers — where would we authors be without you? You are a creative and inspiring force in the world of books.

Lastly, thank you to my readers. Musician and author Andrew Peterson wrote in his book *Adorning the Dark* about how surprising it is — whether you're a writer of books or a singer of songs — that an audience will give you not only their money but their *attention*. He says the act of giving that attention is a "profound generosity in a culture that clamors for every second of our attention already." So, thank you, dear readers, for making space for my books, both on your bookshelves and in your hearts. I treasure every message and email you send me, and it's truly the highest honor to write books for you. My prayer is that they continue to bring you hope and beauty, humor and encouragement.

# DISCUSSION QUESTIONS

1. Do you have any knowledge of or connection to the Alabama Gulf Coast? If so, did this story and its setting in the area around Bon Secour, Alabama, stir any memories for you?
2. Is there a particular character you identify with? What about one you didn't understand or whose choices you disagreed with? Was there a character who had any trait you admired?
3. Lily Bishop finds a kind of fresh start in the shady streets and welcoming neighbors of Safe Harbor Village. Have you ever experienced a season of life when you had to start over from scratch? If so, what or who helped you through it?
4. What defines *home* for you? Has it ever been something other than the place where your family resides? Discuss the idea of finding *home* in a person or people instead of in a physical place.

5. Coach tells Rose that all the villagers at Safe Harbor have struggles they keep inside. Could you identify with any of the villagers' struggles? Have you ever been in a situation where you had to cover up your pain in order to move forward with your life?

6. Rawlins tells Lily that being out on the water is the best way to forget your troubles. Similarly, former psychiatrist Kitty mentions water's healing properties. How do you see characters in the story coming to the water to relieve their hurt? Do you feel like being near the water does something similar for you?

7. Lily tells Rose her life feels unraveled, as if the death of her mother pulled a string, and each painful event after has yanked the string a little bit more. Can you relate to the idea of painful events or struggles seeming to come in waves?

8. Rose is surprised to find that her brother, Jim, is willing to "forgive and forget." How do you think he was able to do that? Should he have required more from her before he asked her to sit at his kitchen table? Have you ever had an old wound you chose to forgive because you missed the person more than you were angry at him or her?

# ABOUT THE AUTHOR

**Lauren K. Denton** is the author of the *USA TODAY* bestselling novels *The Hideaway* and *Hurricane Season.* She was born and raised in Mobile, Alabama, and now lives with her husband and two daughters in Homewood, just outside Birmingham. Though her husband tries valiantly to turn her into a mountain girl, she'd still rather be at the beach.

LaurenKDenton.com
Instagram: LaurenKDentonBooks
Facebook: LaurenKDentonAuthor
Twitter: @LaurenKDenton
Pinterest: LKDentonBooks